REMEDIES

IN A NUTSHELL®

FOURTH EDITION

WILLIAM M. TABB
David Ross Boyd Professor
Judge Fred A. Daugherty Chair in Law
University of Oklahoma

RACHEL M. JANUTIS
Professor of Law
Capital University Law School

WEST
ACADEMIC
PUBLISHING

The publisher is not engaged in rendering legal or other professional advice, and this publication is not a substitute for the advice of an attorney. If you require legal or other expert advice, you should seek the services of a competent attorney or other professional.

Nutshell Series, In a Nutshell and the Nutshell Logo are trademarks registered in the U.S. Patent and Trademark Office.

© 2005 Thomson/West
© 2013 Thomson Reuters
© 2017 LEG, Inc. d/b/a West Academic
© 2021 LEG, Inc. d/b/a West Academic
   444 Cedar Street, Suite 700
   St. Paul, MN 55101
   1-877-888-1330

West, West Academic Publishing, and West Academic are trademarks of West Publishing Corporation, used under license.

Printed in the United States of America

ISBN: 978-1-64708-220-8

To Elaine W. Shoben, our wonderful mentor and friend, for all her kindness and support.

PREFACE

This Nutshell on Remedies provides an overview of judicial remedies. It explores the substantive requirements for major remedies at law and in equity as well as the practical considerations that aid with context and application. The study of Remedies is challenging because it arises in all areas of law— statutory, constitutional, and common law. The questions of remedial availability and effectiveness are among the most important issues in law because the potential remedy in a case reflects the extent to which the right may be vindicated. One of the central themes in this book is the relationship between "rights" and "remedies" and how a right is only as great as the remedy that protects it.

In most law schools, Remedies is a capstone course that builds on the study of first year subjects in torts, property, contracts, and civil procedure. It assumes familiarity with the substantive doctrines that form the basis for establishing rights under those areas of law, such as whether negligence exists or a contract breach has occurred. The issue of remedies arises when one or more legally recognizable right exists and has been violated. The question then becomes determining what remedies may be available to enforce, vindicate, redress or compensate that right.

Other major themes in this book include the selection of the most effective remedy when alternative remedies may be available and the relationship of multiple remedies to each other. For example, the victim of embezzlement may seek either damages or restitution, but not both. In contrast, someone who has suffered an injury to land for repeated trespasses may have multiple and compatible remedies. In many cases involving injuries to land, the innocent landowner may seek compensatory damages for the harm suffered and may also seek equitable relief to prevent invasions in the future. The study of remedies includes the entitlement and measurement of damages, the principles guiding equitable relief, and the process by which law and equity may be applied for the benefit of the landowner in such a case.

The organization of the book reflects the four classifications of remedies: injunctions, damages, restitution and declaratory relief. The major remedial alternatives are examined within each classification. Therefore, the study of injunctions considers the various types of temporary orders, permanent injunctions, and specific performance. The study of compensatory damages for contract breach evaluates both the common law rules and those under Article II of the Uniform Commercial Code.

In order to gain more insight into the practical application of each area, the book also evaluates the important defenses, exceptions, limitations, and adjustments to the basic remedies. Thus, the study of equity becomes more fully understood by evaluating the requirements of civil and criminal contempt to enforce equitable decrees. The examination of damages is completed by matters such as the doctrine of avoidable consequences and the rules of discounting to present value for lump sum awards in personal injury cases. The exploration of equitable restitution similarly includes the limiting doctrines of tracing, change of position, volunteers and the bona fide purchaser for value rule.

We have sought to provide a book that can provide a general survey of the subject for any reader. We have also tried to produce a useful accompaniment to any casebook for law students. The materials provide references to leading cases in each substantive area, Restatement provisions, or statutory citations in order to facilitate understanding and application. The authors wish to note our debt to our students for making the challenge of teaching this subject such a rewarding one.

WILLIAM M. TABB
RACHEL M. JANUTIS

February, 2021

ACKNOWLEDGMENTS

American Law Institute

OUTLINE

TABLE OF CASES

References are to Pages

REMEDIES
IN A NUTSHELL®

FOURTH EDITION

CHAPTER 1
INTRODUCTION TO REMEDIES

The study of remedies answers the question that is most important to the victorious party in a lawsuit: What does a substantive victory mean in practical terms? A plaintiff may seek monetary recovery or an equitable order to restrain certain activities of the defendant. Conversely, a defendant wants to limit liability or be protected by recovery under a bond if wrongfully enjoined. Both parties want to know about the availability of attorneys' fees, if any, to the prevailing litigant. By definition, a remedy is the means by which rights are enforced or the violation of rights is prevented, redressed, or compensated.

The subject of remedies complements the study of both substantive law and procedure. Substantive contract law determines whether or not a valid contract is formed, and substantive tort law sets forth standards for negligence. The question of remedies is a second stage inquiry. For example, assuming that a breach of contract has occurred, or a tort is established, what sort of relief should the injured party receive and how is that accomplished? Procedural issues may affect that answer. For example, must a claimant post a bond as a condition to obtaining a temporary restraining order? Constitutional issues also may apply, such as the doctrine of abstention that restricts the ability of federal courts to enjoin matters in state court proceedings.

Several basic themes recur in the study of remedies. One is the distinction between entitlement and measurement of relief. For example, whether a party may receive attorneys' fees through a federal fee-shifting statute is a question of entitlement, but how those fees are calculated is a question of measurement. Similarly, the nature of the defendant's conduct determines entitlement to the discretionary remedy of punitive damages, but the evidence relevant to assessing punitive damages is a measurement question. Another theme is the interrelation of remedies when there are multiple remedial options in law and equity. For instance, assume that a manufacturing plant emits noxious fumes that cause damage to an orchard located on a neighboring landowner's property. The landowner may successfully maintain an action for nuisance. Remedies may include damages for past and/or future injuries, as well as injunctive relief to prohibit future invasions. The availability of an injunction includes evaluation of many factors: the adequacy of the legal remedies, the irreparable nature of the harm, the balance of hardships, the public interest, and the supervisory role of the court. The subject of remedies explores whether damages, injunctive relief, or both may redress the wrong.

The law of remedies also considers various defenses, limitations and adjustments to claims. Fundamental issues of fairness between the parties affect all aspects of remedies law.

The interests of third parties, the public, and the courts are also relevant. Similarly, the practicality of framing, enforcing and supervising an injunction influences a court in deciding whether to issue the order and how to most effectively write it.

There are four basic types or classifications of remedies: (1) coercive remedies, (2) damages, (3) restitution, and (4) declaratory relief. The processes and principles by which the most effective remedies are selected, and the relationship of alternative remedies to each other, are the central themes of this book. Remedies are defined and limited by the source of the right, whether by statute, common law, or Constitution. (Chapter 2)

(A) COERCIVE REMEDIES

Coercive remedies include injunctions (Chapter 3) and specific performance (Chapter 4). They are available only from a court of equity, where a judge determines whether the plaintiff is entitled to the "extraordinary relief" of an order commanding the defendant to do or refrain from doing specific acts. These remedies, like all equitable ones, are subject to the equitable defenses, including unclean hands, laches, estoppel, election of remedies, and unconscionability. (Chapter 5)

Upon a compelling showing by the plaintiff, the court may issue a coercive order even before full trial on the merits. A preliminary injunction gives the plaintiff temporary relief pending trial on the merits. A temporary restraining order affords immediate relief pending the hearing on the preliminary injunction. Both of these types of interlocutory relief are designed to preserve the *status quo* to prevent irreparable harm before a court can decide the substantive merits of the dispute. Such orders are available only upon a strong showing of the necessity for such relief and may be conditioned upon the claimant posting a bond or sufficient security to protect the interests of the defendant in the event that the injunction is later determined to have been wrongfully issued. (Chapter 6)

Injunctions and specific performance remedies are called "coercive" because they are backed by the contempt power of the court. A court can coerce disobedient defendants with a civil contempt order, such as one designed to compel a party in an ongoing lawsuit to furnish discovery documents. The sanctioned party can purge themselves of that order by compliance with the underlying order. A court may impose incarceration and fines, and award damages to compensate the plaintiff for losses incurred by the willful disobedience of the order. Further, a court may summarily impose criminal contempt to protect the orderly administration of the judicial proceedings, provided certain procedural safeguards are followed. (Chapter 7) Injunctive decrees are also characterized as "extraordinary" remedies because courts hesitate to issue an equitable order that binds a party *in personam* knowing that disobedience of the order could lead to a contempt sanction. As a consequence, courts developed a type of hierarchy whereby legal remedies are preferred over equitable orders unless the remedy at law is deemed "inadequate" to address the claim asserted.

Courts traditionally categorized injunctions as preventive, but in the latter part of the twentieth century courts of equity in the United States adapted to modern needs with the development of other types of injunctions: structural, restorative and prophylactic injunctions. A structural injunction, such as a school desegregation order or prison reform order, derives its name from the involvement of the courts in the institutional policies and practices of the defendant entities. A restorative injunction operates to correct the present by undoing the effects of a past wrong, such as by a reinstatement order when an employer fired an employee for reasons that violate public policy. It focuses not only prospectively, as does the traditional preventive injunction, but retroactively. A prophylactic injunction seeks to safeguard the plaintiff's rights by ordering behavior not otherwise required by law so as to minimize the chance that wrongs might occur in the future. (Chapter 8)

Cases involving prior restraints of speech, abatement of nuisances orders, and injunctions against crimes create special problems with fashioning injunctive relief. Common law limitations, constitutional constraints, and legislative enactments affect the process of judicial discretion in these areas and others. (Chapter 9)

(B) DAMAGES

The damages remedy compensates plaintiffs for losses sustained in violation of their personal, property, or contractual rights. Once a plaintiff establishes both the claim in substantive law and the entitlement to a particular type of damages, the problem of measurement remains. For example, what is the proper measure of damages if a contractor fails to follow specifications in building a house? If the parties attempted to set damages in advance through the contract, will a court enforce the provision? The law of contract damages governs both questions. (Chapter 10)

Considerations of entitlement and measurement apply also in tort cases. What if a beautiful old tree in front of a house is destroyed by negligence? Is the owner entitled to damages even if the tree did not have any value separate from the land? Is the appropriate measure of damages only any diminution in fair market value of the land, or can damages include the cost of replacement, the loss of enjoyment by the owners, or some other measure? In calculating compensatory damages, tort law takes into account a number of policy factors, with the overarching goal of making the injured party whole by restoring them financially to their pre-tort position. Additionally, damages serve to deter anti-social behavior, protect valuable resources, shift costs to the responsible actor and avoid economic waste. Chapter 11 examines these concepts.

Once the appropriate measure of damages is ascertained, certain adjustments may be made to the award. Courts account for the use and changing value of money by awarding interest and by reducing awards of future losses to present value. (Chapter 12) Common law also imposes limitations on damages awards. Awards cannot be too remote, speculative, or uncertain. Other forms of limitation come from rules such as the collateral source rule and the doctrine of mitigation or avoidable consequences. Thus, for example, historically, an injured party in a car accident could sue the tortfeasor for medical costs even if insurance paid for those costs. The common law applied this "collateral source" rule regardless of whether the insurance policy provides for subrogation. This rule has been a frequent subject of change by tort reform. Another rule that limits recovery, the avoidable consequences rule, excludes damages that the plaintiff could have reasonably avoided, such as exacerbation of injury by failing to seek medical attention in a timely manner. (Chapter 13)

Another limitation exists on the types of losses a plaintiff can claim because not all losses are compensable. The law imposes restrictions on the recovery of mental distress damages and on recovery of purely economic losses. (Chapter 14)

All the topics already noted relate to the primary goal of damages: fair compensation of loss. The only exception for this goal occurs in punitive damages, or exemplary damages. They function to punish and deter wrongdoers in cases involving particularly egregious or malicious conduct. Because these damages play a different societal role under the guise of civil damages, there are constitutional due process constraints on the ability of states to award them. (Chapter 15)

(C) RESTITUTION

Restitutionary awards prioritize a different goal than compensatory damages. The role of restitution at law and in equity is to restore property to its rightful owner or to disgorge from a defendant any unjust enrichment occasioned by the wrong to the plaintiff. (Chapter 16) The substantive basis which may justify restitution is not limited to wrongdoing, however, but may include restoration of benefits received by another as a result of mistake.

In contrast with compensatory damages that serve to make a plaintiff whole after a tort or grant expectancy in contract, the measurement of restitution is the defendant's gains rather than the plaintiff's losses. For example, an embezzler who purchases appreciating collectibles with the misappropriated money is not allowed to keep any profit from the investment. A plaintiff may receive the property itself by imposition of a constructive trust if the embezzler still holds the property. If it has been sold and money profits can be traced, the plaintiff can recover the profits. Because the law of restitution prevents the intentional wrongdoer from profiting from the wrong, the plaintiff thus may receive more than was lost in the original embezzlement.

Certain limitations apply. For example, there is no disgorgement when the defendant is a bona fide purchaser for value. Likewise, no disgorgement is permitted when the plaintiff acted as an officious intermeddler. (Chapter 17)

(D) ATTORNEYS' FEES AND JURY TRIALS

Two other notable remedies issues affect litigants: the right to a jury and the availability of attorneys' fees. These two topics can dictate important aspects of resolving cases.

The Seventh Amendment governs the right to a jury trial in federal court. This constitutional amendment guarantees the right to a jury trial in actions at law where the amount in controversy exceeds twenty dollars. The phrase "at law" refers to courts sitting at law rather than in equity. Thus, litigants enjoy a right to a jury trial in federal legal cases but not equitable ones. Although the Seventh Amendment does not apply to the states, many state constitutions contain similar provisions. Thus, the states generally follow that same distinction. Differences between federal and state law occur in some areas such as cases where there are mixed claims of law and equity. (Chapter 18)

Attorneys' fees, when available, are awarded as "costs" of the suit. The Supreme Court has noted that they are a type of remedy, at least in public interest cases, which gives the plaintiff an additional tool for asserting rights. Evans v. Jeff D., 475 U.S. 717 (1986). As a general rule, however, attorneys' fees are not recoverable in most claims. The "American Rule" on attorneys' fees is that parties must bear their own costs of litigation. There are a few common law exceptions to this rule, and several important statutory ones. The major areas of statutory change providing fee-shifting to the prevailing party are evidenced in the areas predominantly implicating public interest values, such as in environmental protection and civil rights.

(E) DECLARATORY REMEDIES

The purpose of a declaratory remedy is to obtain a declaration of the rights or legal relations between the parties. This remedy is often used to determine the constitutionality of a statute or to construe a private instrument so that the interested parties may obtain a resolution of the dispute at an early stage. Federal and state statutes provide that declaratory relief is to be liberally administered, but the parties must demonstrate a justiciable controversy rather than one of a hypothetical or advisory nature.

Nominal damages also serve to declare the relative rights of the parties. Courts award nominal damages when a plaintiff establishes a substantive claim but cannot establish damages. Nominal damages are important because they can provide a basis for attorneys' fees and punitive damages. Like declaratory judgments, their primary function is to signify rights, such as the right to control property, even in the absence of a substantial remedy. (Chapter 20)

CHAPTER 2
THE SIGNIFICANCE
OF REMEDIAL
CHARACTERIZATIONS

The relationship between "rights" and "remedies" is critical to understanding the availability and efficacy of various types of judicial relief. The study of remedies begins with the assumption that the plaintiff established a substantive right. That right may be (1) based upon a statute, (2) derived from the common law, or (3) permitted directly from the Constitution. The court need not decide the question of remedy if the plaintiff does not demonstrate the existence and infringement of a right under one of those sources of law. Beyond that truism, even after the plaintiff prevails with a substantive right, it does not automatically follow that a desired remedy is available for the violation of that particular right. Not every right supports all possible remedies. Just as rights must have a source in the law, remedies also must derive from common law or statute.

Assuming that one or more remedies is available, a plaintiff must then establish the requirements for the particular remedy. In some instances, a plaintiff may have multiple remedies available for the same operative core of facts. The question then becomes which remedy most effectively addresses the particular harm presented. For example, if a defendant fraudulently induces a contract for the sale of land, the buyer plaintiff may wish to keep the land and receive damages or may wish to rescind the transaction. If damages are desired, there are two ways to measure compensatory damages. Under the out-of-pocket measure of loss, the plaintiff receives the difference between the contract price and the fair market value of the land. Under the benefit of the bargain approach, the plaintiff receives the difference between the contract price and the value of land if it were as represented, which usually results in a higher dollar recovery. If the facts support punitive damages, that award would be in addition to the compensatory damages. If rescission is the remedy, then the parties must make restitution of benefits exchanged. The availability of each of these remedial possibilities turns first on whether the plaintiff prevails with a tort claim or a contract claim or both and then on whether the plaintiff can establish the requirements for each remedy. The difference in the source of rights not only affects these remedies but also affects other practical matters, including the statute of limitations, the availability of attorneys' fees, and the right to a jury trial.

Future chapters examine remedial requirements and evaluate remedial choices. This chapter examines the significance of whether a remedy is legal or equitable in nature, and then how the source of a right may impose a limitation on the remedy.

(A) REMEDIES AT LAW AND IN EQUITY

The term "to do equity" in everyday speech implies that a decision-maker has reached a fair and impartial result in a conflict. An "equitable result" usually means a resolution that does not come from established principles but simply derives from common sense and socially acceptable notions of fair play. In the judicial system this popular concept of equity is not the essence of equitable decision-making. Instead, "equity" refers to a system of jurisprudence distinguishable from the system "at law." Each have their own specific characteristics and attributes, even following the merger of law and equity in modern law. Although the judge sitting in equity retains discretion to allow a particular remedy, that process is guided by principles established by *stare decisis*.

The origin of equity as a separate system of law began in fourteenth century England. The King's common law courts were incapable of doing justice in some circumstances because of the procedures and writs. Not all litigants could conform their cases to the rigidity of the pleading requirements. Alternative relief was sought from the King's Chancellor, who possessed a greater freedom to do justice. For example, a suitor could seek relief from the King, through his Chancellor, for fraud. Because the common law did not recognize fraud as a defense to a contract under seal, the contract would be enforceable but for the Chancellor's intervention. With the increase in such claims, equity became a separate court system that afforded relief to petitioners who had no adequate remedy at law because of a harsh application of legal doctrine.

The King's Chancellor did not provide remedies in the same manner as the courts of the King's Bench.

As a religious figure, the Chancellor operated on the conscience of the defendant. Thus, equity had jurisdiction over the person of the defendant rather than his property and could jail disobedient defendants. In modern law, equity similarly enforces its orders through the contempt power.

The Seventh Amendment of the Constitution provides a right to trial by jury for causes "at law." No similar right to trial by jury exists for actions in equity. In the federal system, this constitutional right has been interpreted to mean that causes of action seeking legal remedies as opposed to equitable ones must be afforded trial by jury. An action seeking only equitable remedies may be tried by the judge without a jury, although an advisory jury can be impaneled.

The cases entertained by Chancery historically fell into two main categories: (1) those where the suitor had some remedy at law, but not an adequate one, and (2) those where a remedy at law was unavailable because the cause of action was not one recognized at law. In modern law, the first category is reflected in cases where the suitor seeks an equitable remedy such as an injunction or specific performance on the grounds that the damages remedy at law is inadequate. "Inadequacy" has a special meaning in the law of equity because it is a shorthand expression for the policy that equitable remedies are subordinate to legal ones. They are subordinate in the sense that the damage remedy is preferred in any individual case if it is adequate. Although scholars have attacked this rule as outdated, the usual policy reasons for it are judicial efficiency and fairness. The efficiency argument notes that equitable remedies generally require more judicial supervision and the fairness argument is based on the fact that equity acts *in personam* on the defendant and punishes disobedience with contempt.

The second category of cases before the Chancellor in old England included those where the King's Courts would not recognize the action. In modern law, this category is called "substantive equity." The most notable examples of this category include equitable trusts and liens, as well as stockholders' derivative actions. There is a split among jurisdictions concerning the availability of a jury trial in cases involving substantive equity if the remedies sought are otherwise legal ones. The Supreme Court held in *Ross v. Bernhard,* 396 U.S. 531 (1970) that in federal courts, the nature of the remedy controls the right to a jury trial rather than the historical accident of a claim being one of substantive equity. Most states have elected not to follow the federal approach and retain the old rule that claims in substantive equity do not support a right to a jury trial.

Historically, some petitioners came to equity for protection from the legal enforcement of contracts. Concepts such as promissory estoppel and unconscionability originated in equity. Today those historically equitable doctrines have been incorporated into legal jurisprudence as well. Despite the diminished importance of recognizing the substantive contributions of equity, the concept of equitable remedies distinct from legal ones remains important. Equitable remedies include flexible coercive orders such as injunctions and specific performance orders. Some restitutionary remedies are equitable, such as constructive trusts or rescission and restitution in contract. The hallmark of equity is discretion. Courts retain considerable discretion both with respect to determining if an equitable order should be issued and also how it should be fashioned.

The most prevalent legal remedy is damages. Some restitutionary remedies are also legal, such as quasi-contract. In a merged system of law and equity, a plaintiff may seek both legal and equitable remedies in the same claim. The importance of the distinction between legal and equitable remedies, however, lies with the availability of a jury trial. The Supreme Court held in *Dairy Queen, Inc. v. Wood*, 369 U.S. 469 (1962), that if a plaintiff presents a mixed claim of law and equity, the legal issues must be tried first by the jury and any remaining equitable issues may be tried by the judge in a manner not inconsistent with the jury verdict. Both plaintiffs and defendants possess jury trial rights, which they may waive.

In state court systems the right to trial by jury is often different. The Seventh Amendment has not been held to apply to the states. Some states have constitutional provisions of their own affecting the right, but others rely entirely upon historical precedent. Cases in which the plaintiff seeks only legal remedies usually entitle the parties to trial by jury; cases seeking only equitable remedies do not. In a merged state court system, a mixed claim of legal and equitable remedies may not entitle the parties to a jury trial if the primary character of the case is equitable. The doctrine of "equitable clean-up" may control whereby the judge as trier of fact in equity may decide also any incidental damages issues.

(B) LIMITATIONS ON REMEDIES

Once the plaintiff establishes a substantive right, the available remedy will rest on the same source. That source may impose limitations on the remedy itself. Consider the provision governing unconscionable contracts in the Uniform Commercial Code. Section 2–302 provides:

If the court as a matter of law finds the contract or any clause of the contract to have been unconscionable at the time it was made the court may refuse to enforce the contract, or it may enforce the remainder of the contract without the unconscionable clause, or it may so limit the application of any unconscionable clause to avoid any unconscionable result.

The remedy here is a limited one. The court may refuse enforcement of all or part of an unconscionable contract but it may not grant compensatory or punitive damages that may otherwise be justified. In *Cowin Equipment Co. v. General Motors Corp.*, 734 F.2d 1581 (11th Cir. 1984) the plaintiff, a car dealer, tried to sue the manufacturer for losses occasioned by its refusal to let the dealer return cars that the dealer couldn't sell during a recession. The dealer alleged that the no-return clause was unconscionable and that as a result of the manufacturer's enforcement of that clause the dealer suffered losses when it had to sell the cars below cost. The court held that regardless of any unconscionability in the provision, the remedy sought was not permissible under the statute. Damages were not available even if they flowed directly from the claim.

An action at common law typically permits the plaintiff to recover any type of common law remedy. Courts consider remedial efficacy in whether to permit a new cause of action at common law. If a meaningful remedy cannot be afforded in the usual case, then the jurisdiction may consider that problem as a reason to deny expansion of common law duties. Many states include this reason as a justification for denying claims for educational malpractice, for example.

Similarly, claims brought directly under the federal Constitution support all common law remedies. For several policy reasons including the expansiveness of the remedies, courts do not permit such claims when there are other avenues of redress.

The relationship between rights and remedies is circular in the sense that a right is only as great as its remedy and remedies are limited by the rights they protect. Thus, for example, when the legislature creates a new statutory right and defines a remedy such as $500 per violation, then a wrongdoer may repeatedly violate if he or she is willing to pay the limited amount of damages. Unless the court is willing to expand the remedies beyond the statutory scheme and allow for an injunction, the remedial limitation diminishes the right.

Most courts are unwilling to assume that a legislature intended for courts to expand upon a specific statutory provision, such as the $500 remedy in the previous example. One case which famously did so is *Orloff v. Los Angeles Turf Club*, 180 P.2d 321 (Cal. 1947). In that case a California statute prohibited racial discrimination in certain public places and provided simply for a damage remedy. This statute predated Congressional action in the Civil Rights Act of 1964 which ended racial segregation in public places as a matter of federal law. The California case arose almost twenty years before and court was asked to permit an injunction against a race track that wanted to discriminate on the basis of race in admission. The California Supreme Court looked beyond the literal wording of the remedial provision in order to give effect to the apparent purpose of the legislature as reflected in the objects of the Civil Code. By issuing an injunction that bound the defendant *in personam*, the court could ensure compliance with the law. An award of damages would not necessarily affect future behavior because a liable party could theoretically continue to violate rights and simply pay compensation for the resulting harm. In contrast, disobedience of the equitable order could trigger sanctions through the contempt power of the court. This case illustrates the general principle that a right without a meaningful remedy is a "paper tiger" which cannot vindicate a violation.

Procedure also limits and defines remedies. A remedy is more effective in some situations if a class action is permissible to provide redress widely.

Congress famously limited remedies through a denial of jurisdiction to federal courts in matters of labor disputes. The Norris-LaGuardia Act prohibits federal courts from issuing injunctions in such cases. The Supreme Court explained in *Boys Markets, Inc. v. Retail Clerks Union, Local 770*, 398 U.S. 235 (1970):

> The Norris-LaGuardia Act was responsive to a situation totally different from that which exists today. In the early part of this century, the federal courts generally were regarded as allies of management in its attempt to prevent the organization and strengthening of labor unions; and in this industrial struggle the injunction became a potent weapon that was wielded against the activities of labor groups. * * * Congress, therefore, determined initially to limit severely the power of the federal courts to issue injunctions 'in any case involving or growing out of any labor dispute * * *.

Courts have had to interpret this limitation on federal jurisdiction in light of other federal statutes that grant jurisdiction over related matters. The general principle, however, is that the legislature may limit the discretion of courts through statute.

Finally, remedies are limited by the prohibition on double recoveries. Generally, injured parties may only recover one remedy for each distinct loss. This does not mean that a plaintiff is limited to recovering only a single type of remedy in a case or on a single claim. Instead, all relief awarded to the plaintiff must be complementary rather than duplicative. For example, in a private nuisance action, a plaintiff may be awarded both damages and an injunction. The injunction will issue to protect against future harm from the nuisance. Thus, any damages awarded must be to compensate the plaintiff only for those losses which have already occurred and cannot be to compensate the plaintiff for future losses. Likewise, in a personal injury action, if the injured party recovers for damages such as lost future wages, the injured party's spouse or child cannot recover damages for loss of economic support if the injured party would have provided the economic support from the lost future wages. Some exceptions to this rule exist. Most notably, the collateral source rule allows an injured party to recover damages from a wrongdoer even if the injured party has received compensation from a third party such as an insurance carrier.

CHAPTER 3
PREVENTIVE INJUNCTIONS

(A) OVERVIEW OF PREVENTIVE INJUNCTIONS

The term "equity jurisdiction" refers to the appropriate exercise of a court's discretion in granting equitable relief. The use of the word "jurisdiction" by modern courts is confusing because it does not refer to the power of the court in the way that subject matter jurisdiction and personal jurisdiction concern the court's authority. Although there was an historical justification for the use of the term "jurisdiction" by the Chancery, the term "equity jurisdiction" today refers to the propriety of equitable relief as a matter of remedial equity. Thus, if a court incorrectly concludes that equitable relief should be granted, it is merely an erroneous order that must be appealed and not a void order from a court lacking jurisdiction.

The classic form of injunction in private litigation is the preventive injunction. By definition, a preventive injunction is a court order designed to avoid future harm to a party by prohibiting or mandating certain behavior by another party. The injunction is "preventive" in the sense of avoiding harm. The injunction most commonly is framed in prohibitory terms ("Do not trespass") but also may be mandatory ("Remove the obstruction"). Because mandatory orders are considered harsher and more intrusive, they are generally less favored by courts.

This chapter covers the traditional requirements for a preventive injunction. Recall that the plaintiff must establish the substantive claim as a precondition for asserting any remedy. For purposes of equitable relief, the right can stem from statute, common law, or constitutional sources. Modern equity will act to protect both personal as well as property interests, although historically equity required plaintiffs to demonstrate a property interest.

The traditional test for issuance of a preventive injunction requires a plaintiff to demonstrate: (1) that she has suffered an irreparable injury; (2) that remedies available at law are inadequate; (3) that, considering the balance of hardships between the plaintiff and the defendant, a remedy in equity is warranted; and (4) that the public interest would not be disserved by a permanent injunction. *See* eBay Inc. v. MercExchange, 547 U.S. 388 (2006). Injunctions are often characterized as "extraordinary" in the sense that equitable remedies are disfavored and subordinated to law. The rationale for that hierarchy of remedial preference is judicial efficiency because injunctions bind parties *in personam* and are backed by the contempt power of the court. Thus, courts exercise discretion in determining the propriety of issuing injunctions based upon a determination that legal remedies, even if available, are inadequate to protect fully the rights asserted and the claimant has demonstrated a sufficient showing of projected hardship if an injunction is not granted.

(B) INADEQUACY OF THE REMEDIES AT LAW

1. INADEQUACY OF REMEDIES AT LAW—GENERALLY

The first element of equity jurisdiction requires an inadequacy of the remedy at law. History explains the rule better than logic, but the rule still has force to restrict the availability of equitable remedies. The inadequacy rule was originally applied by the Chancellor in the sixteenth century to determine whether to take a case or to leave the petitioner to go to the law courts with a writ for relief. *See* W. Blackstone, *Commentaries* 46–55; F. Maitland, *Equity* 7 (1930). In modern law, courts frequently invoke the rule as a shorthand explanation for granting or denying equitable relief.

That requirement is met if damages would be too speculative or if multiple damage actions would be necessary because of the nature of the invasion of the plaintiff's rights. Thus, in one well-known case, *Wheelock v. Noonan*, 108 N.Y. 179 (1888), an injunction was granted to require the defendant to remove great boulders which he had left on the plaintiff's property beyond the term of the license to do so. The plaintiff could not easily remove the boulders and sue for the cost of removal of the trespassing rocks because of their size and weight and the unavailability of an alternate location in which to store the boulders. Likewise, the court recognized that the plaintiff could maintain an action in trespass but would only be able to recover damages for the trespass to the date of trial. The plaintiff would be required to maintain successive actions to recover damages until the defendant removed the boulders. Thus, although damages were available, the court deemed them "inadequate" and issued an injunction requiring the defendant to undertake removal of the rocks.

An illustration of the inadequacy prong for injunctive relief involved claims by the United States and certain Indian Tribes in the Pacific Northwest that the State of Washington violated fishing rights possessed by the Tribes in a series of treaties, known as the Stevens Treaties, which dated back to 1854– 1855. U.S. v. State of Washington, 853 F.3d 946 (9th Cir. 2017). The claimants contended that the State's construction and maintenance of extensive barrier culverts blocked rivers and streams and impeded salmon from returning from the ocean to their spawning grounds, which consequently detrimentally affected the Tribes' fishing rights under the Treaties.

The federal district court found that an extensive reparative equitable order was appropriate because the injury to fishing rights was ongoing and prior State efforts to correct the barriers had been insufficient. Thus, the Tribes lacked an adequate remedy at law as monetary damages would not fully and effectively compensate the Tribes and their individual members for the harms. The Tribes relied upon salmon as a dietary component for subsistence, used the fish in religious and cultural ceremonies, and also harvested salmon commercially.

The Ninth Circuit Court of Appeals affirmed the district court's issuance of a permanent injunction which mandated that the State of Washington correct the obstructing culverts over a 17-year period as an appropriate remedy to correct the State's violation of the Treaties. Further, the court observed that public interest would be served by improving fishing for the Tribes. Also, the restorative injunction would benefit the public by protecting resources, increasing economic returns, and enhancing environmental benefits of salmon habitat restoration.

In other circumstances, courts generally find the remedy at law to be adequate if the harm can be easily and accurately ascertained in a single action. This is most common when the plaintiff has suffered the entire injury by the time of trial and the condition giving rise to the harm has abated. Thus, in *Thurston Enterprises, Inc. v. Baldi*, 519 A.2d 297 (N.H. 1986), the court reversed an order granting an injunction where the defendant's trespass had caused injury to the plaintiff's land. By the time of trial, the damage to the plaintiff's land had been sustained and the conditions necessitating the defendant's entry onto the plaintiff's land had ceased. Thus, the court concluded that the plaintiff's remedy at law was adequate.

In one class of cases, the inadequacy rule does not apply. Claims invoking substantive equity, as opposed to remedial equity, may be brought without regard to the adequacy of the remedy at law. Substantive equity allows a cause of action in equity for certain types of interests like trusts, mortgages, bankruptcy, and stockholders' derivative actions. Historically these interests were recognized only in Chancery, as described in Chapter 2, *supra*, so there was no further consideration of the adequacy of the remedy at law. In contrast, remedial equity refers to cases where the subject matter of the claim lies in law, such as for tort or breach of contract, but the remedy sought is available only in equity.

2. INADEQUACY OF REMEDIES AT LAW IN TRESPASS CASES

When a trespass has abated by the time the plaintiff landowner brings suit, the property owner could sue for damages measured by the rental value of the land. Difficulty arises when the trespass is continuing at the time the landowner brings suit or when the potential for repeated invasions exists. Damages are inadequate to prevent future invasions such as these. If the defendant were permitted to pay damages in order to continue to use the plaintiff's land, the defendant would become the forced tenant of an unwilling landlord. Further, the plaintiff landowner would be required to bring multiple lawsuits to seek compensation for each successive future trespass. Thus, the remedy at law is inadequate to remedy future invasions.

That being said, equity will not act to prohibit future harm that is considered remote or speculative. Courts do not issue "be good" orders but instead require proof of immediate and probable harm. This limitation avoids wasting judicial resources, but it

CH. 3   *PREVENTIVE INJUNCTIONS*

also protects the defendant. Because equitable orders are backed by the contempt power, an individual who commits a wrong such as trespass, faces a greater potential penalty from violating a prohibitory injunction than the usual criminal and civil sanctions for the wrong. As such, an injunction must be based on the court's prediction that the alleged threatened harm is imminently likely to occur. The plaintiff must provide sufficient probative evidence to demonstrate to the court's satisfaction that the defendant is reasonably likely to continue or repeat the invasions.

A plaintiff may establish that future harm is likely in several ways. First, where a continuing trespass exists, the plaintiff may establish that the defendant has not honored a demand to vacate. Thus, for example, an injunction was appropriate under this rule when a patient would not vacate a hospital room because her husband refused repeated demands to transfer her to a nursing home. Whether the plaintiff has communicated a request to stop trespassing is also relevant to establish whether a repeated trespass is likely to occur because the defendant may not repeat the trespass once on notice of the plaintiff's objection.

A plaintiff, likewise, may demonstrate the likelihood of future invasions on the basis of past behavior or on other grounds. For example, if a defendant has engaged in a repeated pattern of behavior regularly, the likelihood of repeated trespass is shown from the pattern. Thus, in one case, the court found a likelihood of future invasions where the defendant had engaged in a pattern of parking on the plaintiff's property regularly. Such repeated violations also have been shown likely to recur in one case where a neighbor's construction project kept knocking into the neighbor's hedge and in another where a duck hunter made annual trespasses on neighboring land. This can be particularly useful where the plaintiff faces the possibility of *repeated* trespasses.

3.   INADEQUACY OF REMEDIES AT LAW TO PROTECT CONSTITUTIONAL RIGHTS

Other special circumstances may warrant extraordinary relief as well on the grounds that law cannot provide an adequate remedy because of the nature of the right involved. Constitutional claims, such as for school desegregation, involve rights that require equitable intervention. The Supreme Court discussed the necessity of flexible equitable powers in its second opinion in *Brown v. Board of Education of Topeka, Kansas*, 349 U.S. 294 (1955) addressing remedial issues for the correction of the violation of equal protection where public schools were intentionally segregated on the basis of race. Similarly, equity intervenes to correct unconstitutional situations such as prison systems that violate the Eighth Amendment guarantee against cruel and unusual punishment. *See* Hutto v. Finney, 437 U.S. 678 (1978). The Supreme Court recently reaffirmed the courts' responsibility to remedy unconstitutional prison conditions, including through orders limiting the size of prison populations. *See* Brown v. Plata, 563 U.S. 493 (2011).

4.   INADEQUACY OF REMEDIES AT LAW IN INTELLECTUAL PROPERTY CASES

Traditionally, courts recognized the inadequacy of remedies at law to protect intangible business interests such as patent rights and copyrights. Because these rights included a right to exclude others from using the intangible property, courts found money damages inadequate to remedy infringement. Money damages without an injunction potentially permitted a defendant who was willing to pay damages to continue to infringe on the plaintiff's intellectual property rights. This, in turn, weakened the value of the property to the injured owner. Indeed, the U.S. Court of Appeals for the Federal Circuit, which holds exclusive jurisdiction to hear appeals in cases involving patents and trademarks, created a general rule that a permanent injunction should issue upon a finding that a patent was valid and had been infringed. *See* Odetics v. Storage Technology Corp., 185 F.3d 1259 (Fed. Cir. 1999).

In *eBay Inc. v. MercExchange*, 547 U.S. 388 (2006), the Supreme Court expressly rejected the Federal Circuit's presumption. The Court concluded that the decision to grant or deny an injunction rests within the sound discretion of the trial court and that the court was required to exercise its discretion in a manner consistent with traditional equitable principles. The Court held that those principles required a plaintiff to satisfy the same four-factor test that has always applied before a trial court could grant an injunction. In a concurring opinion, Justice Kennedy instructed lower courts to consider changes in the nature of the property interest being protected by the patent and the economic function of the patent holder. Specifically, he instructed courts to consider whether the patent holder intended to bring the patented invention to market itself or intended to license the patent rights to others; whether the patented invention was but a small component of the defendant's product and whether the patented invention was a traditional invention or a business method patent which he characterized as vague and of "suspect validity." Following the *eBay* decision, lower federal courts have still often recognized the province of equity as particularly well-suited to protect valuable intellectual property rights. SiOnyx LLC v. Hamamatsu Photonics, 981 F.3d 1339 (Fed. Cir. 2020).

(C) IRREPARABLE HARM

Most jurisdictions list irreparable harm as a second, separate requirement for coercive relief, but this element is often subsumed in the inadequacy rule. As a general matter, the remedy at law is inadequate precisely because the harm is irreparable and damages do not suffice.

The requirement of irreparable harm, however, does play a distinguishable role. Such harm must be great in nature and not trivial. Some courts define irreparable harm as a continuing injury that results in substantial prejudice. Equity routinely protects some interests, such as trespass to land, because of the inadequacy of the remedy at law. The irreparable harm requirement, however, prevents the court from exercising its extraordinary powers in equity if the harm involved is trivial. An irreparable harm also may be seen as qualitative in nature, such as involving invasion of privacy claims in tort.

The Court reaffirmed the importance of irreparable harm for purposes of issuance of preliminary injunctions in *Winter v. Natural Resources Defense Council, Inc.*, 555 U.S. 7 (2008). In *Winter*, the Court held that the movant must demonstrate that irreparable injury was likely, not merely possible, in order to support equitable relief.

Irreparable harm may be demonstrated in some circumstances even when the pattern of past invasions has been varied and unpredictable. An illustration is *Galella v. Onassis*, 353 F. Supp. 196 (S.D.N.Y. 1972), aff'd in part, rev'd in part, *Galella v. Onassis*, 487 F.2d 986 (2d Cir. 1973). In that case, the wife of the former president of the United States sought an injunction to restrain a professional free-lance photographer from violating her rights of privacy. The evidence showed that the photographer had repeatedly engaged in harassing behavior of the Onassis family in order to obtain pictures, but each time the invasive behavior was different. Based upon the pattern of past conduct, the court concluded that the photographer's behavior would continue indefinitely in the future. The evidence of future invasions was very strong because the photographer had even sent an advertisement to customers announcing future anticipated pictures of Onassis. Even though the pattern of behavior was varied in the types of invasive conduct, the overall nature of it was consistently harassing. With sufficient evidence, even an unpredictable pattern can establish the likelihood of future invasions.

(D) BALANCE OF HARDSHIPS
AND PUBLIC INTEREST

Injunctions are discretionary and not a matter of right. In the exercise of that discretion, a judge weighs the relative hardships to the parties and considers any problems of practicality in enforcing an order and the public interest. These factors, along with the determination of the inadequacy of the remedy at law and irreparable harm, form the "equities" of the case. On appeal, the trial judge's assessment of the equities can only be overturned upon a finding of abuse of discretion.

The factors of practicality and hardship can affect the case in two ways. First, they make up elements in the determination of the equities. No injunction will issue unless practical and unless the balance of hardships tips in favor of the plaintiff. The judge weighs the relative hardships—how much the plaintiff would benefit by the injunction against the burden to the defendant.

Second, the judge may consider practicality and hardship in determining the scope of the order. In a nuisance case, for example, the court may order limited abatement. Offensive animals may be reduced in number but not eliminated or excessive noise from a neighboring business operation may be restricted during certain hours. The court asks, then, not whether a hardship can be entirely avoided or eliminated but rather which party should bear the burden and why.

In some instances, courts have recognized competing public interests which must be weighed in the balance of equitable discretion. In the recent decision, *Roman Catholic Diocese of Brooklyn, New York v. Cuomo*, 141 S. Ct. 63 (2020), the Supreme Court considered a constitutional challenge to an Executive Order issued by the Governor of New York which placed certain restrictions on attendance at religious services in specified areas in response to the health issues presented by the COVID-19 pandemic. The Court upheld an injunction against the restrictions imposed by the Order, finding a strong countervailing public interest in the preservation of religious liberties. The Court found that the State of New York failed to show that public health would be endangered by less intrusive measures.

The defendant may often face economic burdens, but it need not be a dollar loss. Justice Cardozo explained in *Yome v. Gorman,* 24 N.Y. 395 (1926) that it is not possible to formulate a rule but only to "exemplify a process." In that case the plaintiff sought to move the remains of loved ones from one cemetery to another after a change in her religious affiliation. The judge could not quantify the interests in any objective way and was required to balance the sentiments as much as possible.

Another example of a noneconomic burden that a court must balance is a restraint on speech. The value of what is protected by the injunction must be balanced against the value of rights guaranteed by the First Amendment. The Supreme Court considered such an injunction against abortion protestors at a health clinic in *Madsen v. Women's Health Center, Inc.*, 512 U.S. 753 (1994). The Court held that an injunction restraining speech is permissible if the judge carefully balances the rights of the parties and narrowly tailors the injunction. The Constitution permits states to issue injunctions that protect a woman's freedom to seek lawful medical and counseling services, but such injunctions must also protect the protestors' right of speech. The injunction in that case established a 36-foot buffer zone around the clinic and surrounding private property. It also imposed limited noise restrictions and provided for a 300-foot no-approach zone. The Court held that the provisions establishing the buffer zone around the clinic and noise restrictions did not violate the First Amendment, but that the buffer zone on private property and the no-approach zone burdened more speech than necessary.

Public interest values may be evidenced by the status of the litigants and the nature of the rights asserted. In *Kansas v. Nebraska*, 574 U.S. 445 (2015) the State of Kansas sought disgorgement of gains and injunctive relief against the State of Nebraska for alleged violations of an interstate water Compact and accompanying Settlement agreement. A special master recommended an equitable remedy of partial disgorgement of Nebraska's excess gains for knowingly exceeding its proper allowable water consumption. The master rejected the claim for an injunction to force Nebraska to comply with the Compact and Settlement prospectively.

The Supreme Court approved the award of partial disgorgement based upon equitable principles but rejected Kansas's request for injunctive relief. Kansas had argued that an injunction was justified due to the pattern of past violations by Nebraska, and sought an equitable order to ensure future compliance, contending that it could seek contempt sanctions for any future breach. Justice Kagan, writing for the Court, reasoned that Kansas had failed to show a sufficiently "cognizable danger of recurrent violation" to support injunctive relief. 574 U.S. at 466.

The public interest also affects the decision whether to grant an injunction as well as the scope and nature of it. Relevant considerations include public health and safety as well as public economic interests. The public interest in the continued operation of a major employer was relevant in the famous case of *Boomer v. Atlantic Cement Co.*, 26 N.Y. 219 (1970). In this case landowners sued a neighboring cement plant for injury from its pollution. Under New York law, an injunction was the usual remedy for nuisance, but the problem lay with the potential injury to the larger community because of corresponding loss in jobs.

The court in *Boomer* declined to enjoin the multi-million dollar operation and instead conditioned an injunction on the failure of the defendant to pay the plaintiffs permanent damages. The practical effect of this approach was to allow only damages and no equitable relief. The dissenting opinion characterized the result as an inappropriate inverse condemnation because the permanent damages allowed the company a "servitude on the land" to continue its pollution. The taking of property for public purposes, the dissenting judge reasoned, is appropriate only when the public is primarily served in the taking or impairment of property and he saw no such public use or benefit in allowing a company to continue to pollute.

Boomer is a favorite topic of authors in the area of law and economics, who generally approve the result. In the absence of a court order specifying the amount that the company must pay the landowners, the parties could negotiate the amount that the landowners would take in exchange for the right of the company to pollute. Theoretically, if the pollution were very significant, the amount of money necessary to purchase the right to pollute would be so high that excessive polluters would be driven out of business by the market force.

The court in *Boomer* refused to grant an injunction that would have enjoined the operation of the nuisance unless the pollution were abated within eighteen months. The court noted that if there were no new technological advances in that time to allow the abatement within reasonable cost, the landowners would be in the position to extort an unreasonable settlement. If the company elected instead to close at the end of the eighteen months, the community would lose an important part of its economy.

Parties can demonstrate public interest by statute as well as under common law. In some situations, both parties can point to public interest factors that favor their position. For example, in *Boomer* the factory argued successfully that their operation serves the public interest by contributing jobs and taxes to the local economy. The competing public interest was the environmental pollution and widespread interference with neighboring landowners. This 1970 opinion slightly predated the era of federal legislative activism in environmental law. Numerous statutes now reflect the strong public interest in protecting the environment and human health from excessive risks of harm, such as through pollution or exposure to hazardous chemicals.

(E) NATIONWIDE OR UNIVERSAL INJUNCTIONS

The scope of an injunction is generally limited to the parties before the court. Thus, for example, the enjoined party is ordered to do or refrain from doing something to the party seeking the injunction. Occasionally, however, in cases involving widespread public interests such as immigration, environmental concerns, public health or land regulations, courts may issue injunctions that have widespread applicability beyond the parties seeking the injunction.

Thus, for example, in *Roe v. Department of Defense*, 947 F.3d 207 (4th Cir. 2020), several HIV-positive enlisted Air Force personnel challenged Air Force and defense department policies that, when applied together, required the categorical discharge of certain HIV-positive service members. The district court granted a preliminary injunction prohibiting the Air Force from applying the challenged policies to discharge not only the plaintiffs but also all similarly situated HIV-positive service members.

In affirming the scope of the preliminary injunction, the Fourth Circuit affirmed the authority of lower courts to extend injunctive relief to those who are similarly situated to the litigants in the case before it if necessary to "meet the exigencies of the particular case." The Fourth Circuit noted that, in balancing the equities, courts should focus "specifically on the concrete burdens that would fall on the parties and on the public consequences of an injunction." In this case, the Fourth Circuit noted that the categorical nature of the policies and the small number of affected service members supported the nationwide injunction.

This practice of issuing so-called "nationwide" or "universal" injunctions has come under increasing scrutiny recently, including from members of the Supreme Court. In *Department of Homeland Security v. New York*, 140 S. Ct. 599 (2020), the Supreme Court stayed enforcement of one such nationwide injunction, pending appeal. In their concurring opinion, Justices Gorsuch and Thomas raised several objections to nationwide injunctions. The Justices questioned whether nationwide injunctions exceeded the scope of judicial power under the "cases and controversies" clause of Article III. The Justices also noted the potential for conflicting orders if different plaintiffs sought injunctions in different courts. Finally, the Justices noted the unfairness of the asymmetrical nature of the situation. Specifically, if litigants filed claims in multiple courts challenging the same government policy, the government would have to be victorious in all actions in order to implement the challenged policy. In contrast, the plaintiffs need only prevail in any one action to block implementation of the challenged policy. If the plaintiffs obtained an injunction prohibiting enforcement of a challenged policy in any court, the government would be prohibited from enforcing the policy under that order even if it was victorious in every other court.

Other courts and commentators have raised additional concerns about nationwide or universal injunctions. Some of the objections include the following:

(1)   the injunctions may exceed the geographic boundaries of the issuing court;

(2)   litigation involving one or a small number of plaintiffs lacks the procedural safeguards available in class actions;

(3)   injunctions against sovereign entities may run afoul of sovereign immunity;

(4)   nationwide or universal injunctions are inconsistent with the nature of equity which demands narrowly tailored relief;

(5)   such orders invite forum shopping among federal courts;

(6)   nationwide injunctions contribute to the increased polarization of the courts and

undermine public confidence in the judiciary; and

(7) the injunctions prohibit the organic development of the law by limiting the opportunity for multiple lower courts to consider a given issue.

Conversely, advocates of universal injunctions contend that such orders are necessary to provide comprehensive relief to address the scope of the problem presented, particularly in matters involving significant public interest such as involving immigration laws. See East Bay Sanctuary Covenant v. Trump, 950 F.3d 1242 (9th Cir. 2020).

CHAPTER 4
SPECIFIC PERFORMANCE

Specific performance is an equitable discretionary remedy that is issued to enforce contractual rights and duties. The normative remedy for breach of contract is damages, so specific performance requires a showing that the claimant's rights and expectations pursuant to the agreement necessitates equitable intervention. The role of the court in ordering prospective performance is simply to carry out the original bargain intended by the parties. The remedy, like other types of injunctions, binds the party enjoined *in personam*. Therefore, disobedience of the equitable order may be punishable by contempt. Specific performance is available both at common law and, in a liberalized form, under the Uniform Commercial Code governing transactions involving the sale of goods. The equitable defenses, like laches and unclean hands, may preclude specific performance. If a court denies specific performance, the non-breaching party may still seek any available legal remedies.

Courts consider several basic requirements in deciding the propriety of specific performance: (1) the existence of a valid contract with definite and certain terms, (2) whether the claimant is able and ready to perform their own duties and has satisfied all conditions under the agreement, (3) whether the breaching party is able to render performance, (4) no adequate remedy at law exists, and (5) the balance of interests and relative hardships favors the claimant.

Additionally, the court of equity will take into account potential issues in fashioning, supervising or enforcing the order.

(A) REQUIREMENTS

1.   DEFINITE AND CERTAIN TERMS

The contract terms must be clear, definite, and certain for a court to issue a specific performance order. This requires a higher level of certainty and definiteness of terms than what the law requires to support a finding of contract formation and therefore damages at law. The elevated role of certainty aids the court in framing the decree and ensures that the party enjoined understands with appropriate clarity the nature of the obligations expected. The latter consideration is critical because disobedience of the order could subject the party to potential contempt sanctions. Therefore, if significant contract terms are vague or ambiguous and not capable of reasonable interpretation through resort to extrinsic evidence, the court will decline equitable relief. While courts cannot write contract terms for parties, in some cases a court may supply a minor missing detail of performance, such as time for delivery or total quantity in an output contract in order to authorize specific performance to carry out the parties' expectations. However, a specific performance order must maintain fidelity to the bargain entered into by the parties. In the recent decision, *Porter v. Williamson*, 2020 WL 3478540 (Ala. 2020), for example, the court reversed an award of specific performance of a shareholder repurchase agreement because the trial court had determined share valuation using an evaluation method which was inconsistent with the process set forth in the agreement.

2. ABILITY TO PERFORM

A court will only issue an order for specific performance upon a showing that it will serve a useful purpose and that both parties are ready, able, and willing to satisfactorily perform remaining contractual duties. Claimants, as a matter of fairness, must also show that they have completed all of their own duties under the contract. If a defendant is unable to comply with the order, such as where she already transferred the subject matter of the contract to a bona fide purchaser or substantially destroyed the property, then an equitable decree would be futile. *See* Restatement (Second) of Contracts § 357, cmt. c (1981) ("[A] court will not order a performance that is impossible.")

A court will try to approximate, as closely as possible, the balance of respective rights and duties embodied in the original contract. In certain cases, however, a party cannot deliver the exact performance bargained-for but the non-breaching party still seeks specific performance. An illustration of the problem is where a seller in a land sales contract does not possess complete title to the full acreage subject to the contract.

Several remedial options exist for the court in such situations, each of which will carry out the intentions of the parties. For a minor discrepancy that does not impair the contract substantially, the court may find that no breach occurred and still order specific performance with no adjustment in price. If the court finds a slight defect, it may decree specific performance with an abatement in the purchase price proportionate to the deficiency. Where the defect is considered substantial, either quantitatively or qualitatively, the court may award damages for the breach or order rescission and restitution. A specific performance order may be inappropriate if it requires a major rewriting of the contract.

3.   INADEQUATE REMEDY AT LAW

The most important factor affecting the decision of specific performance typically is whether an award of damages would constitute an adequate legal remedy. The preference for legal remedies over equitable orders exists for several reasons. First, since a specific performance order is essentially a specialized type of injunction, the doctrine of subordination of equitable remedies is followed. The law views equity as a harsher avenue of relief because it binds parties *in personam*. Second, equitable orders may require more extensive judicial resources of supervision and enforcement. Finally, the nature of contract bargaining itself reflects a strong sense that parties ordinarily expect either performance or payment as a substitution for lost performance. The theory of efficient breach of contract provides that it maximizes economic resources to allow a party to breach and pay damages for losses caused by the breach in order to move goods to a higher bidder. An equitable order commanding a breaching party to perform, then, must overcome the traditional contract view of seeing damages as the norm for breach.

A well-recognized instance in which courts will find an inadequate remedy at law for specific performance purposes occurs where the non-breaching party cannot reasonably obtain a substitute for the subject matter of the contract and has an objectively justifiable basis for expecting performance. The most common illustration of this principle is the historical view that every parcel of land is inherently unique; therefore, an aggrieved vendee may seek an equitable decree to force conveyance of the land from a breaching vendor. Some courts apply the same principle and use equity to allow a non-breaching vendor to force conveyance of a land sale to a breaching vendee. Another view declines equitable relief on the basis that the contract expectation of the seller was to receive payment for the realty, which can be accomplished through a substitutionary monetary award.

The inability to reasonably effect cover due to the uniqueness or scarcity of other non-fungible goods, such as heirlooms or works of art, may similarly satisfy the standard of an inadequate remedy at law. Further, such items may present problems in valuation and proving damages with reasonable certainty. Finally, an inadequate remedy at law may arise where the claimant faces difficulties in collecting the damages awarded, such as where the breaching party is insolvent. *See* Restatement (Second) of Contracts § 360 (1981).

The court will also look to the purposes and expectations of the parties in the bargain in deciding adequacy of legal remedies. For instance, if a buyer of certain property is a dealer and has a primary interest in reselling for a profit, a court may decide that the expectation interest is adequately satisfied with a money judgment. On the other hand, if the buyer of land planned to occupy and farm the tract of land, then the court may readily conclude that the property was unique and irreplaceable and order specific performance.

4.   BALANCE OF HARDSHIPS

The court, in the exercise of its discretion, will balance the equities and relative hardships of the parties in deciding entitlement to specific performance as well as the manner in which the order is framed. Whether the order is issued or denied, one party will presumably experience some degree of hardship. Thus, the court considers the relative degree of the burden on the parties and how equities affect which party should bear the hardship.

A variety of factors may be considered in the balancing calculus, including the likely extent of judicial supervision, the complexity of the obligations remaining to be performed, and potential difficulties with enforcement. Also, the court may consider whether the contract potentially implicates third party contracts or the public interest. Finally, the court may deny specific performance in situations involving mistake, grossly disproportionate consideration, duress, or other unreasonable hardship. Even if those factors may not rise to the level of independently avoiding the contract as a matter of substantive law, they influence the court's discretion in granting or shaping equitable relief.

In *Davis v. Harmony Development, LLC*, 460 P.3d 230 (Wyo. 2020), for example, the court upheld the trial court's award of specific performance to a vendor against a prospective purchaser of a lot in a subdivision. The court considered various factors, including the adequacy of consideration, the relative hardships and benefits to the parties, whether performance was impossible, and the adequacy of remedies at law, among others. In balancing the hardships, the court found that the vendor would be particularly harmed unless specific performance was ordered because they had made substantial improvements to the property and the purchaser was an anchor tenant for the subdivision. Conversely, the buyer—a sophisticated developer—would not experience an undue hardship because they would simply receive the property they bargained for.

Although substantive contract law does not inquire into the adequacy of consideration for purposes of contract formation, a significant disparity in consideration exchanged can affect equitable relief. The court may not invalidate the contract as unconscionable yet may determine that damages would adequately compensate for a breach rather than impose equitable relief to enforce a hard bargain. The evaluation of the reasonableness of the consideration exchanged is made at the time of contracting rather than based upon subsequent events.

Similarly, a unilateral mistake of fact made by one contracting party may influence a court to decline equitable relief if the effect of the order would heavily burden the mistaken party. Although the mistake may not be sufficient to prevent formation of the contract, it may affect equitable discretion. The sympathy of a court with respect to consideration of a mistake is heightened where it was induced by misrepresentations or unfair practices by the other contracting party. *See* Restatement (Second) Contracts § 364(1)(a) (1981).

Finally, a court will consider potential problems associated with supervising a complex equitable decree. If the court would incur a significant burden of time and resources or if the nature of the subject matter affected by the decree calls for technical expertise, a court may decide that damages are a more appropriate remedy. *See* Restatement (Second) of Contracts § 366 (1981).

(B) MUTUALITY OF REMEDY

Historically, a lack of mutuality of remedy sometimes impeded the availability of specific performance. The rule held that specific performance would only be available to one party if it was equally available to the other contracting party. The mutuality of remedy argument rests on a pure fiction in that it asks a theoretical question of the availability of a remedy if the other party had breached. Although the symmetry and apparent fairness of the doctrine reflected equity's traditions of justice, the rule worked unsatisfactorily in certain instances. Additionally, the doctrine fails to consider that parties bargain for different things.

For example, if parties contracted to convey land in exchange for services rather than money, the mutuality rule could potentially foreclose specific performance in the event of a breach. An illustration of the application of the mutuality doctrine is shown in *Henderson v. Fisher,* 236 Cal. App. 2d 468 (1965). In that case, an 86-year old man named Baker contracted to convey a deed to his home in exchange for receiving care and support from the plaintiffs during his lifetime. At the time of making the contract Baker was in reasonably good health. The plaintiffs moved into the home and provided the personal services contemplated by the agreement, but Baker died just 18 days later. The trial court denied the plaintiff's claim for specific performance of the realty, partially on the basis that the contract lacked mutuality, but granted a small sum under quantum meruit. The trial court reasoned that since constitutional restraints against involuntary servitude would prevent the seller from hypothetically obtaining an equitable decree to demand performance of personal services, then the remedy was also unavailable to force conveyance of the land. The appellate court reversed, finding that the mutuality rule did not apply when the contract was fully performed.

The case reflects a growing dissatisfaction by courts with the potential for hardship or inequity resulting from strict adherence to the rule. Courts have recognized various exceptions to the rule or simply rejected it completely. As illustrated in *Henderson v. Fisher*, the mutuality rule did not apply when the contract was fully executed. Other exceptions appear where the party seeking specific performance substantially performed or the court was assured of continued performance in the future. Also, some courts limited the rule to the time equitable relief was sought rather than when the contract was formed. Several states have enacted statutes which codified the developing common law limitations on the mutuality rule. A companion doctrine that historically affected contract formation, mutuality of obligation, was also expressly rejected by Restatement (Second) Contracts § 79(c) (1981).

The modern view treats mutuality of remedies as just one factor in deciding the propriety of specific performance. Courts may consider mutuality to ensure that both sides will fully perform if an equitable order is given. *See* Restatement (Second) Contracts § 363, cmt. c (1981). In that sense, the doctrine provides security to the party in breach that they will not be compelled to perform without adequate assurance of receiving return performance from the non-breaching party. In summary, because parties typically have different expectations in the bargain, courts no longer require that the remedies potentially available to them must correspond or mirror each other.

(C) PERSONAL SERVICES

The traditional rule in equity is that courts will not order specific performance of contracts for personal services, such as contracts with professional athletes or artistic performers. Several policy considerations support this judicial approach: (1) an adequate remedy at law exists unless the services are unique, (2) such orders are difficult to supervise and enforce, and (3) and the constitutional prohibition of involuntary servitude. Fashioning an order with sufficient specificity is essential since the decree would be enforceable with contempt. Moreover, courts are disinclined to force someone to work in a hostile environment. Similarly, employers are rarely required to accept personal services tendered under a contract unless subject to a statutory requirement, such as in fair employment acts or a collective bargaining agreement.

Although equity will not compel performance of personal services, the court may grant a negative injunction to prohibit rendering the same services for another. The Restatement (Second) of Contracts § 367 comment b states that the character of a personal service is one which is "non-delegable", meaning that the contracting party retains certain unique abilities to perform the contractual obligations. If the court delegated or assigned the duties to a third party, the non-breaching party would not receive the benefit of their bargain.

In the leading case, *Lumley v. Wagner*, 42 Eng. Rep. 687 (Ch. 1852), an opera singer entered into an exclusive contract to sing for the proprietor of a

London theater for a period of three months. Another London theater persuaded the singer to break the contract and perform for their opera production instead. The court granted an injunction restraining her from performing for the competing production. On appeal, the Lord Chancellor upheld the prohibitory injunction but acknowledged that the court could not force compliance with the original contract.

Negative injunctions work to protect the contractual bargain because damages in these unique situations are considered an inadequate remedy at law. The inadequacy lies in the difficulty of measuring the harm and the inability to obtain a suitable substitute performer because of the special skills involved. The non-breaching party cannot use equity to compel performance but may restrain the breaching party from performing under another contract.

Traditional common law has allowed contractual restrictive covenants on the practice of a profession, business or trade to protect an employer's legitimate competitive business interests, provided the restrictions were reasonable in duration, geographical area and the scope of subject matter of employment or line of business. Such restrictive covenants may also be implied when the contract makes clear the parties' intent. Courts have recognized that an employer's difficulty in calculating damages attributable to loss of customers, loss of goodwill and potential impact on competitive market position can constitute irreparable harm to justify injunctive relief but must be established by concrete evidence rather than conjecture. Some states, though, have modified or rejected outright the common law rule of reasonableness and enacted statutes restricting or abolishing covenants not to compete, recognizing a strong public policy in favor of open competition and employee mobility. *See* Cal. Bus & Prof. Code § 16600; Edwards v. Arthur Anderson LLP, 189 P.3d 285 (Cal. 2008) (noncompetition restraint in employment agreement void under California statute).

(D) UNIFORM COMMERCIAL CODE

1.   UNIQUE GOODS

The Uniform Commercial Code § 2–716(1) provides that specific performance may be an appropriate remedy when goods are "unique or in other proper circumstances." The Code espouses a "more liberal attitude" than common law with respect to authorizing equitable relief. *See* § 2–716, cmt. 1. The rationale for expanding the availability of specific performance may reflect the recognition that such commercial transactions generally involve relatively sophisticated parties and that replacement goods may be difficult to obtain through cover.

The concept of "uniqueness" carries forward in restated fashion the common law tradition of considering whether the non-breaching party has an adequate remedy at law. Therefore, goods may satisfy the test of uniqueness where no commercially reasonable substitute is readily available without undue expense, difficulty, or delay. Other factors that may suggest uniqueness could include difficulties in valuation, prospective problems in collection of damages, and the potential of multiplicity of suits to obtain the benefit of the bargain. Most commonly, however, the critical factor is whether or not the non-breaching party can enter the market and obtain cover to replace the contract goods. Where goods are relatively fungible, such as most commodities, damages would ordinarily be a satisfactory remedy for breach of contract.

The comments to § 2–716 admonish that the test of uniqueness must be made based upon the "total situation which characterizes the contract." *See* § 2–716, cmt. 2. For example, output and requirements contracts are acknowledged as potentially proper subjects for specific performance because alternate sources or markets may not be readily available.

2.   OTHER PROPER CIRCUMSTANCES

The general term "in other proper circumstances" expresses the broader application of the standard for equitable relief. This alternative portion of the test amplifies the issue of uniqueness and also considers the type of contract involved. Comment 2 to § 2–716 suggests that the buyer's inability to cover serves as strong evidence of "other proper circumstances" and may justify specific performance. For example, in *Kaiser Trading Co. v. Associated Metals & Minerals Corp.*, 321 F. Supp. 923 (N.D. Cal. 1970) the court found that because the subject matter of the contract involved a scarce material, the buyer could not readily cover. Further, since the material was an important substance used in the company's manufacturing process, damages would not be an adequate remedy and specific performance was necessary to protect its expectation interest. Also, in *Eastern Air Lines, Inc. v. Gulf Oil Corp.,* 415 F. Supp. 429 (S.D. Fla. 1975), the court recognized the problems associated with product shortages and specifically enforced a contract for supplying aviation fuel to an airline company during the 1973 Arab oil embargo.

3. OUTPUT AND REQUIREMENTS CONTRACTS

Certain types of agreements, such as output and requirements contracts, may be considered more likely to support a grant of specific performance because of the particular needs of the parties and the nature of the markets involved. *See* U.C.C. § 2–716, cmt. 2. Not all such contracts are necessarily proper subjects for equitable enforcement, however, and courts will evaluate the commercial alternatives to an assured source of supply, the reasonable and justifiable expectations of the contracting parties, difficulties of supervision, and the respective hardships if specific performance was granted or withheld.

For example, in *Laclede Gas Co. v. Amoco Oil Co.,* 522 F.2d 33 (8th Cir. 1975), the court enforced a long term requirements contract which involved the shipment of propane gas to a utility company for distribution to its customers through specific performance. The court found damages inadequate and potential arrangements with alternative suppliers infeasible without the utility company incurring substantial costs. The lack of a time requirement for performance in the contract did not preclude equitable relief and the court recognized a strong public interest in maintaining the utility company's ability to furnish propane gas to its retail customers.

4.   ACTION FOR THE PRICE

The U.C.C. provides a framework of approximately equivalent remedies which may be available to non-breaching buyers and sellers to protect their respective interests in contracts for the sale of goods. The counterpart to a buyer's remedy of specific performance under § 2–716 is called an action for the price under § 2–709 (also see discussion in Chapter 10, *supra*). While specific performance sounds in equity and accordingly is backed by the contempt power of courts, an action on the price is an action at law for damages.

Specific performance requires actual fulfillment of the contract, such as delivery of the goods to the buyer, but an action for the price only provides monetary damages to the aggrieved seller for the contract price. Sellers also may recover incidental damages, if applicable. The purpose of § 2–709, then, is to place the non-breaching seller in as good a position financially as if the buyer had fully performed under the contract.

Just as entitlement to specific performance considers whether the non-breaching buyer may reasonably effect cover by procuring substitute goods in the market, an action for the price contemplates an impracticability on the part of the seller in accomplishing a reasonable resale of the subject goods following breach.

The most common scenario in which sellers may resort to § 2–709 arises where goods are objectively not reasonably resalable because no ready market practicably exists, such as in defective goods or those specially designed for a particular buyer. Other recognized circumstances in which an action on the price may apply include where a buyer has accepted goods or where risk of loss has passed to the buyer and the goods are subsequently lost or destroyed.

(E) REPLEVIN

Apart from specific performance, another civil remedy available to parties seeking recovery of specific goods is replevin. The remedy is used to force the conveyance of possession of personal property to a party who can demonstrate superior title over a party in possession. The remedy traces its origins to ancient common law writs but today is principally codified by state statute and in Article 2 of the Uniform Commercial Code. Fuentes v. Shevin, 407 U.S. 67, 78–79 (1972). The inability of the non-breaching buyer to reasonably obtain replacement goods through cover affects entitlement to specific performance and replevin under the Code; however, the remedy of replevin also requires that the claimant identifies the goods to the contract. U.C.C. § 2–716(3).

Although replevin shares some history with the tort of conversion, it offers certain advantages because the remedy includes an order mandating transfer of the property itself as well as potentially awarding damages sustained by the rightful holder associated with the wrongful possession. State statutes vary in their formulation of the requirements for replevin but generally they involve a showing of ownership or rightful possession of the property, the value of the property, and that the defendant has wrongfully withheld or detained the property. Abbott Laboratories v. Feinberg, 2020 WL 7239617 (S.D.N.Y. 2020). State replevin statutes often require claimants to post a bond. In some jurisdictions the bond serves to indemnify the official executing repossession for costs incurred if the claimant fails to prosecute the action diligently. A replevin surety bond also provides a source of funds to compensate the party being forced to transfer the property for damages incurred, such as if the property is damaged and the court later determines that replevin should not have issued.

The remedy has been used historically for a wide variety of items of tangible personal property, such as jewelry, cars, pets, and artwork. For example, in the recent decision *Mueller v. TL90108, LLC*, 938 N.W.2d 566 (Wis. 2020), an owner of a vintage automobile successfully maintained an action for replevin to force conveyance of possession of the vehicle from a subsequent purchaser of the property which had been wrongfully converted by a third party. The court also awarded compensatory damages for detention of the car. Replevin is conditioned upon the defendant presently retaining possession of the subject property; consequently, where an ex-fiancé sold a diamond ring after an engagement was broken their former fiancé could not maintain a replevin action to recover possession of the ring. *See* Liceaga v. Baez, 126 N.E.3d 682, 689 (Ill. App. 2019). The principal inquiry in replevin is determining which party has rightful possession; therefore, if the court finds that the personal property was originally conveyed unconditionally as a gift, then replevin will be denied.

CHAPTER 5
EQUITABLE DEFENSES

This chapter concerns defenses that a defendant may raise to equitable relief. Such defenses are independent of any defense to the substantive claim itself, such as privilege. Recall that to obtain an equitable order a plaintiff must first establish the substantive claim for a right to relief and then must establish the requirements for the equitable order itself, as seen in Chapters 3 and 4.

The equitable defenses covered in this chapter are laches, unclean hands, *in pari delicto*, estoppel, unconscionability, and election of remedies. They share a common origin in the old English courts of equity as reflected in the Chancellor's laws of conscience. The Chancellor would not give relief to a suitor whose behavior was somehow "tainted" with respect to the claim. The Chancellor had discretion to deny equitable relief if the claimant had engaged in unconscionable or otherwise wrongful conduct in securing the right being asserted, or if the defendant had been prejudiced by prior inconsistent conduct or by undue delay by the suitor in pursuing the claim. In such cases, the plaintiff would be sent from equity back to law to seek whatever damages remedy was available for the substantive right in dispute. Even in a case where the defendant's behavior was much worse by comparison, the Chancellor was unsupportive of rights tainted by improper conduct and the plaintiff would be forced to seek redress from a court of law. One principle that remains in modern law is that a court sitting in equity will not sully itself by lending aid to someone who has a questionable moral posture with regard to the claim. Another central principle is that the court maintains considerable discretion to grant, deny, or shape equitable relief based upon reference to the claimant's own conduct, even where a claim might be otherwise meritorious.

These defenses have been preserved even in the merged system of law and equity. Modern equity still possess a moralistic foundation: a court will not grant equitable relief if the plaintiff behaved in a way prejudicial to the defendant or offensive to public policy. An equity court today is guided by discretion that is more constrained by principles of *stare decisis* than the Chancellor's original courts of equity, but its orders still bear the name "extraordinary relief." Whenever the plaintiff seeks equitable remedies, the court may apply the doctrines of laches, estoppel, unconscionability, unclean hands, or election of remedies.

(A) LACHES

1. OVERVIEW

Laches bars a suitor in equity who has not acted promptly in bringing the action. It is reflected in the maxim: "Equity aids the vigilant, not those who slumber on their rights." The doctrine serves to promote diligence on the part of the claimant in asserting rights, to prevent the enforcement of stale claims, and to provide an end to conflict and uncertainty that may surround a dispute. The Supreme Court gave the following description of the doctrine of laches:

> The doctrine of laches is based upon grounds of public policy, which requires for the peace of society the discouragement of stale demands. And where the difficulty of doing entire justice by reason of the death of the principal witness or witnesses, or from the original transactions having become obscured by time, is attributable to gross negligence or deliberate delay, a court of equity will not aid a party whose application is thus destitute of conscience, good faith and reasonable diligence.

Mackall v. Casilear, 137 U.S. 556, 566 (1890). The equitable defense of laches contains two basic requirements: (1) the claimant had an unreasonable delay in asserting rights, and (2) the delay would operate to unduly prejudice the defendant. There are no mechanical rules for proof of these elements because each case turns on its individual facts, unlike the statute of limitations. The Federal Rule of Civil Procedure consider laches an affirmative defense, therefore the defendant bears the burden of proof. Fed. R. Civ. Pro. 8(c). The defense of laches will bar equitable claims but legal remedies remain unaffected. For example, a plaintiff who is denied specific performance because of laches may still seek contract damages, if otherwise available.

2.   DELAY

In contrast with a statute of limitations, the delay necessary for laches is not determined rigidly by the passage of a specified period of time. Rather, the evaluation of the reasonableness of the delay in instituting an equitable claim is a highly fact-intensive, flexible inquiry.

If a claimant lacks material information relevant to support a claim and, in the exercise of reasonable diligence could not have obtained the necessary facts or documents in a timely manner, courts will generally excuse a delay in seeking equitable relief. Courts may consider additional factors in assessing the reasonableness of delay, such as if the claim arose out of a confidential or family relationship, other efforts to seek relief, ongoing negotiations between the parties, incapacity, and the lack of financial means to bring suit.

The Supreme Court recently examined the relationship between the laches defense and statute of limitations in the intellectual property context. In *Petrella v. Metro-Goldwyn-Mayer, Inc.*, 572 U.S. 663 (2014), the owner of a screenplay sought damages for copyright infringement and the defendant asserted the laches defense, even though the claim was brought within the three-year window established by the Copyright Act. The Court concluded that laches cannot bar the damages claim brought within the statute's limitations period, reasoning that "courts are not at liberty to jettison Congress' judgment on the timeliness of suit." Recognizing that the equitable defense of laches historically applied as a gap-filler device, the Court observed that laches served as a guide when no statute of limitations controlled the claim. The Court also observed, however, that in extraordinary circumstances laches may be invoked to limit the relief equitably awarded. Thus, when Congress speaks directly to the issue of timeliness of claims, courts must give fidelity to that determination.

In a similar vein, in *SCA Hygiene Products Aktieboiag v. First Quality Baby Products, LLC*, 137 S. Ct. 954 (2017) the Court held that laches could not be asserted as a defense against damages for alleged patent infringement which occurred within the statutory limitations period. The Court reasoned that enactment of the statute of limitations reflected a Congressional policy decision that the timeliness of covered claims should be governed by a bright line rule rather than a fact-specific judicial determination that occurs when a laches defense is asserted.

Even if not directly applicable, an analogous statute of limitations may provide some evidence of the reasonableness of a delay in seeking equitable relief. *See* Doyle v. Huntress, Inc., 513 F.3d 331 (1st Cir. 2008)(three year statute of limitations for unpaid wage claims used as guideline in applying laches defense to admiralty claim for wages against vessel owners).

Laches can bar a claim even when a prejudicial delay was caused by an administrative agency rather than the plaintiff. In *Whitfield v. Anheuser-Busch, Inc.*, 820 F.2d 243 (8th Cir. 1987), for example, a ten year delay of the Equal Employment Opportunity

Commission did not bar the complainant's claim under the statute of limitations because it did not start to run until after administrative exhaustion. Nonetheless, the delay barred the individual's claim in equity because the defendant's witnesses no longer recalled the event.

3.   PREJUDICE

Laches does not preclude equitable relief solely because of an unreasonable, unexcused delay in instituting claims. Instead, the party asserting the defense must also demonstrate that it suffered prejudice as a consequence of the delay. The nature of the prejudice may be economic or affect the ability of the defendant to bring a defense to the equitable claim. For example, due to the passage of time the defendant may no longer have access to evidence, witnesses may be unavailable, property may change, or third party rights affected. Also, prejudice may be principally economic, such as where the party conducted business, made hiring decisions, and committed investments based upon a justifiable expectation that its interests were protected.

In *Osage Nation v. Board of Commissioners of Osage County*, 399 P.3d 1224 (Okla. 2017) objectors challenged zoning ordinances and conditional use permits approving the construction and operation of a wind energy facility. The court found that the challenge seeking declaratory and injunctive relief was untimely and barred by laches because the request for relief was instituted three years after the project was approved and construction had commenced. The delay was unreasonable and unexcused because the claimants had knowledge of the permit issuance. The court further determined that the defendants would suffer material economic prejudice if an injunction halted completion of the project at a late stage.

(B) ESTOPPEL

The doctrine of estoppel is deeply ingrained throughout law and equity and is based on the principle of fairness and justice that a party should not be allowed to profit from their own misconduct which would result in undue prejudice to another. The defense of equitable estoppel holds that a court will not grant equitable relief to a claimant where an innocent party detrimentally relied upon the claimant's prior misrepresentations or actions. Equitable estoppel precludes a party, then, from maintaining inconsistent positions which would likely result in substantial hardship to an innocent party relying upon such words or conduct. The defense operates to bar a party from asserting a right that it otherwise could have held but for its own inappropriate conduct. Most courts treat equitable estoppel as a shield rather than an independent claim, which serves to protect the party in justifiable reliance from the grant of equitable relief sought by the wrongdoer.

Equitable estoppel historically was premised upon some deception or fraudulent inducement designed to influence another into believing and acting upon an understanding of certain facts which were erroneous.

Despite its origins in the prevention of fraud, assertion of the defense is not dependent upon proving fraud or illegality. Estoppel may also arise where a party negligently concealed information and may involve affirmative statements, admissions, conduct, silence when under a duty to speak, or the failure to act consistently with a claim later asserted.

While courts impose varying requirements, the elements for an affirmative defense of equitable estoppel typically include: (1) the intentional misrepresentation of material facts to another, (2) the party making the representations or withholding information knows the true facts, (3) the statements are intended to and do induce reasonable, good faith reliance by the other party, (4) the party in reliance lacks knowledge of the true facts and cannot ascertain the facts in the exercise of reasonable diligence, and (5) the party claiming estoppel would sustain undue prejudice if the other party was permitted to take an inconsistent position from the facts originally asserted.

The type of detriment that may support application of estoppel may take many forms, including serious personal or financial hardship or inconvenience or the loss of substantial legal rights. The principle of avoiding prejudice through estoppel is consistent with laches but the defenses vary in the remaining elements. Laches also considers unreasonable delay in asserting an equitable claim, while estoppel involves actions inconsistent with the rights the plaintiff subsequently asserts. The classic example of estoppel is that a plaintiff cannot ask equity for an order to remove a neighbor's fence built over the lot line if the plaintiff stood by and watched the fence construction in full knowledge of the location of the lot line. The plaintiff's silence with knowledge of the facts is an action inconsistent with the right asserted in court.

Courts traditionally do not apply laches and equitable estoppel with the same force to government entities as with regard to private actors. The rationale for such liberalized deference recognizes that the sovereign bears responsibility to further the public interest; consequently, courts generally protect the government from equitable claims brought by private parties.

The rule is not absolute, however, and some courts have applied equitable defenses against the government where its agents act outside the scope of authorized police powers or where the government affirmatively mispresented or concealed a material fact. *See* Ramírez-Carlo v. United States, 496 F.3d 41, 49 (1st Cir. 2007). Also, courts occasionally apply the defense to estop the government where it would otherwise result in highly inequitable or oppressive circumstances, or where government actors engaged in affirmative misconduct. For example, in *Water-Haskins v. Human Services Department*, 210 P.3d 817 (N.M. 2009), a person received government food stamp assistance for a number of years and regularly complied with the requisite filing and disclosure requirements for maintaining eligibility in the program. After a period of years, the state agency discovered its own error in calculating benefit eligibility and sought repayment of the amounts of the mistaken benefits paid. The court applied equitable estoppel to preclude the government from recovering the overpayment sums, finding that the recipient had relied in good faith on its eligibility status and that forcing repayment would offend the principle of "right and justice."

(C) UNCLEAN HANDS AND IN PARI DELICTO

Unclean hands and unconscionability are sometimes called "conscience defenses" because they operate to bar relief to plaintiffs whose claims the court deems morally tainted in some way. The foundation of these defenses developed because it is beneath the dignity of the court to grant equitable relief to unworthy suitors. In contrast with other equitable defenses, unclean hands aims to preserve the integrity of the judicial system and the interest of the public rather than the legal rights of the parties. The unclean hands defense is reflected in the maxim, "He who comes into a court of equity must come with clean hands."

A party may raise unclean hands as an affirmative defense in the pleadings, or the court may raise it *sua sponte*. The court may exercise its discretion to deny equitable relief to a claimant through the unclean hands defense when two conditions are met: (1) the claimant has engaged in "serious misconduct" which is (2) directly related to the same transaction forming the basis upon which relief is sought. The defense is not based upon the merits of the underlying claims and, if applied, may result in the loss of otherwise viable equitable claims. Also, unlike laches and equitable estoppel, there is no requirement that the defendant be prejudiced in any way. The unclean hands defense only affects the equitable claim. When the unclean hands doctrine bars the plaintiff from equity, she may nonetheless retain possible actions at law.

The nature of the misconduct which bars equitable relief must be sufficiently egregious but it does not necessarily demand a showing of fraud, illegality, or other actionable wrong. Most courts require a showing of serious, intentional wrongdoing that evidences willfulness, bad faith, or shocks the moral sensibilities of the court. The tainted conduct must be specifically related to the matter before the court and not collateral, however. It is often said that "equity does not require its suitors to lead blameless lives." In other words, the court only looks to the plaintiff's moral posture with respect to the matter at issue before the court and any questionable behavior concerning unrelated matters is not relevant. Courts typically apply the defense sparingly, therefore requiring a direct nexus between the offensive conduct and the equitable claim. For example, if a claimant transferred property to shield it from the reach of creditors a court may apply unclean hands to bar the claimant from later seeking a constructive trust to regain title to the property. *See* Senter v. Furman, 265 S.E.2d 784 (Ga. 1980).

A closely related defense to unclean hands is called *in pari delicto*, which means "in equal fault". The doctrine applies to situations in which both parties engaged in some serious misconduct related to the claims asserted. The predicate for the defense is that each party bears substantially equal responsibility. In those cases, courts may exercise discretion to decline awarding relief to either party. As a public policy matter, courts do not want to become entangled in resolving disputes among wrongdoers. Further, the denial of relief may help to deter future illegality.

(D) UNCONSCIONABILITY

Unconscionability is closely related to unclean hands but holds distinct characteristics. The doctrine of unconscionability boasts roots both in law and equity, and both common law and the Uniform Commercial Code embrace the doctrine. *See* Restatement (Second) of Contracts § 208 (1981); U.C.C. § 2–302. The defense is limited specifically to contract remedies.

The court makes determinations of unconscionability as a matter of law based upon the time the contract is made. Because the term "unconscionability" itself is not defined under the Uniform Commercial Code, courts retain considerable flexibility in applying the doctrine to limit or exclude contract terms considered too oppressive or one-sided. If the court finds that the contract or specific terms amount to unconscionability, it can either: (1) invalidate the entire agreement, (2) enforce the remainder of the contract without the offending clause, or (3) limit the application of the terms to avoid an unconscionable result.

The determination of unconscionability is purely defensive in character as it does not amount to breach of contract nor give rise to a cause of action for damages. Unlike the concepts of illegality or fraud, unconscionability will not necessarily invalidate the entire contract. A judge who applies the unconscionability defense, either as an equitable defense or under the statutory authority of the U.C.C., acts in a supervisory role to preserve the integrity of agreements while protecting against unscrupulous practices.

The doctrine of unconscionability involves consideration of both substantive and procedural factors. The substantive issue focuses on whether the bargain reflects "unreasonably favorable terms", such as where a substantial difference exists in the consideration exchanged for the nature of the product or services rendered. In *Jones v. Star Credit Corp.*, 59 Misc. 2d 189 (N.Y. Sup. Ct. 1969) the court found that a contract where welfare recipients agreed to purchase a freezer for $900 that possessed a retail value of just $300 was unconscionable. Although courts do not inquire into the adequacy of consideration for purposes of contract formation, an excessive disparity may indicate that the contract is unconscionable. The evaluation of unconscionability is made at the time of contract formation. Therefore, subsequent changes in market conditions that may make a contract bargain unfavorable to one party do not affect the issue of unconscionability.

A court may similarly consider terms substantively unconscionable by referencing custom or standard practices in the industry. The U.C.C. allows consideration of the commercial setting and the purpose and effect of the contract to aid the court in making its determination regarding unconscionability. *See* § 2–302(2). The lack of readily available alternatives, such as the inability to obtain housing, goods, or services, may also indicate unconscionability. A significant risk of default by the economically weaker party, however, may justify contract terms that reflect the higher degree of risk assumed by the party with the stronger bargaining position.

Procedural unconscionability is often characterized by the "lack of meaningful choice" by the party with lesser bargaining strength. Although even gross inequality in bargaining power alone does not necessarily make a contract procedurally defective, it may influence a court to scrutinize the manner of formation closely to ensure appropriate appreciation of the risks involved. Courts may find contract formation suspect in situations where an adhesion contract contains fine print or is the product of sharp practices, such as high-pressure sales tactics, or where contract terms are written in unduly complex or a foreign language.

The lack of meaningful appreciation of risk undermines the basic assumption of mutual assent in contract law. Therefore, if the court determines that one party would not have entered into the contract had they reasonably understood the risks, the court may find the contract unconscionable. The Restatement (Second) of Contracts § 208 comment b explains the standard as a contract that "no man in his senses and not under delusion would make and no honest and fair man would accept." The U.C.C. expresses the principle that the doctrine serves to prevent "oppression and unfair surprise." *See* § 2–302, cmt. 1. Courts also may consider whether the economically stronger and more sophisticated party took advantage of the lack of understanding by the other party.

In a famous unconscionability case at common law, *Campbell Soup Co. v. Wentz*, 172 F.2d 80 (3d Cir. 1948), the court refused to enforce a contract between a major soup producer and a farmer because it contained overreaching terms. Campbell Soup entered into a contract with the defendant farmer, Wentz, to purchase at thirty dollars a ton all the carrots produced on a certain acreage. The contract provided that Wentz had to sell all the carrots to Campbell but that Campbell was not obligated to purchase them. Furthermore, if Campbell did not want the carrots, Wentz could not sell them to a third party without obtaining prior permission from Campbell. This one-sided arrangement reflected the vastly superior bargaining power of Campbell.

The price of carrots subsequently rose to ninety dollars per ton and Wentz violated the contract by selling them on the open market rather than to Campbell at the lower contract price. Campbell needed the carrots and was forced to cover on the open market—possibly purchasing Wentz's contract carrots indirectly at the much higher prices in the open market where Wentz took them.

Campbell sought specific performance of the contract on the grounds that the unique quality of these Chantenay red cored carrots made them particularly suitable for use in vegetable soup. Wentz successfully defended with unconscionability because the court found that the contract was so one-sided as to be unenforceable in equity. Notably, the court found the entire contract unenforceable even though the unconscionable part of the contract was invoked.

(E) ELECTION OF REMEDIES

The doctrine of election of remedies provides that when an injured party has two available but inconsistent remedies to redress a harm, the act of choosing one constitutes a binding election that forecloses the other. A classic illustration of the doctrine is that a defrauded party must choose or "elect" between disaffirming a contract through rescission or affirming the contract and seeking damages. The rule developed historically to promote traditional equitable principles against double recovery and undue prejudice of a defendant. Although the policy justifications for the doctrine appear sound, some courts have applied the rule rigidly and produced unexpected and occasional harsh results. The doctrine may operate to extinguish a substantive cause of action even prior to filing suit and under circumstances where the plaintiff never intended to make a true election of remedy.

For example, assume that fraud occurs in a transaction to purchase an automobile. The buyer returns the car to the dealer. The election of remedies doctrine may effectively hold that the buyer now "elected" to disaffirm the contract to purchase the car, which would preclude an action for damages. Conversely, if the buyer had sent a letter to the dealer demanding damages associated with the fraud, the doctrine may deem that conduct an affirmance of the transaction. In either situation, the buyer may be bound by their initial action even if the dealer has not been prejudiced and no double recovery has occurred. Further, the election may be considered irrevocable even before the aggrieved buyer files suit or seeks legal advice.

Consider the following recent illustrations of application of the doctrine. In *Kaste v. Land O'Lakes Purina Feed, LLC*, 392 P.3d 805 (Or. App. 2017), operators of a dairy farm purchased feed which caused harm to a number of their cows. The farmers brought claims against the seller alleging both contract claims for breach of warranty as well as various tort claims for negligence and strict liability. The court held that the plaintiffs were not required to elect between the contract and tort remedies because they served different purposes and would not result in a double recovery.

Compare *Teutscher v. Woodson*, 835 F.3d 936 (9th Cir. 2016), where an employee brought wrongful termination legal and equitable claims under state and federal law against a former employer. The legal claims included compensatory and punitive damages and the equitable claim sought reinstatement. The court found that when the jury awarded the employee damages for front pay, the election of remedies doctrine precluded the equitable claim for reinstatement. The court reasoned that both reinstatement and front pay were alternative remedies for wrongful discharge and the employee had waived the right to reinstatement by affirmatively electing to seek front pay damages.

The rule has come under sharp criticism for its potential for harsh results and historical basis in formalism rather than substance. Rather than following a literal application of the rule, some courts consider whether double recovery in fact would occur or use principles of estoppel, merger or res judicata to analyze the claimant's actions.

The Restatement (Second) of Contracts approaches the issue of election among remedies from the perspective of estoppel. Section 378 provides that the manifestation of a choice of inconsistent remedies does not bar another remedy unless the other party "materially changes his position in reliance on the manifestation." A change of position is considered "material" if allowance of a switch in remedies would be "unjust." *See* § 378, cmt. a.

Further, according to the Restatement, the potential for preclusion only occurs where the remedies in fact exist and they are inconsistent with one another. *See* § 378, cmt. d.

For example, a party cannot obtain specific performance of a contract affirming the bargain and also seek damages for total breach of contract. Some remedies are complementary, however, and serve different purposes because they address different protectable interests in the bargain. Thus, a party may be able to receive restitution and damages in some instances in order to be made whole.

The Uniform Commercial Code specifically rejects the doctrine of election of remedies as a "fundamental policy." U.C.C. § 2–703, cmt. 1. Instead, U.C.C. remedies are deemed cumulative in nature and include all of the available remedies for breach. Whether the pursuit of one remedy bars another depends on the facts of each individual case rather than on formalistic or mechanical rules. The U.C.C. remedies are to be "liberally administered." § 2–711, cmt. 3; 2–703, cmt. 4. A clear illustration of the more liberal approach of the Code is reflected in § 2–721 regarding remedies for fraud. That provision states that neither rescission of a contract of sale nor a rejection or return of goods bars or is considered "inconsistent" with a damages claim or any other remedy.

CHAPTER 6

PRELIMINARY INJUNCTIONS AND TEMPORARY RESTRAINING ORDERS

(A) NATURE AND PURPOSE OF INTERLOCUTORY RELIEF

Interlocutory relief includes equitable orders available in special circumstances when a plaintiff needs immediate court action to avoid irreversible losses while waiting for the trial on the merits. By definition interlocutory relief is expedited relief for a short term that a court may give before final adjudication of a case on the merits.

Temporary restraining orders and preliminary injunctions are the two main forms of interlocutory relief. Generally, a party must make the same substantive showing to entitlement regardless of whether the party seeks a temporary restraining order or a preliminary injunction. The speed of acquisition, the duration of the orders, and the procedural formalities observed during the issuance of the orders are the primary differences between temporary restraining orders and preliminary injunctions.

The focus of this chapter is on the federal rules related to these remedies. Federal Rule of Civil Procedure 65 governs preliminary injunctions and temporary restraining orders in federal courts. Many states have identical or similar rules, but other states vary slightly in the names, procedures, and requirements for preliminary injunctions.

These injunctions are considered "extraordinary" relief that require a strong showing of necessity. The principal concern underlying issuance of interlocutory relief is that immediate and irreparable harm will occur during the interim period before the dispute between the parties can be resolved at a full trial on the merits. The interlocutory injunction may issue to prevent commission of an act which threatens injury to the plaintiff's interests respecting the subject of the action or which will render the judgment ineffectual. For example, a court may issue a restraining order to prevent a defendant from removing or disposing of property at issue in a lawsuit between the plaintiff and the defendant.

A common characterization of the purpose of interlocutory injunctions is "to preserve the status quo" until a hearing on the merits can be held. The "status quo" may be characterized as the last actual peaceable uncontested status of the parties to the controversy. It does not alter the legal relations of the parties but instead serves to maintain their relationship for the duration of the order. The status quo can be active or passive. For instance, it can be a condition of action, such as ordering the defendant to continue supplying goods pursuant to a distributorship agreement. An illustration of a passive order would be an order restraining a developer from razing a building pending resolution of a dispute regarding whether the structure qualified for preservation as a historical landmark under a statute.

A plaintiff must be prepared to compensate a wrongfully enjoined defendant for losses caused by the expedited order regardless of the plaintiff's good faith in seeking it. Unless the plaintiff is ultimately victorious in the underlying case, the plaintiff will be liable for the defendant's proven losses associated with the interlocutory order. Courts generally are reluctant to act when there has not been time for careful deliberation of the full facts of a case.

(B) PRELIMINARY INJUNCTIONS

1.   PRELIMINARY INJUNCTIONS— TRADITIONAL TEST

Neither the federal Judicial Code nor the federal rules of civil procedure impose any substantive requirements or standards for obtaining preliminary injunctions. Therefore, federal courts have interpreted the federal rules of civil procedure to incorporate common law substantive requirements traditionally governing equitable orders. The traditional test for a preliminary injunction required a movant to demonstrate: (1) a likelihood of success of the merits; (2) an irreparable injury if the relief is delayed; (3) a balance of hardships favoring the movant, and (4) a showing that the injunction would not be adverse to the public interest. Winter v. Natural Resources Defense Council, Inc., 555 U.S. 7, 20 (2008). Under the traditional test, the burden of proof on each of these four elements rested with the movant. Further, the movant must establish these elements independently from one another. Thus, the movant was required to establish that she was more likely to prevail on the merits than not prevail regardless of the degree to which she would suffer irreparable harm in the absence of a preliminary injunction.

The application of these requirements is illustrated in a case involving a patient who wanted his health insurance to cover a liver transplant. In *DiDomenico v. Employers Coop. Ind. Trust*, 676 F. Supp. 903 (N.D. Ind. 1987), the plaintiff sought a preliminary injunction to keep the defendant health insurer from denying coverage for the procedure. The health plan specifically excluded "experimental" liver transplants but the plaintiff's doctors testified at the hearing that adult liver transplants recently had become accepted and were no longer considered experimental by the medical community. The operation was medically necessary to save the patient's life and he could not afford it without the insurance coverage. The district court found that the plaintiff had satisfied each of the traditional requirements for issuance of a preliminary injunction. The most difficult element was irreparable harm because the problem essentially involved a monetary issue. The plaintiff successfully proved that he could not get the operation to save his life in the absence of insurance coverage and that he could not wait to get relief until the end of a full trial on the merits, which might be several years in the future.

2. PRELIMINARY INJUNCTIONS—
ALTERNATIVE TEST

Many federal circuits have adopted an alternative, more flexible standard which evaluates the movant's likelihood of success on the merits in relation to the gravity of the irreparable harm the movant will suffer if a preliminary injunction is not granted. Under the alternative test, the movant must show either a likelihood of success on the merits and some irreparable harm or "a serious question on the merits" and "that the balance of hardships tips *decidedly* in its favor." Alliance for Wild Rockies v. Cottrell, 632 F.3d 1127, 1135 (9th Cir. 2011). The flexible test operates as a sliding scale such that the greater the degree of gravity of the irreparable harm to the movant and the clearer the balance of hardships weighs in favor of the movant, the lesser the required showing of strength on the merits of the case. The alternative test, then, may be successfully used where the movant has a relatively weak case on the merits but the potential harm would be extremely serious absent equitable intervention.

Conversely, under this alternative test, a movant with a strong substantive claim can receive a preliminary injunction with a lesser showing of irreparable harm and balance of hardships. The movant would still bear the burden of proving her case on the merits at trial. Likewise, to receive a permanent injunction after trial, the movant would still need to establish irreparable harm. The interlocutory order would give the movant the opportunity to establish her claim without sustaining the harm.

Judge Posner famously stated this flexible test as a mathematical formula:

If $(P \times H_p) > (1 - P) \times H_d$ then the preliminary injunction should be granted.

In Judge Posner's equation, P is the probability that the movant will prevail on the merits at trial. H_p is the harm to the movant if the preliminary injunction does not issue. H_d is the harm to the opposing party if the preliminary injunction does issue. Judge Posner posited his formula as the procedural counterpart to Judge Learned Hand's famous negligence formula in *United States v. Carroll Towing Co.*, 159 F.2d 169 (2d Cir. 1947). *See* American Hosp. Supply Co. v. Hospital Prods. Ltd, 780 F.2d 589 (7th Cir. 1986).

One early case using this alternative approach provides a good illustration of its application. In *Chalk v. U.S. District Court*, 840 F.2d 701 (9th Cir. 1988) a teacher was reassigned to an administrative position after he was diagnosed with Acquired Immune Deficiency Syndrome (AIDS). He sought a preliminary injunction for reinstatement with a classroom assignment and lost at the district court level. The trial judge found that the teacher suffered no irreparable harm because the administrative position paid the same salary as the classroom assignment. On appeal to the Ninth Circuit, this finding was reversed as clearly erroneous.

The Ninth Circuit in *Chalk* noted that the plaintiff had established a strong likelihood of success on the merits because medical testimony established that there was little risk of his infecting the children with the virus in the classroom setting. Irreparable harm was also present. The appellate court found that the lack of monetary loss was only one aspect of irreparable harm and that the trial court should have focused also on the nature of the alternative work. The plaintiff was a special skills teacher who derived great personal satisfaction from working closely with his small class of hearing-impaired children. In contrast, the reassigned administrative work involved writing grant proposals for which he had no special training nor interest.

The Court of Appeals further addressed the balance of hardships in *Chalk*. The opinion notes that this element is satisfied even though it was unnecessary under the alternative test to find that the balance of hardships favored the plaintiff after the strong showing of success on the merits and irreparable harm. The public expressed fear about the risk of AIDS exposure in schools. The Court of Appeals held that the trial court could retain jurisdiction to remove the teacher from student contact at whatever point qualified medical opinion might determine that his condition poses a risk to the children. For example, if the teacher contracts an opportunistic infection capable of transmission, he can be removed from the classroom. Until then, the preliminary injunction should preserve the *status quo* with the classroom teaching assignment pending the full trial on the merits of the case.

3. PRELIMINARY INJUNCTIONS— IRREPARABLE HARM REQUIRED UNDER ALTERNATIVE TEST

Some courts employing the alternative test permitted a movant who made a particularly strong showing of probable success on the merits to show only the "possibility" of irreparable harm to obtain a preliminary injunction. In *Winter v. Natural Resources Defense Council, Inc.*, 555 U.S. 7 (2008), the Supreme Court rejected this approach. The Court reversed the federal appellate court, holding that the possibility standard was "too lenient." The Court ruled that a movant must establish that "irreparable injury is *likely* in the absence of an injunction." The Court also concluded that the lower court erred in ordering an injunction to issue because the harm to the opposing party and the public interest outweighed any potential irreparable injury to the movants.

In reaching its holding in *Winter*, the Court noted that:

A plaintiff seeking a preliminary injunction must establish that he is likely to succeed on the merits, that he is likely to suffer irreparable harm in the absence of preliminary relief, that the balance of equities tips in his favor, and that an injunction is in the public interest.

Winter, 555 U.S. at 20. After *Winter*, it is clear that courts employing the alternative test must find some irreparable harm to the moving party before issuing a preliminary injunction even if the movant raises a strong likelihood of success on the merits. However, the issue of whether courts employing the alternative test can continue to issue a preliminary injunction based on a 'serious question on the merits' when the movant shows grave irreparable harm and that the balance of the equities tips heavily in the movant's favor remains an open question. The Second Circuit, the Seventh Circuit and the Ninth Circuit have all concluded that courts may continue to employ the flexible test to issue a preliminary injunction when the movant raises only a serious question on the merits but also demonstrates grave irreparable harm and that the balance of equities weighs heavily in its favor. *See, e.g.,* Alliance for the Wild Rockies v. Cottrell, 632 F.3d 1127 (9th Cir. 2011); Citigroup Global Markets, Inc. v. VCG Special Opportunities Master Fund Ltd., 598 F.3d 30 (2d Cir. 2010). Meanwhile, the Fourth Circuit has concluded that *Winter* precludes the use of the alternative test and that the movant must establish a likelihood of success on the merits.

4. THE ROLE OF PUBLIC INTEREST

Under both the traditional and the alternative tests for temporary restraining orders and preliminary injunctions an important consideration is the potential effect on public interest. This factor principally takes into account the interests of non-parties, and is often couched in the negative, i.e. whether the grant of an equitable order will be "adverse" to the public interest. *See* Woodhouse v. Maine Comm'n on Gov't. Ethics & Election Practices, 40 F. Supp. 3d 186, 197 (D. Me. 2014)(public interest favored preliminary injunction mandating the state to permit campaign contributions consistent with Equal Protection requirements). The problem faced by courts and litigants in interpreting this factor is that the notion of public interest does not connote any uniform or constant formulation, but rather may be evidenced by reference to statutes, the nature of the subject matter in dispute, or by judicial determination that certain topics—like protecting the environment or civil rights—traditionally are seen in a favorable light regarding the public interest.

Often claimants point to competing public interest factors and courts will balance those respective considerations. In *League of Wilderness Defenders/ Blue Mountains Biodiversity Project v. Connaughton*, 752 F.3d 755 (9th Cir. 2014), environmental organizations sought a preliminary injunction to halt timber-cutting in mature forests, alleging violations of certain federal environmental statutes. The defendants contended that an injunction halting the project would be adverse to the public interest because the planned logging would mitigate the risk of forest fires and reduce insect infestation. Further, the project would provide economic benefits to the local community in added jobs, increased school funding, and improved health services. The court granted the injunction, determining that a countervailing public interest in preserving an elk habitat in the forest outweighed the other considerations.

In contrast, in *Alliance for Wild Rockies v. United States Forest Service*, 2016 WL 3349221 (D. Idaho 2016), the court denied injunctive relief by environmental organizations against logging operations and a road construction proposal, finding a strong public interest in increased economic and recreational benefits to the local citizenry, watershed restoration, and reduced wildfire risks.

5.   PROCEDURAL REQUIREMENTS FOR ISSUING A PRELIMINARY INJUNCTION

Federal Rule of Civil Procedure 65 addresses the procedural requirements for issuing a preliminary injunction. Rule 65(a) provides:

(1)   *Notice.* The court may issue a preliminary injunction only on notice to the adverse party.

(2)   *Consolidating the Hearing with the Trial on the Merits.* Before or after beginning the hearing on a motion for a preliminary injunction, the court may advance the trial on the merits and consolidate it with the hearing. Even when consolidation is not ordered, evidence that is received on the motion and that would be admissible at trial becomes part of the trial record and need not be repeated at trial. But the court must preserve any party's right to a jury trial.

Thus, a preliminary injunction may not issue without notice to the opposing party. Federal courts have also concluded that Rule 65(a) requires the court to hold a hearing before a preliminary injunction may issue.

Rule 65 requires all orders granting interlocutory relief to state the reasons why the order issued and state the terms of the restraint specifically as well as describe in "reasonable detail" the acts to be restrained or required. Federal Rule of Civil Procedure 52 requires the court to make findings of fact and conclusions of law when issuing an interlocutory injunction. Finally, 28 U.S.C. § 1292 grants parties a right to immediate appeal from interlocutory orders granting or denying preliminary injunctions.

(C) TEMPORARY RESTRAINING ORDERS

1.   BASIC PRINCIPLES

A temporary restraining order (TRO) is a stop-gap measure for a truly urgent situation to preserve the status quo long enough for a preliminary injunction hearing. After a court has had time to hold a hearing, the TRO will be dissolved if not justified, or replaced with a preliminary injunction to continue holding the status quo until the full trial on the merits of the claim.

Generally, the substantive standard for issuing a TRO mirrors the standard for issuing a preliminary injunction. The most significant differences relates to timing, speed of acquisition, the duration of the orders, and the formalities observed during the issuance of the orders. Because the TRO is in place during the period before the court can hold a hearing on a motion for a preliminary injunction, the moving party must show that the irreparable harm is immediate. That is, the moving party must show that the harm will occur before the court can hold a hearing on a preliminary injunction.

Federal Rule of Civil Procedure 65 contains specific procedural requirements for issuing TROs. For example, a TRO also may only last for a limited duration. Federal Rule of Civil Procedure 65(b) provides that the order can last only 14 days, with a second 14 day extension for good cause or if the other party consents to an extension. The court must set a time for a preliminary injunction hearing as soon as possible in order to minimize the time of restraint without such a hearing. In contrast, a preliminary injunction lasts until trial or modification, which means that it could possibly last for years. Additionally, Rule 52(a) requires the court to state its conclusions of law and findings of fact that constitute the grounds for its action.

2.   APPEAL

Although preliminary injunctions are appealable under 28 U.S.C. § 1292(a), an order granting or denying a temporary restraining order is generally not appealable. Several reasons support the distinction. First, unlike a preliminary injunction, a TRO is not a final decision under 28 U.S.C. § 1291. Also, on a practical level, because a TRO is of a short duration and terminates with a ruling on a preliminary injunction, an appeal is not necessary to protect the rights of the parties. *See* Nutrasweet v. Vit-Mar Enterprises, Inc., 112 F.3d 689, 692 (3d Cir. 1997).

In some circumstances, however, a temporary restraining order may be essentially transformed into a preliminary injunction and consequently subject to appeal under 28 U.S.C. § 1292(a). Where the duration of a TRO is extended beyond the permissible limits of Rule 65, for example, it will be treated as a preliminary injunction. Sampson v. Murray, 415 U.S. 61, 86–88 (1974). Additionally, when the relief contemplated by the order goes beyond the purpose of preserving the status quo, it may become immediately appealable.

Courts consider the purpose and effect of a TRO when determining whether it should be treated as a preliminary injunction for purposes of appeal. In *Pearson v. Kemp*, 2020 WL 7093408 (11th Cir. 2020), a group of Presidential Electors obtained a temporary restraining order enjoining various Georgia officials from erasing or altering forensic data on voting machines in three counties, asserting election misconduct. Before a preliminary injunction hearing, the claimants sought to appeal the TRO, seeking broader relief.

The Eleventh Circuit Court of Appeals observed that appellate jurisdiction over TRO decisions was ordinarily reserved for matters which could have a serious, irreparable consequence such as when a prisoner was set to be executed or a patient removed from life support. The court denied the appeal, finding that the TRO would preserve the status quo by precluding the voting machines from being erased and finding that other alleged harm was not imminent.

In contrast, in *Hope v. Warden York County Prison*, 956 F.3d 156 (3d Cir. 2020), the court determined that a temporary restraining order effectively functioned as a preliminary injunction and therefore was immediately appealable. A group of immigration detainees housed at a prison facility sought and obtained their immediate release based on alleged serious health concerns incident to their detention from risks associated with COVID-19 exposure. The Third Circuit Court of Appeals found that the TRO was immediately appealable because the relief granted in releasing the detainees went beyond preserving the status quo and granted them mandatory, affirmative relief.

3.   NOTICE

One of the most notable differences between a TRO and a preliminary injunction pertains to notice. Unlike a preliminary injunction, a TRO may be entered *ex parte,* but only upon a specific showing that immediate and irreparable harm will result before the opposing party could be notified and heard. This most commonly occurs when the opposing party is located some distance from the moving party such that service cannot be effectuated quickly. In limited situations, a court may properly issue *ex parte* orders of brief duration and narrow scope to protect the status quo. *See* Granny Goose Foods, Inc. v. Teamsters, 415 U.S. 423, 438–39 (1974).

Federal Rule of Civil Procedure 65(b) codifies these limits on *ex parte* TROs for cases pending in federal court. Although states generally are free to adopt procedures that differ from the federal rules, in *Carroll v. President and Commissioners of Princess Anne*, 393 U.S. 175 (1968), the Court recognized constitutional limits on the issuance of an *ex parte* TRO under state law, at least when First Amendment rights are at stake. In this case speakers belonging to an extremist organization held a rally which included racially provocative remarks. Town officials obtained an *ex parte* TRO to prohibit a second rally because they feared an explosive confrontation. The Supreme Court found that the TRO was procedurally defective because the officials had failed to attempt to give notice of the proceedings to the defendants. The Court explained that when First Amendment rights are at stake, it is particularly important to have all parties present to assure that the equitable order is fashioned as narrowly as possible to protect all interests affected.

Finally, the limitations on TRO have been strictly applied by the federal courts. It is an extraordinary remedy to enjoin a party when there has been very little opportunity to receive evidence in the matter.

(D) INJUNCTION BONDS

Federal Rule of Civil Procedure 65(c) states security must be provided by the applicant before a court issues a TRO or preliminary injunction. The security required by Federal Rule of Civil Procedure 65(c) can be either a bond or guarantee from the movant.

The provision of Rule 65(c) is broad:

(c) Security. The court may issue a preliminary injunction or a temporary restraining order only if the movant gives security in an amount that the court considers proper to pay the costs and damages sustained by any party found to have been wrongfully enjoined or restrained. The United States, its officers, and its agencies are not required to give security.

Posting of a bond is ordinarily not considered to be a jurisdictional prerequisite to the validity of a preliminary injunction. *See* Aoude v. Mobil Oil Corp., 862 F.2d 890 (1st Cir. 1988). In *Popular Bank of Florida v. Banco Popular de Puerto Rico*, 180 F.R.D. 461 (S.D. Fla. 1998) a defendant argued that it was not bound by the terms of a preliminary injunction and consequently could not be held in contempt because it had not violated an enforceable order because the court had not ruled on posting of security pursuant to Rule 65(c). The court disagreed and held that the equitable order could be enforceable through contempt.

In *Coquina Oil Corp. v. Transwestern Pipeline Co.*, 825 F.2d 1461 (10th Cir. 1987), however, the court held that it lacked jurisdiction to decide an appeal of a preliminary injunction order because trial judge had not ruled on the bond requirement. Thus, the express language of the Rule stood as an absolute condition precedent to issuance of a preliminary injunction and the failure to require posting of a bond renders the equitable order without operative effect.

The prevailing view in federal courts is to follow Rule 65(c) closely and require the posting of security, and some authority holds that the failure to post a bond may constitute reversible error. Some courts acknowledge that although the language of the Rule is couched in mandatory terms, they retain discretion to waive posting of security for temporary restraining orders or preliminary injunctions in exceptional circumstances. Illustrative circumstances in which courts have waived the requirement of posting a bond are for indigent plaintiffs, where the injunction does not subject the restrained party to compensable monetary losses, and where the costs to post a bond would effectively prevent enforcement of important rights affecting the public interest. *See generally* Temple Univ. v. White, 941 F.2d 201, 219 n.26 (3d Cir. 1991). For example, in *Youth Justice Coalition v. City of Los Angeles*, 2017 WL 396141 (C.D. Cal. 2017) the court waived the bond requirement in a civil rights claim on the basis that the movant had a high degree of probability of success on the merits, the City had not submitted any evidence of damages potentially suffered as a consequence of the injunction, and the bond would negatively impact the movant's constitutional rights.

Requiring a claimant to post bond or supply security provides redress for wrongfully enjoined defendants. The bond assures that the defendant will be compensated for any losses occasioned by the order in the event that the plaintiff does not ultimately prevail in the underlying case. The funds in the bond will therefore indemnify the party enjoined from actual, provable damages directly resulting from a wrongfully issued injunction.

Since courts issue interlocutory injunctions based on a liberalized showing of probable rights and probable harms, the defendant may sustain losses caused by the injunction and may later prevail in a trial on the merits. The bond assures that the defendant will be compensated for any losses occasioned by the order in the event that the plaintiff does not ultimately prevail in the underlying case. The bond provides a convenient repository of funds against which the wrongfully enjoined party can collect actual damages such that the enjoined party does not have to run the risk that the plaintiff is judgment-proof.

Because the claimant must incur costs in posting the bond, this requirement also serves as a check on the zealousness of plaintiffs in instituting litigation. The bond requirement indirectly preserves the dignity of the court and reflects the hesitation of our judicial system to permit orders without time for the judge to hear all the evidence and to reflect on the just result. Therefore, the function of the security requirement is to guarantee that plaintiffs will compensate defendants for losses caused by that hasty decision.

The court has discretion in setting the amount of a bond, but the enjoined party may request that it be increased in order to more fully protect its interests during the interim period of the interlocutory order. For instance, in *DeVos v. Cunningham Group*, 297 So.3d 1176 (Ala. 2019), the court awarded a preliminary injunction to a medical center to enforce restrictive covenants in an employment agreement against two doctors who left their practices. The trial court required posting just a $25,000 surety bond. The doctors argued that the bond should be substantially increased to redress their potential damages and attorney fees if they were later found to be wrongfully enjoined. The court agreed, finding that the estimated compensation the doctors would receive far exceeded the bond amount.

The amount of the bond is generally regarded as a ceiling on the measure of damages potentially recoverable by the restrained party unless the bond was an "open" one or unless security was given without a limitation to recovery. Some courts recognize an exception whereby a claimant may obtain damages in excess of the bond against the plaintiff in "exceptional" cases where the injunction was secured by fraud or malice. The surety always has limited liability.

If the enjoined party subsequently prevails on the merits at trial, the presumption favors some recovery of damages against the bond. The enjoined party must still bear the burden of proving actual losses suffered as a result of the wrongfully issued injunction with specificity. Compensable losses include measurable harms caused specifically by the wrongful order, not including distress and humiliation. The bond does not function as a type of forfeiture or liquidated damages, but rather serves as a repository of funds to pay provable compensatory damages directly caused by the wrongfully issued injunction. Courts generally employ a presumption that damages will be recoverable against the bond upon a showing that the defendant prevailed on the merits and does not require a showing that the movant exercised bad faith in seeking the equitable order.

CHAPTER 7
CONTEMPT

(A) OVERVIEW

Courts possess the inherent authority to issue contempt orders to maintain the orderly administration of the judicial system and to ensure proper respect and compliance with their orders. The contempt power of state and federal courts, though, is largely governed by statutory directive and civil and criminal procedural rules.

The significance of contempt becomes particularly relevant in equitable proceedings because the court must act in both a lawgiver capacity and a quasi-law enforcement capacity. A decree in equity, such as an order to pay child support or an injunction mandating disclosure of documents, binds the party affected *in personam*. The effectiveness of equitable orders is directly related to the authority to enforce such orders through the contempt power. When a party is bound by a specifically detailed equitable decree, has proper notice of the order, and has the ability to comply but refuses to obey its terms, the disobedience may be punishable as contempt. The range of punishments available to the court through contempt can potentially include substantial fines and incarceration of the party found in violation of the court's order. In contrast, even the willful failure to pay damages awarded in a civil judgment can only result in an order executing satisfaction against the property of the defendant.

Contempt orders may be categorized as either civil or criminal, with the difference principally based on their purpose and function. A civil contempt order typically serves a remedial or compensatory function—generally seeking to coerce the bound party into compliance prospectively, as demonstrated by daily fines or imprisonment. When the party chooses to conform their conduct to satisfy the court's directive, the sanctions cease. The purpose of civil contempt protects the opposing party in an underlying lawsuit, as illustrated by the situation where a court orders discovery of documents and the defendant refuses to comply. Civil contempt can afford compensation associated with the disobedience as well as coercing the defendant into furnishing the documents ordered by the court. Civil contempt is classified as compensatory and coercive.

Criminal contempt, on the other hand, is punitive in nature. The purpose of criminal contempt is primarily to ensure proper respect for the court and the administration of justice. Criminal contempt need not arise out of a criminal proceeding, but rather is used to vindicate the court's interest in its own authority to enforce order and decorum and promote obedience to court orders regardless of the nature of the underlying action. Criminal contempt is classified as direct (or summary) and indirect (or constructive).

The different types of contempt vary in form and function, but sometimes a court order will contain both civil and criminal characteristics, making it difficult to categorize clearly as one or the other. A noncompliant defendant may be held in both criminal and civil contempt for the same act because the functions are different. For example, if a defendant openly defies an order not to trespass, criminal contempt could punish the defendant for disobedience toward the court; civil contempt could compensate the plaintiff for any damage resulting from the defiant trespass, as well as coerce the defendant by threat of jail or fine to cease from further trespass.

Although federal courts possess the inherent power to enforce compliance with their orders so that they may function properly and with due respect, such power is limited by statute and rules of procedure. Federal courts are authorized to exercise their contempt power in accordance with 18 U.S.C. § 401, which provides:

A court of the United States shall have power to punish by fine or imprisonment, or both, at its discretion, such contempt of its authority, and none other, as

(1) Misbehavior of any person in its presence or so near thereto as to obstruct the administration of justice;

(2) Misbehavior of any of its officers in their official transactions;

(3) Disobedience or resistance to its lawful writ, process, order, rule, decree, or command.

On the federal level, all forms of civil and criminal contempt must fit within the scope of one of the three categories of misbehavior set forth in § 401. Section 401 does not specifically classify criminal contempt as a felony or misdemeanor nor does it designate minimum or maximum penalties for its violation. *See* U.S. v. Cohn, 586 F.3d 844, 848 (11th Cir. 2009)(criminal contempt characterized as *sui generis*, rather than as either a felony or a misdemeanor). Consequently, courts have wide discretion to impose penalties for statutory noncompliance. *See* Frank v. United States, 395 U.S. 147, 149 (1969). Some courts, though, have treated criminal contempt as a Class A felony under the federal sentencing statute, 18 U.S.C. § 3559(a), and therefore have held that the statutory maximum under § 401 for criminal contempt is life imprisonment. Other courts have disagreed, finding that it would be unreasonable to conclude that Congress intended all criminal contempts be deemed Class A felonies. *See* United States v. Carpenter, 91 F.3d 1282, 1284 (9th Cir. 1996).

Judges issuing criminal contempt orders in federal court must also comply with the terms of Federal Rule of Criminal Procedure 42, which sets forth certain notice requirements and jury trial rights, and also outlines specific responsibilities of judges which are applicable to summary orders. The procedural requirements are rigorously applied and interpreted strictly for the benefit of the party subject to the contempt process.

Although the contempt power provides an important mechanism to facilitate enforcement of equitable orders, courts must exercise that power within established substantive and procedural boundaries to protect the interests of persons from unfettered judicial discretion. Problems of determining the appropriate level of procedural safeguards in contempt proceedings also may arise where a court order possesses attributes of both criminal and civil sanctions. The recent trend favors a liberal grant of safeguards to protect the restrained party from potential abuses in the contempt process.

(B) CRIMINAL CONTEMPT

Two different categories of criminal contempt function as mechanisms to enforce the authority of the court. One category is direct or summary criminal contempt, which operates to maintain order in the courtroom, such as punishing disruptive courtroom behavior by attorneys, parties, or spectators, which the judge sees or hears. The direct contempt power also serves to esteem the court's authority by summarily punishing disrespectful behavior that disrupts the orderly administration of the proceedings and diminishes the respect and decorum of the court.

The second type of criminal contempt is indirect or constructive criminal contempt. It is called "indirect" because it concerns behavior that occurs outside the direct presence of the judge. The purpose of indirect contempt is to punish conduct that constitutes defiance toward the court through disobedience of a lawful order.

Both summary and constructive criminal contempt promote respect for the dignity and authority of the judicial system and ensure fidelity to the terms of court orders. Even where the contempt power is unexercised, recognition of the latent power of courts to protect and vindicate their orders achieves a derivative, secondary effect. The potential through criminal contempt for receiving punitive sanctions as a consequence of disobedience of an equitable order provides a powerful incentive for persons to conform their conduct to the terms of the decree.

A person may be held in criminal contempt under multiple federal statutes without triggering the Double Jeopardy Clause, provided the statutes contain an element not found in the other. For example, in *United States v. Westbrooks*, 858 F.3d 317 (5th Cir. 2017) the court upheld separate criminal contempt convictions under two federal statutes where the defendant's failure to adequately respond to a subpoena and obstruction of administration of tax code by submitting false testimony constituted different offenses.

1. SUMMARY CRIMINAL CONTEMPT

A court may exercise its discretion in limited circumstances to issue a summary or direct contempt sanction in order to maintain proper decorum in the courtroom. Summary contempt serves to punish conduct that occurs in the presence of the court. Judges are generally hesitant to wield this power because it consolidates all the traditional functions of judge, jury, and prosecutor and reposes them in a single person. A summary contempt order also departs from the traditional safeguards of notice and a hearing common to criminal proceedings. Therefore, the use of this power is generally reserved for "exceptional circumstances" that significantly interfere with the ability of the court to conduct proceedings in an orderly manner. Harris v. United States, 382 U.S. 162 (1965). The Supreme Court has expressly cautioned against holding attorneys in contempt for vigorously advocating for their clients unless such advocacy actually obstructs the performance of the court's duties. In re McConnell, 370 U.S. 230 (1962). Summary criminal contempt orders are reviewable for abuse of discretion.

Federal courts obtain statutory authority to punish direct contempt through 18 U.S.C. § 401(1), which gives a judge the discretion to punish by fine or imprisonment, or both, the misbehavior of any person in the court's presence which obstructs the administration of justice. The Supreme Court interpreted this authority in *Nye v. United States,* 313 U.S. 33 (1941) to apply to "misbehavior in the vicinity of the court disrupting to quiet and order or actually interrupting the court in the conduct of its business."

Summary contempt proceedings are further governed by Rule 42(b) of the Federal Rules of Criminal Procedure, which requires that for summary contempt in a federal court, the contumacious conduct be committed in the actual presence of the court and be seen by the presiding judge. The rule contains the procedural safeguard that the judge's order must recite the relevant facts, be signed, and be filed with the clerk of the court.

This rule is strictly interpreted in order to protect the rights of the party sanctioned and provide an adequate record for review by an appellate court. Minor misconduct is generally deemed insufficient, such as a scuffle in the back of the courtroom, an inaudible curse, or a slamming of a book on the table.

State courts derive power from state statutes similar to 18 U.S.C. § 401, from constitutional grant, or from the court's inherent power. Some state courts have interpreted "presence" somewhat more broadly than federal courts, punishing through summary contempt an outburst which occurred just outside the courtroom door when the judge was on the bench. Although federal law would not permit the use of summary contempt in that situation, some states would consider it sufficiently proximate to the court to obstruct the administration of justice and permit the exercise of summary contempt power.

2. INDIRECT CRIMINAL CONTEMPT

Indirect or constructive criminal contempt serves to protect the integrity of the court by promoting respect for and obedience of its orders. Acts punishable through indirect criminal contempt undermine the court's authority and activities but typically occur outside of the presence of the court, where a court has no direct, personal knowledge of events.

The requirements for indirect contempt are: (1) a valid order issued by a court of competent jurisdiction enjoining the party to act or refrain from acting in a certain manner; (2) notice by the party of the specific terms of the order; (3) the ability of the party to comply with the order; and (4) intentional or willful noncompliance with the order by the party without justifiable excuse. A party who lacks the ability to pay, for example, will not be held in criminal contempt for the failure to make scheduled child support payments. *See* Turner v. Rogers, 564 U.S. 431 (2011). Some courts, though, have held that failure to seek reasonable employment is itself a voluntary act sufficiently related to the court's order to support a finding of contempt.

The distinction between criminal and civil contempt is important for several reasons, but most notably because of the differences in procedural safeguards required in each. Civil contempt generally only requires the minimal constitutional protections of notice and an opportunity to be heard. Criminal contempt, however, is "a crime in the ordinary sense." *See* Bloom v. Illinois, 391 U.S. 194 (1968). The Supreme Court has explained that "criminal penalties may not be imposed on someone who has not been afforded the protections that the Constitution requires of such criminal proceedings." Hicks v. Feiock, 485 U.S. 624 (1988). Those procedural safeguards include the privilege against self-incrimination, the right to a jury trial, a presumption of innocence, the right to proof beyond a reasonable doubt, and the right to present a defense. Other rights that apply include double jeopardy, notice of charges, assistance of counsel, and summary process.

Constitutional protections for defendants accused of criminal contempt apply only to disobedience of a court's order outside the presence of the court, however. In contrast, lesser procedural safeguards exist when a court sanctions a party summarily or directly for misbehavior in the court's presence. The difference in protection is warranted primarily because of the court's substantial interest in restoring order in summary contempt proceedings, along with the reduced need for extensive factfinding. Summary contempt orders are nevertheless limited by certain substantive and procedural standards set forth in Federal Rule of Criminal Procedure 42.

The right to jury trial in contempt cases depends upon the categorization of the type of contempt at issue. For criminal contempts in federal court, the Sixth Amendment right to a jury trial applies to "serious" rather than petty offenses. The Court has held that serious criminal contempts are those where the maximum sentence authorized by statute or, absent statutory guidance, the penalty actually imposed exceeds imprisonment for six months. *See* Bloom v. Illinois, 391 U.S. 194 (1968). The Court has also held that the aggregation of shorter sentences which collectively would exceed six months' imprisonment also implicates the right to jury trial where the statutory violation did not specify a maximum penalty. *See* Codispoti v. Pennsylvania, 418 U.S. 506, 517 (1974). However, the Court has also held that no Sixth Amendment right to jury trial exists where a defendant is prosecuted in a single proceeding for multiple petty offenses, even though the potential aggregate sentence would exceed six months. *See* Lewis v. United States, 518 U.S. 322, 330 (1996). The distinction, as explained in *Lewis*, turns on whether the legislature had established a penalty; if not, the right to jury trial would depend on whether the sentence actually imposed exceeded six months.

Jury trial rights can also be implicated based on imposition of a "serious" fine. The distinction between serious and petty offenses for contempt is imprecise, however. In *Ravago Americas LLC v. Vinmar International Limited*, 2020 WL 6053350 (5th Cir. 2020), the district court imposed a $50,000 fine against an employee for the violation of a preliminary injunction related to a non-solicitation provision in an employment contract. Although the court characterized the fine as civil, the Fifth Circuit Court of Appeals found that it was punitive because there was no opportunity to purge and was unrelated to the employer's pecuniary injury. Consequently, the court found that the fine was "serious", not petty, and therefore triggered the right to jury trial for the employee.

In civil contempt, the traditional view holds that no right to jury trial exists because the defendant retains the ability to purge themselves of the contempt order by virtue of compliance with the underlying equitable decree. Consequently, a party held in coercive civil contempt may be incarcerated for a term exceeding six months yet still would not be entitled to a jury trial because they can remove the conditional imprisonment by complying with the court's order.

Indirect or constructive criminal contempt promotes the strong policy interest in ensuring respect for and compliance with court orders. In the leading case, *Walker v. City of Birmingham*, 388 U.S. 307 (1967), the Supreme Court held that civil rights workers who refused to obey a facially valid state court order enjoining a public demonstration could be punished for contempt even if the order they disobeyed was unconstitutional. In *Walker*, the civil rights protesters had two days after the lower court's ruling in which to petition for revision or dissolution of the injunction, but instead held a press conference and announced their intent to defy the court. Because there was no indication that such a petition would have been frustrated or delayed, failure to properly petition the court in the interim period did not justify defiance of the court's order. The Supreme Court therefore upheld a contempt sanction on the basis that such defiance is punishable with criminal contempt.

The Court explained the policy justifying imposition of criminal contempt, stating that "respect for judicial process" must prevail and that the rule of law followed reflected a belief that "in the orderly fair administration of justice no man can be judge in his own case, however exalted his station, however righteous his motives, and irrespective of his race, color, politics or religion." A party subject to an injunction issued by a court of competent jurisdiction, then, is bound to comply with the order until it is subsequently dissolved or vacated and cannot attack the validity of the order as a defense to a criminal contempt charge. This "collateral bar rule" thus generally prohibits a party from challenging the merits of an injunction to avoid a criminal contempt sanction for its disobedience. *See* United States v. Hendrickson, 822 F.3d 812, 819 (6th Cir. 2016). The rule is founded on the principle of ensuring respect for the integrity of court orders and to maintain efficiency in the judicial system.

Some very limited exceptions to the collateral bar rule have been recognized by federal courts, however. In *United States v. United Mine Workers*, the Court observed that a party may be able to collaterally attack a criminal contempt order for lack of subject matter jurisdiction if the question of jurisdiction was "frivolous and not substantial." 330 U.S. at 293. Similarly, in *Walker v. City of Birmingham*, the Court intimated that exceptions to the collateral bar rule could apply where the underlying injunctive order was "transparently invalid or had only a frivolous pretense to validity." 388 U.S. at 315. For example, in *In re Providence Journal Co.*, 820 F.2d 1342 (1st Cir. 1986), the court reversed a criminal contempt order because the underlying injunction improperly restrained a newspaper's First Amendment rights and met the "transparently invalid" exception to the collateral bar rule. The nature and contours of those potential exceptions, however, have stirred considerable debate and found mixed application in the lower federal courts, particularly involving challenges to subject matter jurisdiction and where important constitutional guarantees were implicated. When jurisdiction is itself in issue, courts must resolve the dispute and parties must respect the orders issued until the matter is resolved otherwise.

A court's criminal contempt power reaches only to parties bound by the underlying court order. For instance, Rule 65(d)(2) of the Federal Rules of Civil Procedure provides that an injunction is binding upon the parties to the action, their officers, agents, servants, employees, and attorneys, and upon those persons in "active concert or participation" with any of the above, and additionally, that anyone bound by the order must have received actual notice. The Supreme Court interpreted this rule in *Regal Knitwear Co. v. N.L.R.B.,* 324 U.S. 9 (1945) to include not only party defendants but those in "privity" with them, at least to the extent that they aid and abet the defendants in "carrying out prohibited acts."

(C) CIVIL CONTEMPT

There are two types of civil contempt, both of which serve primarily to protect the interests of the prevailing party and only incidentally to protect the dignity of the court. Compensatory civil contempt directly awards a party monetary damages for injuries caused by the opposing party's violation of a court order designed to protect adjudicated interests. Coercive civil contempt, on the other hand, encourages compliance with a court order for the benefit of the prevailing party by designating daily fines or imprisonment if the opposing party fails to comply. Civil contempt and criminal contempt may be imposed together, but the Supreme Court has held that the better practice is to separate the proceedings imposing the two types of contempt to ensure proper procedure and constitutional protections.

1. COMPENSATORY CIVIL CONTEMPT

Compensatory civil contempt compensates a party for losses caused by the opposing party's disobedience of a court order. Since compensatory civil contempt sanctions are inherently remedial, they are distinguishable from conditional fines which are designed to coerce compliance. *See* Gompers v. Buck's Stove & Range Co., 221 U.S. 418, 444 (1911). In some instances, sanctions that were originally imposed for a civil, coercive purpose may develop into criminal contempt if the nature and purpose of the sanction changes.

For example, consider the situation where a court orders the defendant to cease use of the plaintiff's trade secrets but the defendant defies the order and continues to do so. Through compensatory civil contempt the plaintiff may recover damages caused by the continued use of the trade secrets after the court's order. Damages caused before the injunction are recoverable only as damages in tort, but the losses directly traceable to the defendant's defiance of the court order are recoverable as compensatory civil contempt. Like damages in tort, the purpose of the compensatory contempt award is to make the plaintiff whole. the plaintiff must show that the losses were caused by the contumacious behavior, and the plaintiff must prove the resulting compensatory damages with reasonable certainty. Unlike tort damages, however, attorneys' fees and costs are included as a proper element of recovery. The fees must be limited to the pursuit of the contempt claim, however, and do not apply to the underlying claim that produced the order that the defendant disobeyed. Remedial civil contempt sanctions are paid directly to the claimant, in contrast with criminal contempt sanctions which are paid to the court. *See* Lightspeed Media Corp. v. Smith, 830 F.3d 500, 508 (7th Cir. 2016).

2. COERCIVE CIVIL CONTEMPT

Coercive civil contempt is a tool to promote prospective compliance with a court order designed to protect a party's rights. It operates to coerce a resistant opposing party by designating a daily (or other measure of increment) fine or imprisonment until the party begins complying with an order. A coercive civil contempt order becomes moot when the underlying preliminary injunction upon which it is based terminates. *See* Shell Offshore v. Greenpeace, 815 F.3d 623 (9th Cir. 2016).

For example, if a parent refuses to disclose the location of a child to thwart the court's order of visitation rights by the other parent, the court may imprison the non-complying parent until they disclose the information. A contemnor is said to carry the "keys to the jail in his or her pocket" because the imprisonment ends as soon as he or she complies with the court's order. Similarly, if a party refuses to produce a document for litigation despite a court order to do so, the court can coerce compliance by imposing an ongoing fine that accrues until the party produces the document. Fines are usually unrelated to the measure of damages suffered by the plaintiff and are paid to the government. A few courts have tailored the fine to daily losses, usually intangible ones, and ordered it paid to the plaintiff. Such orders are controversial, however, because they blur the line between compensatory and coercive civil contempt.

The Supreme Court has held that the amount of a civil contempt fine should be determined by several factors, including "the character and magnitude of the harm threatened by continued contumacy, and the probable effectiveness of any suggested sanctions in bringing about the result desired." United States v. United Mine Workers of Am., 330 U.S. 258 (1947). Thus, the court should consider the resources of the contemnor and impose a fine that is appropriately coercive in its effect.

One key aspect of coercive civil contempt is that the contemnor has the capacity to end the on-going sanction by compliance with the order. In contrast, if the court has ordered a determinant penalty, such as a specified number of days in jail or a fixed fine, the contempt is criminal, not civil, because the contemnor no longer has any control over the penalty.

Courts must limit the sanction for coercive civil contempt to the period of time when coercion may yield its intended effect. If it is no longer possible to comply with the purpose of the order, civil contempt must end. Because the contemnor can no longer purge the offense by compliance, then the penalty takes on a punitive nature and becomes criminal rather than coercive. For example, if a witness is jailed for refusing to testify at a trial even when granted immunity, the sanction must end when the trial is over because at that point the witness can no longer testify and thus could not purge the contempt.

Another limitation on coercive contempt is that it cannot continue once it becomes clear that it will never achieve compliance. In that situation, the contemnor must be released from the sanction because the court's ability to coerce the conduct has been exhausted. For example, if a spouse elects to spend years in jail rather than reveal the location of an asset in a divorce proceeding, the sanction must end at the point where the court is convinced that the coercion will never work.

The Supreme Court added another limitation to coercive civil contempt in *International Union, United Mine Workers of America v. Bagwell*, 512 U.S. 821 (1994), which involved a labor dispute between the union and two coal companies in Virginia. The union engaged in unlawful strike activities, such as blocking access to facilities, physically threatening employees, and damaging company property. The court ordered an injunction against the unlawful activities but the union violated the injunction shortly after the court's order. The court then announced prospective penalties for future violations: $100,000 if violent in nature and $20,000 if nonviolent. Between the court's contempt order and the end of the strike, the court determined the union committed 400 violations. The cumulative penalties exceeded $64 million, of which $12 million was directed to the coal companies and $52 million to the state.

The Supreme Court held that certain constitutional protections normally reserved for criminal contempt applied to civil contempt in cases where the fact-finding was especially complex and the penalties unusually severe. The *Bagwell* decision stopped short of delineating a bright-line standard in which such heightened safeguards should be applied in coercive civil contempt proceedings. Instead, the Court reserved for future decisions where to draw the line regarding which coercive civil contempt cases would potentially merit application of criminal contempt safeguards. As a result, questions of factual complexity, the preference for safeguards, and the intersection of civil and criminal contempt remain challenging and controversial issues for consideration by federal courts.

In *Federal Trade Comm'n v. Rensin*, 687 Fed. Appx. 3 (2d Cir. 2017), for example, the court upheld a compensatory civil contempt sanction because its purpose was to disgorge money received for violation of consent order and to compensate customers. The court held that additional safeguards for a criminal contempt order were not required, because unlike *Bagwell*, the disobedience at issue did not arise out of a complex injunction.

(D) SIGNIFICANCE OF THE CATEGORIZATION

Contempt frequently defies easy categorization, yet distinction as criminal or civil is necessary for three reasons. First, the distinction affects the procedural rights of the contemnor. Second, whether contempt is criminal or civil affects when the contempt may be appealed. Third, the distinction affects whether the contempt is independent of or connected to the success of the underlying action. Judges do not always label a contempt order properly in light of the form and function of the sanction. Appellate courts are not bound by the trial court's characterization and may overturn a finding of contempt if it was not administered consistently with the standards of its correct categorization.

The different procedural and constitutional safeguards in contempt proceedings are consistent with the differences between civil and criminal proceedings in general; criminal contempt imposes greater safeguards than civil contempt. Thus, if a trial judge labels the contempt order as civil but it is actually criminal in its nature and purpose, the trial court's failure to abide by the greater safeguards afforded a criminal contempt will result in reversal on appeal. Criminal contempt cannot be sustained unless all relevant and necessary procedures were followed.

Criminal contempt is an independent final order imposing penalties on the contemnor. As such, a criminal contempt order is immediately appealable. In contrast, civil contempt is tied to the underlying case and may only be appealed at the time the underlying civil action becomes appealable.

Criminal contempt is a separate offense, independent from the underlying case that produced the contempt order. Therefore, the contempt order survives without regard to the success of the underlying case that resulted in the contempt. Consider, for example, that a court orders a departing employee not to use a customer list taken from the former employer. The ex-employee violates the order and is held in criminal contempt. Later in the case the court rules that the employer does not have a protectable interest in the customer list and therefore the ex-employee wins the case. The finding of criminal contempt still stands because it was imposed to vindicate the court's authority and ensure respect for the integrity of judicial orders.

In contrast, civil contempt sanctions depend upon the ultimate success on the merits in the underlying case. A corollary principle applies if the parties reach an out of court agreement; complete settlement of the underlying action automatically ends all matters involved in the case, including civil contempt orders. In *Shell Offshore, Inc. v. Greenpeace*, 815 F.3d 623 (9th Cir. 2016), an oil company secured a preliminary injunction which precluded environmental activists from interfering with certain shipping operations. When the group continued its activities, the court imposed a contempt order which imposed future sanctions and fines for noncompliance. The oil company subsequently discontinued its exploration operations. As a consequence, the injunction expired because its purpose of protecting the company's activities no longer existed. The contempt order also was vacated because it was predicated on ensuring compliance with the preliminary injunction.

The Supreme Court established this durability principle as an alternative ground to its holding in *United States v. United Mine Workers of Am.*, 330 U.S. 258 (1947). The issue in that case was whether a union could strike against the employer when the United States took over operation of the coal mines pursuant to its emergency powers during World War II. The United States sought an injunction against the strike to keep the mines operating, but the union argued that an act of Congress prohibited federal courts from enjoining labor strikes. The United States countered that it was not subject to that provision of the law. The federal district court issued an injunction forbidding a strike by the union while the court considered the applicability of the statute at issue. The union struck in violation of the order and was held in criminal contempt. The Supreme Court found in favor of the United States on the argument over applicability of the statute, but held as an alternative ground that the union could be punished criminally for violating the court's order regardless of whether the United States prevailed in the underlying action. Distinguishing between civil and criminal contempt, the Court held that the difference in the function of the two contempts justifies the difference in their durability.

CHAPTER 8
STRUCTURAL, RESTORATIVE, AND PROPHYLACTIC INJUNCTIONS

(A) MODERN FORMS AND FUNCTIONS OF INJUNCTIONS

There are four types of injunctions: preventive, structural, restorative, and prophylactic. Chapter 3 discussed the preventive injunction. Whereas the preventive injunction holds deep roots in the common law, the last three were conceived and recognized as independent varieties of injunctions over the past half century.

The purpose of the preventive injunction is to stop the defendant from inflicting future injury on the plaintiff. Preventive injunctions can exhibit either prohibitory or mandatory character, but still focus on abating or ameliorating prospective harms in some fashion. As examined in Chapter 3, to receive a preventive injunction the plaintiff must prove the violation of a legally protected interest, the inadequacy of legal remedies, the imminent likelihood of sustaining irreparable harm absent equitable intervention, and the balance of hardships favoring the grant of equitable relief. The court also considers the public interest, if applicable, as well as its own interest in the ability to fashion and supervise the order.

The three modern types of injunctions share these requirements but differ in their forms and functions.

Due to the nature of the issues presented and the interests of the parties involved, they often contain more complexities than preventive injunctions. Such injunctions may seek to remedy ongoing effects of past harm as well as prevent future harm. They frequently require more extensive judicial supervision than preventive injunctions, such as presented in an equitable order mandating comprehensive prison reform. These injunctions also may raise separation of powers questions and the institutional competency of courts to effectuate institutional change.

The descriptive labels for these types of injunctions—preventive, structural, restorative, and prophylactic—are not necessarily used in opinions themselves. Nevertheless, the labels describe the form and function of each injunction. The terms are useful in understanding the nature of what the court has done and to fit it within a framework of similar cases.

(B) STRUCTURAL INJUNCTIONS

Structural injunctions reflect the fact that courts in certain cases have undertaken supervision over institutional policies and practices where constitutional violations exist in those institutions. Structural injunctions are a modern phenomenon born of necessity from developments in constitutional law where the Supreme Court identified substantive rights whose enforcement requires substantial judicial supervision. These rights concern the treatment of individuals by institutions, such as the right not to suffer inhumane treatment in a prison or public mental hospital. Enforcement of such rights by injunction has become an implicit part of the constitutional guarantee of protecting individual liberties from inappropriate government action.

The structural injunctions began with school desegregation cases following the Supreme Court's second decision in *Brown v. Board of Education of Topeka, Kansas*, 349 U.S. 294 (1955). In the first *Brown* decision in 1954 the Court decided the principle that racially segregated schools violated the guarantee of equal protection. *Brown II* in 1955 addressed the remedial issue of how to correct violations of this right. The Court explained that:

> courts may consider problems related to administration, arising from the physical condition of the school plant, the school transportation system, personnel, revision of school districts and attendance areas into compact units to achieve a system of determining admission to the public schools on a nonracial basis, and revision of local laws and regulations which may be necessary in solving the foregoing problems. They will also consider the adequacy of any plans the defendants may propose to meet these problems and to effectuate a transition to a racially nondiscriminatory school system. During this period of transition, the courts will retain jurisdiction of these cases.

Brown II, 349 U.S. at 300–301.

In the years that followed, federal district courts retained jurisdiction in school desegregation cases and worked through the administrative changes necessary in integrating schools. Each of the items mentioned in the Supreme Court's list in the quoted material was litigated extensively. The injunctions "structured" to address the nature of the constitutional infirmities allowed the order to be written with specificity to correct particular problems while the court retained jurisdiction to supervise compliance with its orders.

In cases involving constitutional violations at the institutional level, defendants are first ordered to submit plans to cure the offensive conditions. When defendants do not respond cooperatively or quickly, then judges often undertake to mandate particular changes. Structural injunctions typically involve long and costly battles, yet the importance of the rights they vindicate justifies the cost and attendant difficulties and frustrations. Structural injunctions reflect the traditional province of equity jurisdiction to exercise discretion to balance hardships and to consider public interest in protecting important constitutional rights.

Controversy surrounds structural injunctions as opponents argue that such injunctions improperly force judges to engage in policymaking through intensive fact-finding when balancing larger public interest concerns more properly is a legislative province. At times, Congress has sought to curtail the authority of federal courts to issue structural injunctions. For example, in 1996 Congress enacted the Prison Litigation Reform Act (PLRA) in an attempt to reduce the number of lawsuits brought by prisoners alleging unconstitutional conditions in federal and state prisons. The PLRA also attempted to limit the power of federal judges to issue structural injunctions governing the administration of federal and state prisons. The PLRA provided that injunctions and consent decrees could extend no further than necessary to correct the violations of the particular plaintiff's rights and had to be narrowly drawn and use the least intrusive means to correct the violations. 18 U.S.C. § 3626(a)(1) (1997).

Despite this push-back, structural injunctions remain a valid tool for curbing unconstitutional prison conditions. Indeed, the Supreme Court reaffirmed the federal courts' responsibility to remedy unconstitutional prison conditions in *Brown v. Plata*, 563 U.S. 493 (2011). In that case, the Court recognized the continued ability of federal courts to issue injunctions to remedy unconstitutional prison conditions, including orders reducing or limiting the size of prison populations.

The Supreme Court and other courts, however, have begun seeking to avoid excessive entanglement in institutional policies and practices by identifying the required outcome necessary to remedy the constitutional defect but allowing the institutional defendant to determine the means to achieve that outcome. Thus, for example, in *Brown v. Plata*, the Supreme Court recognized that while the lower court order set limits on the Defendant-State's prison populations, those limits were tied to design capacity and the State maintained the ability to determine the means by which it would meet the required capacity. In these types of cases, the courts retain jurisdiction to ensure that the institution continues to make progress toward remedying the constitutional violation.

This approach can result in protracted and messy litigation. For example, in *McCleary v. State*, 269 P.3d 477 (Wash. 2012), after years of pre-trial proceedings and an extensive evidentiary hearing, a trial court found that the State of Washington had failed to meet its state constitutional obligation to provide for the education of all children within the State's borders. The trial court found legislative funding levels inadequate and ordered a cost study. The Washington Supreme Court agreed that the State had failed to meet its constitutional obligation but set aside the order requiring a cost study. The Court noted that "the general authority to select the *means* of discharging that duty should be left to the Legislature." The Court also noted that the legislature had recently enacted reforms to the school funding system. The Court retained jurisdiction "to help ensure progress in the State's plan to fully implement educational reforms." In a separate opinion, the Chief Justice of the Court dissented from the retention of jurisdiction. The Chief concluded that the retention of jurisdiction without clearly identified goals was unhelpful and inappropriate.

The Chief's observations proved prescient. The Court retained continuing jurisdiction over the case for more than a decade before finally finding the

State in compliance. Along the way, the Court unanimously held the legislature in contempt and imposed a $100,000-per-day contempt sanction. Three justices faced challenges in judicial elections as a result of the Court's handling of the case. The children of the named plaintiffs were in elementary school when the plaintiffs filed the case. By the time the case concluded, the children were in college.

While courts have grown continually more reluctant to issue detailed structural injunctions, courts continue to ratify detailed, multi-faceted consent decrees negotiated by the parties. For example, shortly after George Floyd, an unarmed African-American man, was killed while in police custody in Minneapolis, a Minnesota state trial court entered a detailed consent decree. The decree had been negotiated and agreed upon by the Minnesota Department of Human Rights and the City of Minneapolis. The consent decree required the Minneapolis Police Department to institute specific policy changes, including instituting a ban on choke holds, imposing a mandatory duty to report fellow officer misconduct, requiring the Chief of Police to approve all crowd control weapons before use and authorizing a civilian review board to review all body camera footage. State of Minnesota v. City of Minneapolis Police Department, 27-CV-20-8182, Stipulation and Order (Minn. Dist. Ct., 4th Dist. June 8, 2020).

Federal Rule of Civil Procedure 60(b)(5) also serves an important role with respect to re-evaluating institutional reform injunctions based upon changed circumstances. Such decrees often remain in place for an extended period of time, so significant changes in the facts or law may justify reconsideration of the order. Although the rule is not limited to injunction orders, it notably provides for prospective relief if it is "no longer equitable." Such grounds for modification reflect the traditional power of courts to modify decrees in light of changed circumstances. United States v. Swift & Company, 286 U.S. 106, 114 (1932).

In *Horne v. Flores*, 557 U.S. 433 (2009), the Court found that the lower courts had erred in characterizing the legal standard for Rule 60(b)(5) motions for reviewing structural injunctions. The injunction required the State of Arizona to institute various reforms to ensure compliance with the Educational Opportunities Act. In *Horne*, the Court endorsed a "flexible approach" to Rule 60(b)(5) motions. The Court explained that the critical question informing possible modification was whether the objectives of the injunction had been achieved. The Court also observed that such institutional reform injunctions often implicate federalism concerns, such as where an injunction issued by a federal court effectively dictates state or local budget priorities. Sensitive federalism issues may arise where structural injunctions intrude into matters of traditional state responsibilities like public education. The party seeking modification of a structural injunction pursuant to Rule 60(b)(5) must still show a significant change in facts or law to support revision of the order. Courts will tailor any modification to the specific changed circumstances.

See Rufo v. Inmates of Suffolk County Jail, 502 U.S. 367, 383 (1992).

(C) RESTORATIVE INJUNCTIONS

A restorative injunction, also called a reparative injunction, functions to correct the present by undoing the effects of a past wrong. The notion of "restoring" means it focuses retroactively and not just prospectively, as does the traditional preventive injunction. For example, while a tainted election process affects future governance, the wrong can only be corrected by turning back time, in some sense, and redoing the election. An early example of this type or injunction was *Bell v. Southwell*, 376 F.2d 659 (5th Cir. 1967), where the court found that a racially tainted election could only be cured by another election.

A reinstatement order in an employment discrimination case is another form of restorative injunction. It returns the plaintiff to the position held before the wrong. In *Vasquez v. Bannworths, Inc.*, 707 S.W.2d 886 (Tex. 1986), for example, a farm worker was fired for complaining to the United Farm Workers union about the lack of clean water and sanitary toilet facilities in the fields, as required by law. The trial court issued a preventive injunction which ordered the defendant not to discriminate against her further in the event she ever worked for the defendant again. This future-oriented injunction had no practical effect when her employer had already fired her and was unlikely to rehire her voluntarily. The appellate court found that a restorative injunction was necessary—namely, an order that the plaintiff be rehired and thus restored to the position held before the wrong.

(D) PROPHYLACTIC INJUNCTIONS

A prophylactic injunction shares the goal of a preventive injunction, to thwart future harm to the plaintiff, but it primarily seeks to safeguard the plaintiff's rights by ordering behavior that is not otherwise required by law. Whereas a preventive injunction prohibits future or ongoing behavior that violates rights, such as prohibiting a repeating or continuing trespass, a prophylactic injunction concerns behavior indirectly related to those rights. For example, a prophylactic injunction related to trespass would require a trucking company to inform its employees about the boundary of the parking lot. Although a company's failure to communicate with employees is not a wrong in itself, such an injunction would seek to prevent the defendant's employees from continuing to park on the neighboring lot of the plaintiff.

Thus, the approach of a prophylactic injunction is to direct the defendant's behavior so as to minimize the chance that wrongs might recur in the future. In one famous case, *Bundy v. Jackson*, 641 F.2d 934 (D.C. Cir. 1981), an employer maintained a work force where the social atmosphere encouraged and perpetuated sexual harassment so pervasively that it violated federal law. Judge Skelly Wright's opinion held that the trial court should order the employer to take specific steps not otherwise required by law, such as educating the employees on their responsibility not to harass co-workers. The lack of such education is not in itself a violation of federal law in the absence of a court order. The court ordered the measures only because it deemed that future infractions of the plaintiffs' rights were likely without extra protections.

CHAPTER 9
SPECIAL ISSUES IN EQUITY

(A) STATUTORY LIMITATIONS ON DISCRETION

A basic hallmark of equity is the court's discretion to grant or withhold relief based upon balancing the equities and hardships of the parties and consideration of the public interest. An injunction is not considered an automatic right, even in situations where the claimant demonstrates a right deserving of legal redress. Although a court possesses subject matter jurisdiction over a dispute, the essence of equitable jurisdiction is that the judge retains wide discretion as to the propriety of granting or denying relief.

Following the determination of entitlement to injunctive relief, the court also holds discretion in the manner of fashioning the remedy given. Assume, for example, that a noise ordinance provides standards for allowable decibel levels for commercial businesses during specific hours. The ordinance further states that an injunction was one of several specifically authorized remedies to abate a violation. If the court decides to issue an injunction, it may tailor the order to prohibit certain offending activities by the business within specified times. The court could include certain conditions upon the enjoined party mandating that it modify its operations to conform to the ordinance requirements. Upon demonstrating compliance, the injunction could be dissolved.

When a claim is successfully brought pursuant to a statute, the court will examine the list of remedies provided to redress the statutory violation. If no remedies are enumerated, the court may imply common law remedies. A statute may be silent with respect to equitable relief but expressly provide for damages. In that instance, the court must determine whether implying equitable remedies would achieve the goals of the statutory scheme. Conversely, when a statute provides for only equitable remedies, the court must assess whether implying damages would carry out the statutory purposes.

The process of statutory interpretation begins with legislative intent, which may be gleaned from legislative history and the plain language of the statute. In some cases, the statutory enumeration of particular remedies and the omission of others have led courts to find a negative implication that only the remedies expressed were intended by the legislature and all others excluded. In some other cases, when courts lack clear guidance from the text or history of a statute, judges have invoked the general policy objectives behind the statute to allow additional remedies.

Claimants seeking an injunction with respect to abating specific conduct, such as environmental injuries, may find statutes a helpful supplement to the common law for several reasons. The court may find that the legislature already balanced public and private interests when proscribing specified conduct, drawing the balance in favor of protecting certain values. Further, the showings of inadequate remedy

at law and irreparable harm may be liberalized by
the presence of the statute depending upon how the
court interprets legislative intent. Although the
presence of a statute may make it somewhat easier
to obtain a prohibitory injunction than at common
law, courts traditionally maintain their equitable
discretion to issue or withhold relief and also to
decide how to tailor an injunction. Claimants still
must meet the common law requirements for
injunctive relief: an inadequate remedy at law,
irreparable harm, balance of hardships favoring the
injunction, and public interest in enjoining the
imminent harm threatened. The claimant must show
that the right asserted fits within the scope of the
statutory scheme and that they are within the class
of persons sought to be protected by the statute. A
generalized interest in advancing the public interest
is insufficient.

The Supreme Court strongly endorsed the
principle of equitable discretion in the provision of
statutory remedies in *Hecht Co. v. Bowles*, 321 U.S.
321 (1944). The case involved price controls during
World War II under the Emergency Price Control Act
of 1942. The governmental Administrator argued
that he was automatically entitled to an injunction
upon showing a violation of the Act. Although a
company violated certain provisions of the Act, it
demonstrated its substantial good faith efforts in
attempted compliance. The Administrator contended
that the statutory language "shall be granted"
required courts to issue an injunction automatically
upon a showing of any violation. The Supreme Court
rejected that argument, finding room for discretion

under the statute to select other more appropriate remedies. The trial court held that an injunction would be ineffective and not in the public interest. The Supreme Court found it unlikely that Congress intended a drastic departure from the traditions of equity by removing discretion from the trial judge. Justice Douglas' opinion for the Court observed: "The historic injunctive process was designed to deter, not to punish. The essence of equity jurisdiction has been the power of the Chancellor to do equity and to mould each decree to the necessities of the particular case. Flexibility rather than rigidity has distinguished it."

There are, nonetheless, a few statutes that courts interpret as removing or significantly limiting their equitable discretion, either by a statutory preclusion of an injunction or by a statutory mandate of one. In either instance, the legislative intent must clearly guide courts in their remedial options.

The most famous example of this category of statute is the Court's interpretation of the Endangered Species Act of 1973 in *Tennessee Valley Auth. v. Hill*, 437 U.S. 153 (1978). The Court determined that the Act required the district court to enjoin the continued construction of a federal dam project once it determined that the project threatened the habitat of a species protected by the Act, in direct violation of specified statutory protections. The species in question was a snail darter, which was technically covered by the definition of endangered species under the Act. The Court held that the absolute language of the Act removed traditional discretion from the trial court to balance the relative importance of this species with the economic significance of the federal project, which Congress explicitly funded and was near completion at the time the snail darter was discovered. The Court reasoned that the language, history, and structure of the Act demonstrated the clear Congressional intent that protection of certain species be given the highest of priorities because their value was "incalculable." The Court further found that because Congress already considered the public interest and expressed its intent favoring protection of endangered species, the doctrine of separation of powers precluded normative judicial balancing of equities and consequently withdrew its traditional discretion.

In contrast with the statutory mandate of an injunction seen in *TVA v. Hill*, a handful of other statutes have been interpreted specifically to prohibit injunctions. In *Sandoz, Inc. v. Amgen, Inc.*, 137 S. Ct. 1664 (2017) the Court interpreted a federal statute, the Biologics Price Competition and Innovation Act of 2009, to foreclose injunctive relief for certain violations of the Act. The Act authorizes the holder of protectable patents of biological products to bring a declaratory judgment action for infringement in certain instances. The Court reasoned that the specific enumeration of the declaratory judgment remedy in the Act's detailed enforcement scheme provided strong evidence that Congress consequently intended to exclude all other federal remedies, including injunctive relief for particular violations of the Act. Further, the Court buttressed its finding of equity preclusion by observing that the Act did provide for immediate injunctive relief as an appropriate remedy for the violation of other rules which governed confidentiality of information.

Another example of limitation of remedies is found in the Internal Revenue Code provision which effectively prohibits injunctions against the Internal Revenue Service from collecting taxes. *See* 26 U.S.C. § 7421(a). Also, the Norris-LaGuardia Act, 29 U.S.C. § 104, prevents federal courts from enjoining labor disputes by removing federal jurisdiction over such issues. On the state level, some jurisdictions have limited anti-injunction statutes where public interest strongly disfavors interference with the operations of certain local industries. For example, some heavily agricultural states have anti-injunction legislation barring issuance of injunctions against normal farming activities. The provisions are often contained within nuisance statutes that allow for the recovery of damages where a farming activity substantially interferes with an adjoining landowner.

(B) ENJOINING SPEECH

Courts are extremely hesitant to issue injunctions to restrain free speech and freedom of the press. The judicial disinclination of prior restraint corresponds to the strong democratic notion favoring the robust exchange of ideas in the marketplace. *See* New York Times Co. v. Sullivan, 376 U.S. 254 (1964). Consequently, a strong presumption exists against prior restraint of speech and a heavy burden of proof is required to justify issuance of an injunction. *See* Org. for a Better Austin v. Keefe, 402 U.S. 415 (1971). When freedom of speech is exercised in a way that seriously interferes with other important rights, a court may restrain it with a narrowly tailored order.

An early expression of the strong judicial deference given to freedom of the press was shown in *Near v. State of Minnesota ex rel. Olson,* 283 U.S. 697 (1931). The Court invalidated a state statute that provided for abatement as a public nuisance any "malicious, scandalous and defamatory" newspaper article concerning political and public figures. The Court acknowledged that freedom of the press is not an absolute right and the state can punish abuses. The court considered the dangers associated with censorship, however, greater than potential sanctions or subsequent punishment. The Court recognized the liberty of the press historically, stating "the chief purpose of the guaranty to prevent previous restraints upon publication. The struggle in England, directed against the legislative power of the licenser, resulted in renunciation of the censorship of the press." 283 U.S. at 713.

The freedom of press must be balanced, in some instances, with other constitutional protections. For instance, in *Nebraska Press Ass'n v. Stuart,* 427 U.S. 539 (1976) the Court invalidated a pre-trial restraining order issued by a state court prohibiting news media from disseminating information about a criminal trial. The Court acknowledged the conflict between the Sixth Amendment right to a fair trial and the First Amendment guarantee of freedom of the press. However, the Court found that the barriers to prior restraint remained high and the presumption against its use invalidated the injunction. The Court reasoned that the burden of showing a "clear and present danger" that pre-trial publicity could impinge upon the defendant's right to a fair trial had not been met. 427 U.S. at 570.

Not all injunctions that burden speech are necessarily subject to the prior restraint doctrine requiring heightened judicial scrutiny. For example, in *Madsen v. Women's Health Ctr., Inc.*, 512 U.S. 753 (1994), a state court order imposing noise and distance limitations on anti-abortion protesters was deemed content-neutral because it focused on proscribing certain conduct. Although the persons subject to the order may have shared a common viewpoint, the burden on speech was considered only incidental to the conduct prohibited. The Court recognized that injunctions carry a greater risk of censorship and discriminatory application than ordinances, but noted that they have the advantage of being specifically tailored to afford more precise relief than a statute. The Court upheld certain restrictions imposed by the state injunctive order but found that others, such as certain buffer zones and blanket prohibitions on images observable, burdened more speech than necessary to serve a significant government interest. 512 U.S. at 771.

In *Schenck v. Pro-Choice Network of W. New York*, 519 U.S. 357 (1997), the Court upheld the constitutionality of an injunction establishing a "fixed buffer zone" prohibiting protestors from interfering with patients and counselors within 15 feet of an abortion clinic, but found that further provisions that imposed "floating buffer zones" burdened more speech than was necessary. Similarly, in *McCullen v. Coakley*, 573 U.S. 464 (2014) sidewalk counselors challenged a Massachusetts statute which established fixed buffer zones only at clinics that performed abortions. The Court found that the government had demonstrated a legitimate interest in protecting public safety, but also recognized that public streets and sidewalks historically served as an important venues for the robust exchange of ideas. Thus, although the statute was deemed content-neutral, the Court found that it violated First Amendment guarantees because it was not narrowly tailored to serve significant government interests.

The judicial hesitancy to enjoin free expression applies even in situations potentially implicating national security. In the leading case, *New York Times Co. v. United States,* 403 U.S. 713 (1971) the Court invalidated a lower court restraint on publication by newspapers of a classified study dealing with Vietnam War policies of the United States. The Court found that, absent statutory directive, the government failed to meet its heavy burden of justification for use of prior restraint.

(C) ENJOINING CIVIL LITIGATION

A court sitting in equity will generally decline to issue injunctions that restrict access to civil courts or to interfere with the operation of the criminal justice system. A strong public policy favors liberal access to courts and provides a degree of latitude to parties who may lack the sophistication or resources to properly marshal a well-crafted lawsuit. The policy is supported by the American Rule that each party bears its own litigation expenses, absent showing of bad faith, contract, or a fee-shifting statute. Therefore, the instances in which a court may exercise its discretion to prohibit filing of an action are reserved for the exceptional cases.

In some situations, a pattern may emerge that indicates a claimant is abusing the judicial system by filing repetitive or frivolous claims or attempting to reopen closed cases. Federal courts have the inherent authority under the All Writs Act, 28 U.S.C. § 1651, to enjoin such vexatious litigants. A court may then be persuaded to issue a prohibitory injunction against filing future suits with respect to the same dispute without first obtaining leave of court.

The determination whether to enjoin future filings ordinarily involves consideration of various factors, including: (1) the party's history of litigation and whether the suits were vexatious, harassing or duplicative, (2) whether the party had a good faith basis for pursuing the litigation, (3) the extent of the burden on courts and other parties from the party's filings, (4) whether the litigant was represented by counsel, and (5) the adequacy of alternative sanctions to protect the courts and other parties. Heath Vincent Fulkerson v. Allstate Ins., 2020 WL 7353335 (D. Nev. 2020); Matter of Carroll, 850 F.3d 811, 815 (5th Cir. 2017)(bankruptcy court issued pre-filing order enjoining debtors based on demonstrated history of bad faith and harassing litigation).

The party seeking equitable relief bears a heavy burden to demonstrate that a pattern of litigation rises to the level of harassment or excessiveness. In *Dix v. Edelman Financial Services, LLC*, 978 F.3d 507 (7th Cir. 2020), the court issued a pre-filing injunction against a vexatious litigant who had a twenty year history of filing frivolous lawsuits and appeals. The court observed that the "common thread" running through all the filings was that they were "stunningly devoid of merit." If such a finding is made, the court would potentially issue an injunction for two reasons. First, the court would issue injunctive relief to protect the party seeking equitable relief from expending valuable time and resources when forced to defend against such actions. Second, the order would be imposed to protect the judicial system itself from being overburdened with handling meritless cases.

Any prohibitory injunction involves a measure of future prediction that the conduct proscribed is threatened and imminently likely to occur absent equitable intervention. Consequently, although no bright line exists with respect to when multiple filings constitute excessiveness for purposes of justifying equitable intervention, courts carefully balance the public policy favoring open access to the judicial system with concerns over abuse of that process and the accompanying transaction costs borne by parties defending repetitive litigation.

Where an injunction is issued against filing civil suits, the court must take care to write the order narrowly and with sufficient specificity that the party enjoined understands the scope of the subject matter of the order. A willful violation of the order would potentially subject the party restrained to an order of contempt. *See* Unitronics Ltd. v. Gharb, 85 F. Supp. 3d 133 (D.D.C. 2015). Additional procedural guidelines often followed by courts when issuing pre-filing injunctions are providing adequate notice and a hearing and establishing a record for appellate review.

(D) ENJOINING CRIMINAL PROSECUTIONS

Injunctions against criminal prosecutions are extremely rare. Historically, courts commonly expressed the view that, absent statutory authorization, an equity court had no "jurisdiction" over the prosecution, punishment or pardon of crimes and misdemeanors. The modern view, however, firmly holds that courts with general equity powers do possess the jurisdictional power to restrain criminal prosecutions but should exercise their discretion cautiously and reserve such orders for exceptional cases.

The policy reasons supporting a general rule of non-intervention focus on the respective purposes and functions of the civil and criminal courts. Courts of equity are not established nor designed to deal with criminal proceedings, lack power to punish persons who violate penal statutes, and do not compensate persons injured as a consequence of criminal statutes.

The exceptional circumstances in which a court may enjoin criminal proceedings, then, generally require (1) a clear showing that an injunction is necessary to adequately safeguard important rights of the accused, such as the party's vested property rights; (2) the remedy at law of defending under the relevant criminal statute is inadequate; and (3) that the order can be imposed without imposing an undue burden upon or show disrespect to the criminal court.

An illustration of where a state civil court may enjoin a threatened or existing criminal case in its jurisdiction is upon a demonstration of improper prosecutorial motivation. An extra-territorial injunction seeking to restrain a criminal prosecution in another state would have the additional problem of impracticality of enforcement against non-resident parties. Principles of federalism further limit the willingness of a federal court to issue an injunction against state court proceedings. The strong policy of judicial restraint reflects respect for the integrity of the state court system. The court, as a general policy, will find that a party has an adequate remedy at law by defending themselves in the criminal cases.

(E) ENJOINING NUISANCES

Nuisance law presents certain unique challenges to courts with respect to determining the propriety of injunctive relief. The nature of nuisance law involves a comparative evaluation of competing land uses. The balancing process occurs on two separate levels. First, the threshold requirements to maintain an action are that the defendant's conduct constitutes a substantial and unreasonable interference with the use and enjoyment of the plaintiff's property or public interests. Not every interference with other land uses will amount to an actionable nuisance, but it must be unreasonable based upon consideration of the benefits of the activity, suitability to the locale, and the gravity of the harm. Once the standards for entitlement are met, the court will also consider if the threatened harm is immediate, the injury constitutes irreparable harm, no adequate remedy at law exists, and the balance of hardships favors equitable intervention. The court will determine the extent to which damages will sufficiently redress the injury and the relevance of public interest factors. The legal consequence of a particular prediction is easily applied only at the two extremes: Equity will not enjoin a completed act but may grant injunctions to halt clearly continuous invasions of an important interest where a remedy at law is inadequate.

Nuisances may be classified as either public or private, although the distinction presents difficulties of application to courts. A private nuisance traditionally focuses on the substantial character of interference with conflicting land uses and seeks to protect the use and enjoyment of property. Accordingly, a private nuisance seldom exists except with reference to another competing land use. In contrast, a public nuisance does not necessarily involve the invasion of a protectable interest in the use and enjoyment of property. Rather, a public nuisance is an unreasonable interference with a right common to the general public, such as involving health and safety. Illustrations include keeping diseased animals, storage or shooting fireworks in public, obstruction of public highways, or widely disseminated offensive odors or smoke. *See* Restatement (Second) of Torts § 821B, cmt. B (1971). The historical development of public nuisance arose out of criminal law and the relationship may still be seen with certain public nuisance statutes carrying modest criminal sanctions. Not every violation of a public nuisance statute necessarily constitutes a criminal transgression, but often statutes will provide for criminal fines as one remedial alternative available to the court.

An important difference between public and private nuisance involves determining the proper party who possesses the requisite standing to bring a claim. Because the origin of public nuisance derived from criminal law, the traditional view is that only a duly authorized public official has the right to institute a public nuisance suit. An exception exists which allows a private party to maintain a suit for public nuisance only where they can demonstrate suffering a harm different in kind from that experienced by other persons. Restatement (Second) of Torts § 821C (1979). It is not sufficient to claim a greater degree of harm or more serious interference, but rather that the harm sustained is qualitatively distinct from others. Assuming an individual can make such a showing, it follows that they could assert both public and private nuisance claims.

Some activities, occupations, or structures are so offensive at all times and under all circumstances, regardless of location or surroundings, that they constitute a nuisance *per se*. Activities that imminently and dangerously threaten the public health fall into this category. It is more often the case, however, that the activities challenged by suitors in a nuisance case fall short of this standard of imminent and dangerous harm. Such activities which cause more remote harm to people or are the source of inconvenience, annoyance, and minor damage to property are labeled "nuisance in fact" or nuisance *per accidens*. These latter activities are nuisances primarily because of the circumstances or the location and surrounding of the activities, rather than the nature of the activities themselves. An otherwise lawful business which conducts its activities in a manner that presents a substantial and unreasonable interference with the use and enjoyment of neighboring land uses will fall within this second category. Also, most air and water pollution, when their effects are only minimally or remotely harmful to the public health, will be nuisances *per accidens*.

Consider the situation where a large factory discharges effluent into a drainage ditch and the waste leaches into an aquifer, resulting in the contamination of crops being raised on adjacent land. The surrounding landowners may successfully bring a claim for private nuisance and collect temporary damages, such as diminished rental value or lost crops for the past invasion of their land. The periodic payment of damages, though, would probably not substantially affect the operations of the factory in the future.

The court would balance the economic and public interest advantages associated with operation of the factory, such as providing jobs and taxes, with the health and safety impact on the landowners. The concern with awarding damages rather than injunctive relief is that it would effectively be licensing a continuing wrong and allow payment of damages as a type of private eminent domain. Since the activity is of an ongoing nature, however, the court may find damages an inadequate and ineffective remedy because the pollution will remain unabated and the landowners would be forced to bring multiple suits for compensation. Further, if the interference is particularly hazardous to human health or the environment, such as polluting with toxic waste, the court will likely issue an injunction to abate the activity.

Ordinarily, a permanent injunction will not lie unless either (1) the polluter seriously and imminently threatens the public health or (2) causes non-health injuries that are substantial and the business cannot be operated to avoid the injuries apprehended. When the offensive activities of an otherwise legitimate business operation fall short of that standard, only the combination of substantial annoyances caused to adjoining property owners plus the impracticability of mitigating the offensive characteristics of the business will ordinarily justify the granting of injunctive relief. In any event, injunctions against a nuisance are never granted automatically nor a matter of right, but the decision rests with the sound discretion of the judge sitting in equity.

An illustration of the difficulties in balancing disparate interests such as economics with health and safety may be found in the famous case, *Boomer v. Atlantic Cement Co.*, 26 N.Y.2d 219 (1970). In *Boomer*, neighboring landowners sought to enjoin the operation of a large cement plant, claiming that the dirt, smoke and vibrations emanating from the plant constituted a nuisance. The court granted an injunction but conditioned its effect on the defendant's payment of permanent damages to compensate for the economic losses to their property. The court considered the social and economic repercussions from shutting down the factory in terms of lost jobs and taxes, balanced with the problems posed by the cement dust. The court, in favoring a legal remedy, expressed deference to the legislature as being in a better position to balance the various public and private interests at stake by promulgating a comprehensive solution to the issues of air pollution.

A zoning ordinance may affect the availability and the nature of injunctive relief. The defendant's compliance with state or local governmental regulations is relevant to the assessment of the reasonableness of the activity and its suitability to the locale. Compliance with all pertinent regulations is not always sufficient to defeat an injunction, however. If a court finds an activity to present an imminent and extremely hazardous danger to public health and safety, an injunction would be issued in the public interest to foreclose the threat.

Some statutes may directly govern public and private nuisances and may include the availability of damages or injunctive relief for violation of the statutory provisions. The statute may denominate certain activities as constituting a nuisance *per se*, which could influence a court to favor issuance of an injunction to abate the ongoing offense. In those instances, though, a court typically retains its equitable discretion with respect to whether damages or an injunction would be the more effective and appropriate remedy. *See* Restatement (Second) of Torts § 821D (1979).

Some jurisdictions have passed anti-injunction acts affecting nuisance cases. The statutes generally preclude courts from restraining business activities that are being reasonably conducted in compliance with zoning regulations. An anti-injunction act does not ordinarily withdraw the court's equitable jurisdiction, but may affect the manner in which it exercises discretion.

A typical injunction case involves some degree of future prediction. The judge must determine both the likelihood and degree of future threatened harm absent the injunction. If the claimant seeks an injunction against an activity that already occurred, the court will deny relief following the maxim that "equity will not enjoin a completed act." To illustrate, a factory malfunction causes noxious gases to escape and damage an orchard located on adjacent land. The factory subsequently repairs the problem and no further incidents occur. A court will not issue an injunction on the basis that the incident is not reasonably imminent to occur; therefore, such an order would be without merit. On the other hand, where an ongoing activity presents a continuous invasion of an important interest an injunction may be proper because the remedy at law is inadequate.

A court is faced with an especially difficult task of prediction when the activity sought to be enjoined is causing no current harm and poses only an uncertain future threat. Ordinarily courts will not issue an injunction absent a sufficient showing that an invasion of legally protected interests is likely to occur. For example, in *Nicholson v. Connecticut Half-Way House, Inc.,* 153 Conn. 507 (1966), residents sought to enjoin the prospective use of defendant's property as a temporary residence for selected parolees from state prison. The plaintiffs claimed that the parolees might commit criminal acts in their neighborhood and that the half-way house would cause their property values to depreciate. The court denied injunctive relief because unsubstantiated fears could not justify the intervention of equity.

Compare *Whipple v. Village of North Utica,* 79 N.E.3d 667 (Ill. App. 2017) where neighboring property owners sought to enjoin a silica sand mine as a prospective nuisance. The court found that the trial court erred in dismissing the complaint because the plaintiffs had sufficiently shown that it was highly probable the operation of the mine would detrimentally affect ground water, crops, and the peaceful use and enjoyment of their property.

Some courts apply a sliding scale to evaluate the issues of likelihood of future harm and the potential severity of the prospective injury. Where the claimant may hold a more difficult burden of demonstrating the imminence of the harm yet makes a more compelling showing on the degree of injury, a court may find equity appropriate to prohibit the threatened harm. Even in those cases, though, a presently existing actual threat must be shown rather than the mere possibility of some remote future injury.

Another issue involving the role of equity in nuisance law deals with reconciling the timing of priority of location of competing land uses. Under the "coming to the nuisance" doctrine, courts historically denied equitable relief to a party who knowingly located adjacent to an existing, lawfully conducted business and then complained that the land use constituted a nuisance. The rationale behind foreclosing equitable relief was that the party either impliedly consented to the offending use or should have reasonably foreseen that the activity would cause a significant interference with their own property interests. Further, the doctrine gives some measure of protection to justifiable investment expectations of the existing land uses. The general rule of shielding the existing use from equitable action has been losing force in modern law, however, and replaced with a multi-factor analysis that treats the timing of location of respective uses as one consideration in the balancing calculus. Restatement (Second) of Torts § 840D (1979).

An early example of the changing trend may be seen in the notable decision, *Spur Industries, Inc. v.*

Del E. Webb Development Co., 108 Ariz. 178 (1972). A major residential development situated outside a metropolitan area slowly expanded such that a number of houses were in close proximity to a large cattle feedlot. The noxious odors emanating from the feedlot interfered with the residents and potential buyers, leading the developer to seek an injunction against the operation as a public and private nuisance. The court granted the injunction and mandated the relocation of the feedlot but conditioned the order upon the developer's indemnification of expenses for the move. Although the feedlot had priority in time over the residential development, the court found that it did not automatically foreclose equitable relief. The court was persuaded that the public interest favored enjoining the feedlot based upon the magnitude of the interference and the inadequate remedy at law.

(F) ENJOINING CRIMES

In some situations, the same conduct may potentially implicate both civil and criminal laws. A common illustration is where certain actions may constitute a public nuisance, which is proscribed under both civil and criminal statutes. If so, and a claimant seeks an injunction through civil courts to abate the offending behavior, the judge sitting in equity faces a dilemma whether or not to exercise jurisdiction. *See* Western Sky Financial, LLC v. State, 793 S.E.2d 357, 368 (Ga. 2016)(State attorney general not precluded from seeking to enjoin illegal conduct of violation of usury laws by out-of-state lenders where statute did not provide an adequate remedy at law).

The historical rule is reflected by the maxim that "equity will not enjoin a crime." The statement itself is somewhat overbroad, however. The civil court certainly retains power to enjoin but often will defer to enforcement of the violation through the criminal justice system.

Several important reasons support such deference. First, if the civil court issued an injunction, the defendant would lose the right to jury trial in an equity proceeding. Second, the standard of proof for issuance of an equitable order is lower than beyond a reasonable doubt under the criminal statutes. Third, the judge may determine that an adequate remedy at law exists in the penal sanctions available through enforcement of the criminal statutes. Finally, the equity court may refrain from acting out of deference and respect to the criminal courts and, in the interests of judicial economy, to avoid duplicative proceedings.

The general notion of restraint embodied in the rule is not followed in all cases, however. If the enforcement of the criminal laws does not appear to effectively abate the conduct, then an equity court may decide that a civil injunction would be an appropriate remedy. Consider a situation, where operation of a gambling house violates provisions of a state or local statute, but the only penalty specified for violation under the statutory scheme is a small fine. Several actions of enforcement of the statute resulted in imposition of fines, but the gambling house continues in operation. At that juncture, the equity court may determine that the criminal statute does not constitute an adequate legal remedy to address the proscribed conduct and issue a permanent injunction.

For example, in *Goose v. Commonwealth ex rel. Dummit,* 205 S.W.2d 326 (Ky. App. 1947), the court issued an injunction against the proprietors of a gambling establishment. The court found that numerous arrests of the operators during a five year period had not been effective in abating the criminal conduct. The state therefore had no adequate remedy at law, and the ongoing activities caused irreparable harm to the public. The court stated: "The ground of the jurisdiction is the ability of the chancellor to give a more complete and perfect remedy by a perpetual injunction. It is a weapon from the arsenal of equity to be used to protect Society—to meet the social need that continuation of the offenses at a given place shall be repressed." 205 S.W.2d at 328.

The outer limit of the intervention of equity courts may be seen in another well known case, *State v. Red Owl Stores, Inc.,* 92 N.W.2d 103 (Minn. 1958). The state requested an injunction to restrain the defendant corporations from selling and distributing certain drugs without obtaining the necessary registration and licenses required by the state's Pharmacy Act. The trial court denied the injunctive relief on the grounds that the exclusive remedy in the Act was enforcement by criminal prosecution. The Minnesota Supreme Court reversed, reasoning that the state lacked an adequate remedy at law to enforce a public health measure. The found the legal remedy inadequate because enforcement through the sanctions in the Act would require a multiplicity of actions, even though the state had not yet instituted any enforcement action of the criminal statute.

Rather than a blanket rule of restraint, the modern approach holds that equity courts will generally decline to exercise jurisdiction where a criminal statute offers a sanction against the conduct at issue. Thus, while equity will certainly not enjoin conduct merely because it also violates a criminal statute, neither is a court entirely precluded from such action. The critical determinant is whether or not the injunction will serve a useful purpose and not inappropriately deprive the accused of important safeguards otherwise available through the criminal justice system.

Conagra Foods, Inc. v. Zimmerman, 846 N.W.2d 223 (Neb. 2014) offers a modern application of this balancing of equities. In that case, a trespasser entered the workplace of his estranged spouse and fired shots at window washers working at the building. The employer sought injunctive relief to bar further trespasses. The trial court initially issued a temporary injunction, then dissolved it and denied the employer's request for a permanent injunction. The Nebraska Supreme Court acknowledged that ordinarily the prosecution of such offenses through criminal law offered an adequate remedy at law. However, finding sufficient evidence that the defendant was likely to "flagrantly violate" the criminal laws of the state, the court granted a permanent injunction to prevent future trespassing onto the employer's property. 846 N.W.2d at 230.

CHAPTER 10
BREACH OF CONTRACT REMEDIES

(A) COMMON LAW CONTRACT DAMAGES

Traditional contract law recognizes and protects the injured party's expectancy, reliance, and restitutionary interests in the bargain. The basic purpose of compensatory damages under both the common law and the Uniform Commercial Code is to place the injured party in as good a position as if full performance had been rendered under the contract. The measure of recovery will vary depending upon which of the interests are asserted, although in some instances a breach may give rise to recovery under more than one of the three interests. The law of contract damages also incorporates additional policy considerations of avoiding economic waste, promoting efficient breach of contract to move goods and services to the highest bidder, and advancing the public interest. Since an award of damages for breach of contract does not require judicial supervision or enforcement in the same manner as equitable decrees, the need for judicial oversight is not a factor in determining entitlement and measurement of compensation.

1. EXPECTANCY

Expectancy damages protect the injured party's bargained-for expectation under the contract. Expectancy damages provide a monetary substitute for the promised but undelivered performance. Stated another way, expectancy damages are measured as the amount necessary to place the injured party in as good a financial position as she would have occupied had the breaching party performed under the contract. For example, assume that Seller agrees to sell Buyer a used car for $10,000 and that the car has a market value of $12,000. Had the parties completed the sale, Buyer would have exchanged $10,000 in cash or the equivalent for a $12,000 car. Thus, Buyer would have realized a $2,000 increase in value. As such, Buyer's expectation or benefit under the contract is the $2,000 "bargain" she has negotiated. Alternatively, if Seller refuses to deliver the car, Buyer presumably will have to pay $12,000 to another seller to purchase a car of comparable value. Thus, Buyer will need $2,000 to be put in as good a financial position as she would have been had the sale been completed. Accordingly, Buyer's expectancy damages would be measured as the difference between the market value of the car and the contract price.

2. RELIANCE

The non-breaching party may seek damages for expenses incurred in reliance upon performance of contractual duties. Generally, reliance damages and expectancy damages are alternative remedies, and only one may be awarded. Because reliance damages are generally a lesser recovery, plaintiffs most often seek reliance damages when they cannot recover expectancy damages for some reason such as when the plaintiff cannot prove expectancy damages with reasonable certainty.

For example, assume that Franchisee entered into a contract with Franchisor to open a new restaurant, but Franchisor breached the contract before Franchisee could open the restaurant. Franchisee's expectancy under the contract would be primarily its lost profits. If Franchisee was unable to prove those lost profits with reasonable certainty, Franchisee would be able to recover any costs it had incurred in preparing to open the restaurant. Those costs might include costs such as advertising, renting space, or purchasing inventory.

A party who has entered into a losing contract will have no expectancy damages. Courts disagree about whether and to what extent a party to a losing contract may recover expenses incurred in reliance upon the performance of duties prior to the contract breach. Some courts reduce a plaintiff's recovery by the amount of any losses the plaintiff would have sustained had the contract been performed. However, the defendant generally bears the burden of proving that the plaintiff would have sustained a loss and the amount of the loss with reasonable certainty.

In rare situations, expenses incurred in reliance upon the performance of contractual duties may be added to the loss of expectancy.

3.   RESTITUTION

Contract law similarly protects restitutionary interests. Confusion sometimes occurs, however, in distinguishing between restitution as an entire field of law that may independently provide remedies from the interest reflected within a bargained-for exchange. The law of restitution boasts a lengthy heritage both at law and in equity, emerging in the dual system of law courts and Chancery courts that developed through the influence of the church in England. Although some of the forms and requirements varied between the two lines of restitution, they shared the common purpose of preventing unjust enrichment. The basic premise of restitution was to serve the ends of justice by properly "restoring" back to the rightful party benefits that a defendant held unjustly. Wrongdoing was not a requirement for disgorging the benefit, as a plaintiff could properly use restitution to restore funds mistakenly paid to the wrong party.

On the equity side, some of the restitutionary remedies included constructive trusts, equitable liens, accounting for profits, subrogation, and cancellation and reformation of instruments. On the law side, the remedies emerged in the form of "common counts", such as "money had and received", "quantum valebant", and "quantum meruit". These were generally called "quasi-contracts" because the court would order a payment of money for either goods or services based on a fictional construct, not an actual contract. The remedy was unrelated to an express contract or implied-in-fact contract but instead was a contract implied-in-law to achieve the result of preventing unjust enrichment.

Completely apart from these formal remedial devices at law and equity, the law also recognized and protected the restitutionary *interest* that was embodied within an express contract. This interest served the same basic function of restoring back to the injured party some benefit that the other contracting party should not retain, through restitution damages.

Consider the following illustration: Buyer pays the full contract price of $10,000 to purchase 1,000 widgets from Seller, but Seller only delivers 800 widgets. Under U.C.C. § 2–712, the Buyer has the right to enter the market and purchase substitute widgets in a commercially reasonable manner to replace the shortfall of 200 widgets and receive the difference between the contract and market price for the goods, plus incidental damages less expenses saved. The Seller should also repay the $2,000 overpayment for the non-delivered goods to protect Buyer's restitutionary interest in the contract. The restitutionary interest in this example would be combined with protecting the Buyer's expectancy interest via the Code provisions on cover to replace the undelivered goods.

The Restatement (Third) of Restitution and Unjust Enrichment (2011) attempts to resolve some of the confusion by delineating separately the principles governing restitution that is based on unjust enrichment and restitution that is based on an enforceable contract. Principles governing restitution for unjust enrichment appear in sections 31–36. Principles governing restitution for breach of an enforceable contract appear in sections 37–38 and are expressly termed "restitutionary remedies for breach of an enforceable contract."

4. GENERAL AND SPECIAL DAMAGES

The common law of contracts classifies damages as either "general" or "special". The importance of distinguishing between them turns on the principle of foreseeability, which found early expression in the English case, *Hadley v. Baxendale*, 9 Ex. 341, 156 Eng. Rep. 145 (Ex. Ct. 1854):

> Where two parties have made a contract which one of them had broken, the damages which the other party ought to receive in respect of such breach of contract should be such as may fairly and reasonably be considered either arising naturally, i.e., according to the usual course of things, from such breach of contract itself, or such as may reasonably be supposed to have been in the contemplation of both parties, at the time they made the contract, as the probable result of the breach of it.

Also see Restatement (Second) of Contracts § 351 (1981). Thus, general damages are those which flow directly and immediately as a natural consequence of the kind of wrongful act by the breaching party. The law conclusively presumes such damages to be foreseen or contemplated by the defendant. Most commonly, general damages are damages that compensate the injured party for damage to or loss of the object of the contract. For example, assume that Contractor and Owner enter into a contract for

Contractor to build an office building according to certain specifications. If Contractor fails to build according to those specifications, general damages will be measured as the cost to correct the defect and conform the building to the contract specifications.

In contrast, special damages do not always follow from the kind of conduct involved. Accordingly, breaching parties are liable only where the evidence shows that they should have reasonably foreseen the kind of harm resulting from their non-performance at the time of entering the agreement. Special damages usually arise from the use to which the non-breaching party intended to put the object of the contract. Thus, breaching parties generally are liable for special damages only where they should have reasonably foreseen the use that the non-breaching party intended to make of the object. For example, as discussed above, in a construction defect case, damages awarded as the cost to correct the defective condition would be classified as general damages and would not require special foreseeability. In contrast, if Owner sought lost profits due to delays in opening the office building due to the faulty construction, those damages would be "special" and necessitate foreseeability by the contractor.

Although the terms "general" and "special" damages have diminished in application in some jurisdictions, the Uniform Commercial Code has embraced the essence of the special damages criteria under § 2–715(2) with respect to the availability of consequential damages to an aggrieved buyer of goods. Section 2–715(2) allows the buyer to recover consequential damages only if the seller, at the time of contracting, had "reason to know" of general or particular requirements of the buyer and the damages could not be prevented by cover or otherwise. General damages are reflected in § 2–714 as providing recovery for the difference in the value of accepted but non-conforming goods compared to the value as warranted.

5.   COST RULE AND VALUE RULE

The common law recognizes two competing measures of damages for loss of the expectancy interest, generally called the "cost rule" and the "value rule." A typical scenario in which these rules may come into effect would involve incomplete or defective construction under a building contract. The cost rule allows the non-breaching party to recover as damages the cost to complete construction or remedy the defective condition to conform to the contract. The value rule measures damages by the diminution in value of the performance received compared to the value as promised.

The difficulty arises where remedying the defective condition may involve expenditures that substantially exceed the diminution in value measure. Although theoretically both measures of damages would provide recovery for the expectancy interest, most courts will award the diminution in value where the cost of repairs would be clearly disproportionate to the value to the injured party of correcting the defect. Most courts will award repair costs that disproportionately exceed diminished value only if the defect frustrates the purpose of the contract.

The policy supporting that result often is stated as avoidance of economic waste that may accrue from making excessively costly repairs. Other courts point to concerns of giving a windfall to the non-breaching party for the cost to repair. The windfall argument recognizes that the injured party may simply choose to retain the damages awarded and forego making the repairs. The injured party is less likely to forego making repairs when the repairs are necessary to effectuate the purpose of the contract.

For example, in the leading case of *Jacob & Youngs v. Kent*, 230 N.Y. 239 (1921), a contractor built a residence, but installed a brand of plumbing pipe which differed from the specifications. The mistake was made in good faith, the replacement pipe was functionally equivalent to the brand specified, and was discovered only after completion of the project. The court held that the proper measure of damages would be the difference in value between the pipe specified and the type actually installed, reasoning that it would result in economical waste to tear down the house just to obtain the small benefit of substituting a different brand of pipe.

A few courts have awarded damages for the higher cost to complete performance on the basis that the defendant breached the contract willfully or acted in bad faith. *See* Groves v. John Wunder Co., 205 Minn. 163, 286 N.W. 235 (1939). The vast majority of courts, though, have focused on the degree of proportionality between the two measures of damages as the controlling factor rather than on the subjective motivation for the contract breach. Additional factors courts have considered in deciding between the cost rule and value rule have included: the degree of variance between the performance promised and the actual performance rendered, the purpose and expectations of the parties, potential hardship or forfeiture to the breaching party, and the extent to which the conduct of the breaching party comported with standards of good faith and fair dealing.

6.   NEW BUSINESS RULE

Courts traditionally have held that new businesses could not recover lost profits for breach of contract. The rationale for precluding recovery was that the lack of sufficient operating history for new businesses necessarily made prospective profits too speculative, contingent, and remote to satisfy the legal standard of reasonable certainty. The distinction drawn between new business ventures and existing operations for awards of future profits became so common that some courts elevated it to virtually a *per se* rule.

A growing trend, however, focuses on whether the damages can be established with sufficient evidence rather than precluding recovery automatically. *Also see* U.C.C. § 2–708, cmt. 2 (not necessary to a recovery of a seller's profit to show a history of earnings, especially for a new venture.) These courts acknowledge that a new business faces a greater burden of proof in establishing the loss of anticipated profits but allow the claimant an opportunity to produce evidence to meet the reasonable certainty standard. Courts recognize two possible methods to prove lost profits. Under the "before and after" theory, plaintiffs introduce evidence of their track record of profits prior to and following the breach of contract. An alternative method, called the "yardstick" test, considers evidence of profits by comparable business operations. The Restatement (Second) of Contracts § 352, cmt. b (1981) takes a more neutral position and provides that the difficulty of proving lost profits should vary depending upon the nature of the transaction.

7.   LIQUIDATED DAMAGES

Parties to a contract may decide to "liquidate" or specify the amount of damages payable to the non-breaching party in the event of a material breach of contract. The use of a liquidated damages clause may offer several advantages, such as allowing the parties to control or limit their economic risk, to curtail the uncertainties associated with proving actual damages, and to avoid the time and expense of litigation. Additionally, the clauses promote judicial economy through reduced litigation and burden on the court system. On the other hand, some critics express concern that private parties should not supplant the role of courts in styling their own remedy, that the potential for excessive damages could deter efficient breach of contract, and that a liquidated damages clause could be the product of unfairness or overreaching in the bargaining process. The balance often drawn is to use a liquidated damages clause in agreements where, at the time of contract formation, the parties anticipate difficulties could exist in proving actual compensatory damages and decide to make a reasoned forecast of losses if a breach occurred. For example, such clauses are used with some frequency in construction contracts, employment agreements, and real estate transactions.

Although parties possess considerable discretion in stipulating in advance an amount of damages, they are still limited by basic principles otherwise governing compensatory damages. Consequently, a liquidated damages provision will be upheld when it meets the standard of a good faith, reasonable pre-estimate of actual damages. In that sense, the clause simply serves as substitutionary measure for performance in the event of a breach. In contrast, in situations where a court determines that the purpose of the clause is to compel performance or to punish non-performance with excessive damages, it will be considered a penalty and thus unenforceable on grounds of public policy. The *in terrorem* effect of an onerous liquidated damages clause transcends the goal of compensation and is viewed in the same judicial light as unconscionable bargains. Unreasonably low stipulated damages for breach of contract may also reflect overreaching by the favored party.

The labels applied by the parties to characterize a provision as an enforceable liquidated damages clause rather than a penalty are not conclusive. Although some courts may assign some weight to the terminology selected by the parties as one factor in interpreting the validity of a liquidated damages clause, most jurisdictions look beyond the intent to the substance and function for determining enforceability.

The law of liquidated damages reinforces the common law policy of allowing efficient contract breach. In that sense, a contracting party should be permitted to pay the liquidated amount as a type of compensatory damages resulting from a breach in exchange for the opportunity to shift goods or services to a different source in order to maximize economic resources. In contrast, a clause that essentially functions to punish or deter a contract breach would be inefficient in economic terms and contradict the principle of fair compensation.

The traditional test to evaluate the validity of a liquidated damages provision is whether, at the time the parties entered into the contract, the stipulated amount bears a reasonable relationship to the anticipated or actual losses caused by a breach, and damages are difficult to determine. *See* Uniform Commercial Code § 2–718(1) and Restatement (Second) of Contracts § 356(1). The U.C.C. adds the factor of "inconvenience or non-feasibility" of otherwise obtaining an adequate remedy as another consideration in evaluating reasonableness.

Parties may show the reasonableness of a liquidated damages clause by evaluating either the anticipated or actual harm from the breach. Since the parties are dealing with various uncertainties of future risks and potential losses at the time of contracting, subsequent proof of actual harm attributable to the breach invariably will be either higher or lower than the specified amount. Because the amount of provable actual damages will almost certainly vary from that stipulated in the contract, the inquiry of reasonableness in estimation is predicated upon the factors objectively contemplated by the parties at the time of contract formation. The very uncertainty in predicting future harm militates against requiring an exact correlation of actual to liquidated damages.

For example, if parties to an employment contract include a liquidated damages clause, they may do so in recognition that a discharge of the employee by the corporation in breach of the agreement may cause the employee certain subjective injuries like harm to reputation, that would be difficult to prove or calculate. Similarly, a new business venture may choose to include a liquidated damages clause in a construction contract because any future lost profits from delays in construction would potentially be speculative. As long as the parties have a reasonable basis for the selection of the amount, such as by reference to market conditions, custom in the industry, prior dealings, or other risk factors, the clause will typically be upheld under principles of freedom of contract. The measure of damages under a liquidated clause is basically an "all or nothing" proposition, as the court will decide whether or not the provision satisfies the standard of reasonableness.

Another aspect to the traditional common law test for upholding a liquidated damages clause is that the potential damages which might accrue as a result of a breach must be uncertain and difficult to ascertain. The Restatement (Second) of Contracts § 356 comment b (1981) approaches the uncertainty of loss factor with a flexible test based on the nature of the harm. So, to the extent that the nature of the transaction would involve a high degree of difficulty in proving actual losses, more discretion may be given to the amount selected by the parties. The Uniform Commercial Code test in § 2–718(1) has reduced difficulty of loss from treatment as a separate factor to serving as one consideration regarding the reasonableness of the clause.

If a liquidated damages clause is deemed invalid, the non-breaching party may still seek to prove actual compensatory damages resulting from the breach. The standard requirements of proving causation, entitlement, and measurement of compensatory damages would apply.

Several issues exist with respect to whether a liquidated damages clause is considered the exclusive remedy for breach of contract or just an alternative course of action. The prevailing view is that a valid liquidated damages clause will be the sole remedy available to the non-breaching party only upon express language evidencing a clear intent to exclude all other remedies. *See* Rubinstein v. Rubinstein, 23 N.Y.2d 293 (1968). Some courts apply a presumption against exclusivity. S*ee* Chesapeake Square Hotel, LLC v. Logan's Roadhouse, Inc., 2014 WL 970189 (E.D. Va. 2014). Consequently, unless the contract unequivocally states otherwise, the non-breaching party may choose whether to rely upon the liquidated sum or seek other remedies at law or equity. *See* North American Consol., Inc. v. Kopka, 644 F. Supp. 191 (D. Mass. 1986)(vendor claim for specific performance not precluded by existence of liquidated damages provision). Another perspective is that the provision is the sole option available. *See* Fisher v. Schmeling, 520 N.W.2d 820 (N. Dak. 1994)(liquidated damages clause in land purchase agreement provided exclusive remedy to vendor).

In the context of equity, the liquidated damages clause becomes the focus for the inquiry whether the damages constituted an adequate remedy at law. In any event, double recovery of the liquidated amount and compensatory damages is precluded by ordinary principles of contract damages.

In summary, the law of liquidated damages reflects a tension between conflicting goals. The law finds it socially desirable for parties to fix damages in the event of breach when the amount bears a reasonable proportion to the probable loss and the actual loss is difficult to estimate with precision. Such a provision, however, should not have the effect of deterring breach through compulsion because of the potential high economic loss.

8.   PREJUDGMENT INTEREST AS DAMAGES

Prejudgment interest may be awarded as an additional item of compensatory damages for breach of contract. *See* Chapter 12, *infra*. The claimant may be entitled to interest on damages where the breach involves a failure to pay a specific sum of money, render a performance with a fixed or ascertainable monetary value, or in other instances where justice requires to achieve full compensation. The party in breach receives an offset against such an award for any deductions to which they would be entitled under the contract. *See* Restatement (Second) of Contracts § 354 (1981).

The claimant effectively became entitled to a specific sum of compensatory damages when performance was unfulfilled, yet she will not receive payment of those funds until the judgment is satisfied or the claim is settled. The primary purpose of awarding interest on damages owed is to compensate the injured party for the loss of use of money for the period of time commencing when the claim for breach of contract accrued until the date of judgment. Further, a prejudgment interest award removes any incentive to delay in settling the dispute or in paying a judgment and eliminates the potential unjust enrichment of the breaching party by earning interest on funds owed to the claimant.

The award is typically discretionary, however, and requires a showing of reasonable certainty in the assessment of the amount of damages associated with the breach as well as determination of the time in which the damages were incurred. The interest awarded is not punitive but rather corresponds to the goal of compensatory damages of placing the non-breaching party in the same position economically as if the contract had been fully performed as promised.

Prejudgment interest should be distinguished from postjudgment interest. Prejudgment interest flows from the common law principles of compensation and is awarded if the claimant demonstrates entitlement. Prejudgment interest compensates the claimant for the loss of the use of the money from the date of the breach until the date of judgment. In contrast, post-judgment interest is awarded routinely by statutory directive. It compensates the claimant for the loss of use of money from the time of judgment until the time the judgment is satisfied.

9. PUNITIVE DAMAGES

Courts generally will not award punitive damages for breach of contract. Some courts recognize an exception in which punitive damages may be imposed where the conduct giving rise to the breach also constitutes the type of tort that could independently support an exemplary award, such as fraud. *See* Restatement (Second) of Contract § 355 (1981). Those instances are not truly an exception to the basic rule, though, because the tortious behavior supports the punitive award and the breach of contract is merely incidental.

Punitive damages serve to punish and deter certain types of behavior, while breach of contract damages seek to compensate the non-breaching party for the loss of promised performance. A party may choose to breach a contract for various reasons, including a decision to pursue more economically advantageous options than fulfilling performance under an existing agreement. Economic efficiency advances the wide use of such choices, whereby the person who values the goods and services most highly may acquire them. Transaction costs in effecting multiple exchanges may impact whether efficiencies are realized, of course, but the principal purpose of contract damages nevertheless looks to compensating the injured party for the benefit of their bargain and not punishing the breaching party for non-performance. If punitive damages were awarded for contract breach, the goals of contract damages would be undermined and potential marketplace efficiencies could be lost.

(B) SALE OF GOODS CONTRACTS

1. BUYERS' REMEDIES

The damages remedies with respect to contracts for the sale of goods are governed by Article 2 of the Uniform Commercial Code. The remedies available to non-breaching buyers essentially correspond to those available to non-breaching sellers. The buyer's expectancy interest is compensated with three principal elements of damages: (1) contract-market differential damages or cover damages; (2) incidental losses incurred as a result of the breach; and (3) consequential losses that are reasonably foreseeable by the breaching party, including items such as lost profits.

Further, Article 2 provides buyers and sellers with corresponding remedies of rescission and restitution [U.C.C. §§ 2–703, 2–711] and specific performance or an action for the price *See* U.C.C. §§ 2–716 and 2–709. The remedies are considered cumulatively available to the non-breaching party, as the U.C.C.

rejects the election of remedies doctrine "as a fundamental policy." U.C.C. § 2–703, cmt. 1. In keeping with the general policy of the liberal administration of remedies, the Code requires that damages be proven with reasonable certainty rather than mathematical exactitude. *See* U.C.C. § 1–305, cmt. 1.

1–(a). Damages for Non-Delivery or Repudiation of Goods

Where a seller breaches by repudiating or failing to deliver goods, or where the buyer rightfully rejects or justifiably revokes acceptance of a seller's nonconforming tender, the buyer is entitled to receive damages as measured by one of two alternative measures.

1–(a)(i). Cover

One of the primary remedies available to a non-breaching buyer under the Code is "cover." That is, following a breach, the Code permits an aggrieved buyer to enter the market and make a reasonable purchase of substitute goods. *See* U.C.C. § 2–712. The aggrieved buyer may then recover the difference between the cost to cover and the contract price plus incidental or consequential damages, less expenses saved.

To meet the requirements for effecting cover, the buyer must (1) act in good faith, (2) without unreasonable delay, and (3) make a reasonable purchase of substitute goods. The buyer need not purchase identical goods. Instead, the acquired goods must be "reasonable" substitutes. Likewise, the cover contract need not replicate exactly the terms of the original contract. For example, the buyer may buy in a single contract or a series and may vary credit and delivery terms. The guiding principle is that the buyer must act in a commercially reasonable manner.

A properly effected, commercially reasonable cover achieves three objectives. First, the affirmative grant of authority to enter the market and obtain needed goods protects the expectancy interest and business needs of the buyer. Second, the seller is also protected in that the buyer is precluded from claiming any consequential damages which could have been reasonably avoided by cover. *See* U.C.C. § 2–715(b). Finally, a commercially reasonable transaction properly effecting cover provides appropriate evidence of the market for the goods for purposes of making calculations of compensatory damages for the non-breaching buyer.

1–(a)(ii). *Market Damages for Non-Delivery or Repudiation of Goods*

A buyer has no duty or obligation to cover. If the buyer elects not to cover or effects an unreasonable cover, the buyer is entitled to receive damages measured by the difference between the market price and the contract price under § 2–713. Damages also may include incidental and consequential damages, less any expenses saved.

Two possible advantages may accrue to a buyer who chooses to enter the market and cover. First, a commercially reasonable purchase of substitute goods in accordance with § 2–712 provides evidence of the market price. Otherwise, such evidence must be introduced to satisfy the requirements of § 2–713. Second, the failure to make a reasonable attempt to cover may preclude recovery of consequential damages under § 2–715 under the principle of mitigation of losses.

The relevant market price for purposes of § 2–713 is the market price at the time when the buyer learned of the breach. Issues may arise when the seller anticipatorily repudiates. Courts disagree about when the buyer "learns" of the breach for purposes of § 2–713. A few courts conclude that the buyer learns of the breach when the seller notifies the buyer that it intends to breach. Other courts conclude that the buyer learns of the breach when the seller fails to perform at the time set for performance under the contract. Most courts hold that a buyer learns of the breach at the expiration of a commercially reasonable time after the seller notifies the buyer that it intends to breach. This approach protects the interests of both the buyer and the seller by preventing the buyer from speculating in a rising market while also ensuring that the buyer has a sufficient time in which to procure substitute goods.

The counterpart to § 2–713 for non-breaching buyers is § 2–708(1), which is available to non-breaching sellers for a buyer's repudiation or failure to accept conforming goods. One difference between the sections is that the time for calculating damages under § 2–713 is when the buyer learned of the breach, while § 2–708(1) marks the market price at the time and place for tender.

1–(b).   Consequential Damages

The Code carries forward the common law concept of special damages for lost profits under the classification of "consequential" damages under § 2–715(2). An aggrieved buyer may recover consequential damages by showing (1) that a loss resulted from the failure of the seller to perform general or particular requirements of the buyer, (2) that the seller had reason to know of those requirements and needs at the time of contracting, and (3) the buyer could not have prevented the losses by cover or otherwise.

The concept of "reason to know" advances the common law doctrine of foreseeability, which can be satisfied by either an objective standard of what a reasonable person in the seller's position would know or a subjective test of what the seller actually knew. *See* R.I. Lampus Co. v. Neville Cement Products Corp., 474 Pa. 199 (1977). The Code rejects the restrictive common law "tacit agreement" test that required a buyer to prove that the seller specifically contemplated and consciously assumed the risk of consequential damages. Modernly, the buyer must only show that the seller reasonably contemplated that the buyer would sustain some lost profits in the event of a breach, not the exact amount. The evidence to sustain consequential damages includes reference to the particular character, condition, or circumstances of the non-breaching party that were reasonably foreseeable by the seller. The types of evidence that may justify lost profits could include prior history of dealing between the parties, industry custom, and specific language in the contract.

The Code incorporates the doctrine of mitigation to preclude or limit consequential damages that could have been reasonably prevented by cover or otherwise. The buyer must only take reasonable steps to mitigate, however, and is not required to incur substantial expenses or assume excessive risk.

1–(c).   Damages from Acceptance of Non-Conforming Goods

A buyer that accepts non-conforming goods may recover damages under § 2–714. To recover, the aggrieved buyer must give proper notice of a claim to the seller. The measure of damages is the difference at the time and place of acceptance between the actual value of the goods as received and the value as warranted.

The damages for non-conformity may include breach of warranties as well as the failure of a seller to perform obligations under the contract. The buyer is authorized to recover for losses in any reasonable manner. The damages available to buyers under § 2–714 for difference in value are analogous to general damages under common law in that they do not require foreseeability but are conclusively presumed based on the nature of the transaction.

2. SELLERS' REMEDIES

Sellers generally have access to the same categories of damages as are available to buyers under the Code, with some differences in nomenclature and application. The Code seeks to balance remedies in an even-handed fashion, so theoretically no particular advantage or disadvantage accrues to either side as a non-breaching party. Each of the basic damages remedies are complemented by the entitlement to incidental damages to reimburse the seller for expenses reasonably incurred as a result of the breach. Any expenses saved as a result of the buyer's breach are subtracted from the total damages awarded. Although sellers are not entitled to consequential damages, they may recover lost profits on the contract with the breaching buyer and reasonable overhead if the ordinary measure of damages under § 2–708(1) is "inadequate to put the seller in as good a position as performance." *See* U.C.C. § 2–708(2).

2–(a). Resale Damages

The most basic damages remedy available to sellers is the mirror image of the buyer's right to cover under § 2–715. After a breach by the buyer, an aggrieved seller may enter the market and effect a commercially reasonable resale of the contract goods. If the seller does so, the seller may recover the difference between the contract price and the resale price, plus incidental damages and less expenses saved. *See* U.C.C. § 2–706(1). An effective resale provides probative evidence of the market price at the time and place where a buyer should have rendered performance. Therefore, the seller must conduct a resale in good faith and in a commercially reasonable manner, either at public or private sale. *See* U.C.C. § 2–706(2). In the event that proof of relevant market prices at the time of tender is lacking, courts possess some flexibility in using a reasonable substitute to make the necessary calculations. *See* U.C.C. § 2–723(2).

If the resale occurs at private sale, the seller must provide reasonable notification to the buyer of the intention to resell. The seller is not accountable for any profits made on the resale.

2–(b).   Market Damages for Non-Acceptance or Repudiation of Goods

Just as a non-breaching buyer is not required to cover, an aggrieved seller is under no obligation to resell goods following a breach. Section 2–708(1) provides a comparable remedy for recovering damages measured by the difference between the market price at the time and place for tender and the contract price, plus incidental damages and less expenses saved. If the seller chooses not to resell the goods, the measure of recovery is the contract price minus the market price at the time and place for tender. The calculation may also include two adjustments by adding incidental damages and subtracting any expenses saved as a consequence of the breach. *See* U.C.C. § 2–708(1). This item of damages essentially mirrors a buyer's damages for non-delivery or repudiation by a seller under U.C.C. § 2–713.

Although the method for measurement of damages under § 2–706 and § 2–708(1) are the same, one practical difference between the sections is that a commercially reasonable resale itself evidences a fair market price for purposes of § 2–706; otherwise, the seller must provide probative evidence of the market with a reasonable degree of certainty to utilize § 2–708(1). On the other hand, where a seller fails to carry out a resale in accordance with the requirements of § 2–706, she may still seek to recover damages under § 2–708(1) by presenting sufficient evidence of market and contract prices.

2–(c).   Lost Profits

Ordinarily, the measure of damages set forth in § 2–708(1), specifically the difference between the market price and contract price, gives the aggrieved seller their benefit of the bargain. In some cases, however, the Code contemplates that the damages available through § 2–708(1) may be "inadequate" to compensate the seller. In such circumstances, the Code allows the seller to recover its lost profit as calculated by the formula set forth in § 2–708(2).

Section 2–708 should be distinguished from the buyer's right to recover consequential damages under § 2–715. Section 2–715 compensates a buyer for the profits that the buyer would have earned on a subsequent resale or other use of the contract goods that the buyer would have made in a transaction with a third-party. In contrast, § 2–708(2) compensates the seller for the profit the seller would have made from the sale to the breaching buyer.

Section 2–708(2) provides that if the measure of damages for market-contract price differential is:

> inadequate to put the seller in as good a position as performance would have done then the measure of damages is the profit (including reasonable overhead) which the seller would have made from full performance by the buyer, together with any incidental damages * * * due allowance for costs reasonably incurred and due credit for payments or proceeds of resale.

To use this provision, a seller must show that the basic market-contract price differential measure of damages is "inadequate." Courts have recognized three common situations in which the market-contract price differential may be inadequate and for which § 2–708(2) may provide an appropriate remedy to a non-breaching seller. Two of these situations are relatively non-controversial.

The first involves "jobbers" or "middlemen" who enter into contracts to purchase goods in order to resell them to the buyer. If the jobber never actually obtains possession of the contract goods before the buyer breaches, the jobber will not be in a position to effect a resale in the market. *See* Blair Intl., Ltd. v. LaBarge, 675 F.2d 954, 960 (8th Cir. 1982). Because the jobber cannot effect a resale, the jobber cannot recover any portion of its anticipated profit through a resale. Thus, the jobber needs to recover its full lost profit from the breaching buyer in order to receive full compensation.

The second situation involves component parts sellers who manufacture or assemble contract goods. If the seller has not completed manufacture or assembly of the contract goods at the time of breach, the seller will not be able to effect a resale in the market. Because the seller cannot effect a resale, the seller cannot recover any portion of its anticipated profit through a resale. Thus, the seller needs to recover its full profit from the breaching buyer to be adequately compensated. Similarly, some courts extend the exception to situations when goods are specially manufactured for which there is no readily accessible market. *See* Purina Mills, L.L.C. v. Less, 295 F. Supp. 2d 1017, 1035 (N.D. Iowa 2002).

The most difficult and controversial issue pertains to "lost volume sellers" who seek recovery of lost profits. The reference to "volume" in this circumstance essentially reflects the situation where the seller has sufficient production capacity or resources to simultaneously perform the breached contract along with other contract opportunities with respect to the same type of goods.

Consider the following hypothetical: ABC Corporation enters into a contract to manufacture and sell 1,000 widgets to XYZ, Inc. for $1.00 per unit. Prior to the date due for delivery, XYZ unequivocally repudiates the contract, and ABC enters into a second contract to sell the 1,000 widgets on the same terms to a third party. If ABC seeks recovery of damages pursuant to § 2–708(1), the differential between the original contract and the resale price would yield zero damages because the prices for the goods remained the same. However, if ABC had the capacity to perform both contracts (i.e. manufacture and sell 2,000 widgets), ABC will argue that it has lost the "opportunity" to make two sales, and correspondingly two profits, instead of one. Following that approach, then, ABC would claim that its damages under § 2–708(1) are "inadequate" because they do not adequately reflect compensation for the lost opportunity to make the second profit.

For example, in *Neri v. Retail Marine Corporation*, 30 N.Y.2d 393 (1972), the seller contracted to sell a new boat, which it ordered and received from its supplier. The buyer then repudiated the contract. The seller subsequently sold the boat to another buyer for the same price. The court relied on § 2–708(2) and awarded the seller its lost profits under the original contract. The court reasoned that market damages would be "inadequate" to put the seller in as good a position as performance under the initial contract. The court drew an analogy to an auto dealer with an inexhaustible supply of cars. A breach of an agreement to purchase a car at a standard price would cost that dealer a sale even though a third party may subsequently buy the car at the same price. In other words, had the breaching buyer performed, the seller would have made two sales instead of one. While the seller in *Neri* was a retailer, the lost volume seller rule is also applicable to manufacturers.

The requirements for asserting lost volume seller status generally are: (1) the seller would have solicited the second buyer even if no breach occurred under the first contract, (2) the second buyer would have purchased the contract goods, and (3) the seller had the requisite capacity to perform under both contracts. This theory has been criticized on the grounds that not every breach of contract necessarily produces a loss and resulting damages. Accordingly, some critics contend that giving recovery for lost volume seller status contravenes the basic goal of compensatory damages of placing the non-breaching party in the same position as full performance of the agreement. Also, some jurisdictions have rejected the lost volume seller theory on the basis that it undermines the non-breaching party's duty to mitigate. *See* Rezro, Inc. v. Maximo Lanfranco, 2016 WL 597205 (Pa. Super. Ct. 2016).

2–(d).   Action for the Price

The legal remedy available to non-breaching sellers that roughly corresponds to the equitable remedy of specific performance for buyers is called an action for the price under § 2–709. This remedy is much narrower in scope and application than others available to sellers so is used sparingly. The situations in which an action for the price may be utilized are: (1) where the buyer has accepted goods, (2) where conforming goods have been lost or destroyed after risk of loss has passed to the buyer, or (3) where goods are identified to the contract and the resale is impracticable.

The principal situation in which a seller may seek an action for the price is where no ready market exists in which the seller can effect a commercially reasonable resale, such as where goods have been specially manufactured to meet a buyer's particular needs. In *Precision Mirror & Glass v. Nelms*, 797 N.Y.S.2d 720 (Civ. Ct. 2005), for example, a seller manufactured a custom-made glass plate to fit the dimensions of an antique table top. When the buyer breached, the court awarded the contract price under § 2–709 where the seller met its burden of proof that it would be commercially impracticable to effect a resale to another consumer who had a table with the identical dimensions.

The action for the price may also be used when a buyer accepts goods and takes possession but fails to pay. In *Weil v. Murray*, 161 F. Supp. 2d 250 (S.D.N.Y. 2001), an art dealer purchased an original painting by Edgar Degas. The buyer inspected the painting, took possession, and then permitted the painting to be cleaned and restored without the original owner's consent. Although the buyer subsequently returned the painting, the court still awarded the contract price under § 2–709, finding that such acts were inconsistent with the seller's ownership.

In contrast with specific performance, an action on the price is a legal remedy that provides a damages award. It is not an equitable decree and does not bind the party *in personam*.

(C) LAND SALE CONTRACTS

Remedies for breach of contract for the sale of land may include either damages or specific performance. The remedy of specific performance has been traditionally available to non-breaching purchasers of land. The rationale for authorizing equitable relief is that every parcel of land is unique, so the remedy at law for damages would be inadequate. Courts retain discretion, however, to determine the propriety of granting specific performance. Therefore, a court may deny equitable relief if the balance of hardships weighs heavily in favor of the vendor. *See* Restatement (Second) of Contracts § 357 (1981).

A practical problem may affect specific performance where the vendor cannot deliver full title to the property. If the nature of the defect is relatively minor, such as with trivial encroachments or a party wall, the court may still order specific performance with an abatement or adjustment to the purchase price. If the defect is major, however, the court may choose not to order a conveyance that is substantially different from the original agreement.

Assuming that specific performance is not granted, non-breaching vendees may seek damages for their expectancy interest. The majority of jurisdictions follow the "American" rule of damages for a vendor's breach which results from a deficiency in title. The rule provides for an award of the benefit of the bargain to a vendee for a vendor's breach of an executory contract to convey title. The general formula for calculating recovery is the difference between the contract price and the fair market value of the land on the date of the breach, plus expenses incurred and reduced by benefits received or expenses saved. The buyer also may be entitled to recover lost profits. The claimant must prove, with reasonable certainty, that such losses were reasonably foreseeable by the seller at the time of the contract. When a sale of land is in gross, or by the tract, the vendor generally will not be liable for a deficiency in acreage absent fraud in the transaction. On the other hand, where the agreement is on a per acre basis, a court will charge the vendor with damages to reflect the deficiency.

A minority of jurisdictions follow the "English" rule which only provides for restitution of amounts paid by the vendee, together with interest and reliance expenses incurred in connection with the agreement. Under the English Rule, the non-breaching vendee cannot recover damages for the loss of expectancy absent a showing of the vendor's bad faith, fraud or deceit. If granted restitution, the purchaser may also receive a lien on the realty to secure recovery of sums previously paid. The vendee can similarly recover damages when the vendor fails to convey the real property under the time stipulated in the contract or when the vendor breaches a contract warranty, delivering the home in a condition below what the vendee bargained-for in the contract.

In the event of a breach by the vendee, the vendor may seek recovery of the purchase price, as a corollary remedy to specific performance. Otherwise, the vendor may look to recovery of the earnest money as a type of liquidated damages clause. Real estate contracts typically contain earnest money provisions that specify an amount payable to a non-breaching vendor in the event of a material breach by the vendee. Courts treat such provisions as liquidated damages clauses, irrespective of the label assigned by the parties. Therefore, the provision will be upheld if meeting the standard of a good faith, reasonable pre-estimate of actual compensatory damages.

In contrast, if the court concludes that the earnest money provision constitutes a "penalty" designed to compel performance and not approximate reasonable compensation, it will be invalidated. Even if the clause is invalidated, however, the non-breaching party may still seek compensatory damages for the loss of benefit of the bargain. The measure of recovery for loss of expectancy is the difference in market price versus contract price at the time of the breach. The amount of damages recoverable through that measure may be less than the sum stipulated in the liquidated damages clause, however. The claimant bears the burden of proving damages with reasonable certainty.

(D) EQUITABLE REMEDIES

1.   RESCISSION

In some instances, one or both parties to a contract may desire to terminate their future obligations under the agreement. The concept of unmaking or avoiding a contract is called rescission, which may be accomplished at law or in equity. When parties have not yet completed performance in a bilateral contract, both sides may mutually agree to discharge or rescind their remaining obligations.

More problems may arise, of course, where just one party seeks to rescind. A party may rescind at law by giving notice of the intent to rescind, offering to give restitution of benefits received, and demanding restoration of benefits conferred. If the other party complies, restitution is accomplished by agreement. See Restatement (Second) of Contracts § 283 (1981). If parties cannot agree, then the contract is deemed rescinded but recovery will depend on appropriate relief through maintaining an action at law. The grounds for rescission may include mistake, fraud, duress, unconscionability, or misrepresentation. Courts will consider the materiality of the grounds for rescission, and will reserve this drastic remedy for the instances in which the basic assumptions of the contract are affected. An action for rescission operates typically as a complete avoidance of the contract. Courts will not order partial rescission unless the contract itself is considered divisible and the parties fairly returned to their original position.

Parties may alternatively obtain rescission through a court of equity. A claimant typically may seek rescission in equity in order to recover specific or unique property. Assuming that the court grants equitable rescission, the property may be conveyed through a restitutionary remedy such as a constructive trust.

2.   REFORMATION

Reformation is an equitable remedy that may be used to conform an agreement to reflect the true intentions of the parties. In contrast with rescission, reformation does not lead to termination of the contract. Instead, the purpose of reformation is to rectify some inaccuracy in the written terms to make it correspond to the original understanding of the parties. A prime illustration of the need for reformation is where a mutual mistake of a material fact occurs with respect to a description or quantity of the subject matter of the contract. *See* Restatement (Second) of Contracts § 155 (1981). The court may correct any errors that occurred in the integration of the agreement to conform to the parties' reasonable expectations. The parol evidence rule does not bar the admission of extrinsic evidence that may be used solely to explain and correct the terms of the contract for reformation purposes, rather than to vary or contradict its terms.

CHAPTER 11
TORT DAMAGES

(A) PURPOSES AND GOALS OF COMPENSATORY DAMAGES IN TORT LAW

The primary goal of tort damages is to compensate an injured party by placing her in approximately the same position she was in prior to the injury. Other goals such as efficiency and avoidance of waste influence the calculation of the loss and subsequent compensation. Tort damages also attempt to promote out-of-court settlement by using the most predictable and objective measures.

In circumstances where a tension develops between apparently conflicting goals, jurisdictions seek to achieve damages rules that reflect appropriate compromises. Because of the subjective competing principles of fairness and efficiency, jurisdictions formulate different rules to resolve conflicting interests. These rules are further subject to exceptions that erode them as the law changes. Tort damages rules thus can appear arbitrary without an understanding of the unifying principles that govern them and the conflicts in remedial goals that change them. This chapter and the ones that follow address those principles and conflicts.

This chapter explores compensatory damages for tort injuries to personal property, real property, personal injury, and wrongful death/survival actions. These make up the most common categories of tort damages. Chapters 12 and 13 present limitations and adjustments to those damages. Chapter 14 explores two other types of injuries for which damages in tort are only sometimes available because they present special remedial problems: emotional distress without personal injury and economic losses without physical injury. Chapter 15, covering punitive damages, completes the subject of damages. Punitive damages differ from compensatory damages because they seek to punish rather than to compensate.

Compensatory damages in tort are designed to make the injured party whole by substituting money for tangible and intangible losses caused by the wrong. In contrast, restitution, which is discussed in Chapters 16 and 17, seeks to disgorge benefits that are unjust for the defendant to retain, rather than to strictly compensate for an injury. The difference in orientation of these remedies frequently produces different dollar amounts.

(B) PERSONAL PROPERTY DAMAGES

1. PERSONAL PROPERTY DAMAGES—GENERALLY

Courts apply four different measures of value in awarding damages for personal property: (1) market value; (2) actual value; (3) emotional or sentimental value; or (4) cost to repair. Which measure of value a court employs depends, in part, upon whether the personal property has been lost or completely destroyed as opposed to merely damaged and, in part, upon the nature of the property. Each of the measures is discussed more fully below.

2. DESTROYED OR LOST PERSONAL PROPERTY—FAIR MARKET VALUE

The usual measure of damages when personal property is lost or destroyed is its fair market value immediately before its destruction or loss. Restatement (Second) of Torts § 928 (1979). Personal property, such as an automobile, will be considered destroyed if repair is physically impossible or if repair is physically possible but the cost of repair exceeds the market value of the chattel. This inquiry is a finding of fact, and legal consequences follow accordingly.

Consider, for example, the destruction of a couple's car by a negligent driver in an accident. To place the couple in a position equivalent to the position they held before the accident, the law attempts to restore that asset on their personal balance sheet. Their compensatory damages will be the fair market value of the car, considering its age and condition, minus any remaining value. Thus, the total value of their assets remains the same before and after the accident. The resulting net effect of the damages award, then, would place the injured party economically in the same position they held prior to incurring the property damage.

In theory, if the couple wants another car they can take the damages and purchase a used car in substitution for the one they lost. In practice, most people find that they cannot replace a lost car with one exactly like it for the same price. Even if they can, there is no compensation for the time and trouble involved in obtaining a replacement. Thus, while the couple is in the same economic position as they held prior to the accident, they may not feel as if they have been made whole as a practical matter.

Despite these deficiencies in the law from the plaintiffs' point of view, fair market value is beneficial as a predictable number that courts can easily ascertain. Fair market value is the price that a willing buyer and seller would find in an arms' length transaction with each party fully informed. Because certain items such as cars are frequently traded, a readily available and easily ascertainable market value exists. Because items such as cars are frequently destroyed and because coverage is typically through the insurance of the negligent party, this measure encourages efficient settlement of the numerous claims. In turn, efficient and predictable settlement of claims facilitates insurance underwriting and helps reduce the cost of insurance.

Problems of measurement arise when the destroyed or lost property fluctuates in value. Examples of property that fluctuate in value include stocks, commodities and precious metals. If a plaintiff is awarded the fair market value of the property at the time of destruction, the plaintiff may not be placed in as good a position as the plaintiff would have held had the property not been lost or destroyed. Theoretically, when property fluctuates in value, the plaintiff loses not only the ability to hold and use the property for her own purposes but also the ability to sell the property at a profit. Practically, by the time the plaintiff recovers the market value at the time of loss or destruction, the plaintiff may be unable to purchase substitute property because the price has risen.

For example, if an unscrupulous financial advisor steals a client's shares of stock in a particularly profitable corporation, the client loses not only the ability to hold that stock for her own use but also the right to sell that stock at a high price and earn a profit on the sale. If the client recovers only the fair market value of her stock at the time the advisor stole the stock, she may have lost the value of the profit she would have been able to earn on the sale of the stock at a higher price. Further, she may be unable to purchase an equal number of substitute shares because by the time she recovers damages from the defendant the price of the stock may have increased. On the other hand, a person who holds property for investment purposes also bears the risk the market price will fall before the person can resell the property.

Jurisdictions have adopted different rules to attempt to fairly allocate the risks and rewards of a fluctuating market between the plaintiff and the defendant. Many jurisdictions adopt the "New York" rule. Under the New York rule, when converted property fluctuates in value, the plaintiff is entitled to recover the greater of either the fair market value at the time of conversion or the highest fair market value between the time the plaintiff learns of the conversion and the expiration of some reasonable period of time in which the plaintiff could purchase substitute property. Restatement (Second) of Torts § 927(1)(b) (1979). The rationales for this rule are twofold. The rule affords the plaintiff some ability to recover the value of the potential profit the plaintiff lost. However, the plaintiff may not speculate on the market without assuming some risk of a losing market. If a plaintiff wishes to recover the entire profit lost, the plaintiff must purchase substitute property and bear the risk of loss as well. This also provides an incentive to the plaintiff to purchase substitute property and mitigate her damages.

3. DESTROYED, CONVERTED OR LOST PROPERTY—ACTUAL VALUE

Problems also arise when the destroyed personal property lacks any fair market value or the available market value does not adequately represent the value to the injured parties. The most common situations involve "unique" personal property, such as family heirlooms and family pets, specially made or handcrafted items, or infrequently traded household goods, such as used furniture or clothing. When personal property holds no real market value, most courts allow the owner to recover the actual value of the property to the owner. *See* White v. Henry, 49 So. 2d 779, 781 (Ala. 1950)(claimants permitted to provide evidence of long family history of ownership of destroyed antique furniture and set of table china).

Courts also allow plaintiffs to recover the actual value of destroyed personal property when the available market value does not adequately represent the value to the injured parties. In some circumstances, courts may also award the actual value when the actual value to the owner exceeds the available market value.

For example, most courts allow the injured property owner to recover the actual value of destroyed personal consumables such as clothes and household goods. Although a person may own used clothes for business purposes, such as the owner of a second-hand shop, most people own used clothes because they consume them. Used clothes do have a fair market value and that measure could be appropriate in certain instances. For an ordinary consumer, however, an award of fair market value for clothes lost in a house fire would be a hardship. As a practical matter, consumers of goods must replace them rather than simply adjust their balance sheets. Therefore, most jurisdictions permit a "value to the owner" measure for items such as clothes and household goods, with consideration of the age, condition, and cost of replacement or repair as additional factors in calculating the damages awarded.

In *Gibson v. Shephard*, 87 N.E.3d 846 (Ohio App. 2017), for example, a tenant brought a claim against a landlord and property management company for the unauthorized removal and subsequent loss of personal property from a storage locker. The personal property included various items of used clothing and household goods. The court allowed the property owner to testify as to the estimated value of the items based on age, condition, and potential replacement cost even though the owner did not have original receipts to show the purchase prices for the goods.

The court awarded damages to the owner, stating that the valuation need only meet a standard of reasonable certainty. *Also See* State v. Martin, 724 N.W.2d 872, 876 (S. Dak. 2006)(measure of damages for loss of household goods should not be limited to secondhand market value but rather includes original cost, depreciation, and actual value to the owner).

"Actual value to the owner" is nonetheless an objective measure and does not include sentimental value. Further, courts generally have rejected replacement cost as a measure of actual value. Instead, replacement cost is merely a factor in determining the value to the owner. Other factors include the original cost, the quality, the age and condition of the property at the time of loss and depreciation. Generally, replacement cost should be reduced by depreciation.

In *Benford v. Everett Commons, LLC*, 10 N.E.3d 354 (Ill. App. 2014) a tenant sought damages against a landlord for harm to various items of clothing and household goods resulting from water damage caused by a faulty radiator pipe. The plaintiff introduced evidence of the original cost of the items and replacement costs. However, because the owner failed to present evidence of current fair market values immediately before they were ruined by the rusty water, damages were denied. The court reasoned that the jury cannot be allowed to speculate on such values and rewarding full replacement cost would result in a windfall to the claimant.

A few courts have recognized that replacement cost may be an appropriate substitute for actual value. One such court noted:

Because the reduced values recoverable by those methods will require the plaintiffs to spend considerable time and effort to find replacement property at used markets or in bargain sales, the plaintiffs are entitled to compensation for other inconveniences caused by the loss of their property including loss of use of the property. In the alternative, the plaintiffs may claim new replacement costs for their destroyed property, without depreciation, if the plaintiffs show that the replacement amount, in total, is more likely than not to be less than the compensation they would recover based on those reduced values.

See McConchie v. Samsung Elec. America, 2000 WL 1507442 (D.N.H. 2000). Owners may use evidence, such as the amount of insurance carried on the item or expert testimony, to establish the actual value of the property.

4. DESTROYED OR LOST PROPERTY— SENTIMENTAL OR EMOTIONAL VALUE

Establishing the value of property where that value consists primarily of the owner's sentimental attachment creates objectivity problems in reference to calculating compensatory damages. Sentimental value is generally not allowed for the destruction of personal property because of inherent concerns that such recovery would be unduly speculative. Thus, if a tortfeasor negligently breaks a vase that had been a treasured gift from a lost friend, a plaintiff cannot gain recovery for the emotional attachment to the property. Instead, the plaintiff is limited to the actual value excluding sentiment. That might be measured as the replacement cost less some amount to account for the age and condition of the vase at the time of its destruction.

The objective measure of value produces a more easily ascertained value. This, in turn, provides more consistency in verdicts and promotes settlement. Courts also fear that permitting damages for the loss of a sentimental item will encourage false claims or lead to overcompensation.

A few jurisdictions recognize a limited exception to the rule prohibiting sentimental value. The exception is for items whose primary value is generally recognized as sentimental, such as trophies and wedding rings. *See* Campins v. Capels, 461 N.E.2d 712 (Ind. App. 1984)(claimant allowed to testify as to personal attachment to converted commemorative championship rings where the items otherwise lacked traditional market value as jewelry). The policy reason for this limited exception is that certain items may be generally capable of generating sentimental feelings, so an objective basis would exist for assessing damages, rather than relying solely on emotions peculiar to the owner.

The prohibition on recovering sentimental value seems particularly deficient from the plaintiff's point of view when the plaintiff's pet has been killed. Although household pets often may have little market value and hold their value primarily in the owner's sentimental attachment, most jurisdictions limit recovery to the fair market value or the actual value at the pet's death. Recovery may also include the reasonable medical costs and other expenses incurred in treating the injured animal. *See* Barking Hound Village, LLC v. Monyak, 794 S.E.2d 664, 665 (Ga. App. 2016).

Some courts have begun to recognize several exceptions to alleviate the harsh results of this rule. For example, a few courts recognize exceptions when the defendant acts intentionally or recklessly or when the defendant has a fiduciary relationship with the plaintiff, such as in cases of veterinary malpractice. A few states have enacted legislation providing statutory damages for the negligent or intentional killing of a pet. Some courts have allowed a plaintiff to recover the full cost of the veterinary treatment required to restore an injured pet to full health despite the fact that those costs exceeded the fair market value of the pet. *See* Hyland v. Borras, 719 A.2d 662 (N.J. Super. Ct. 1998).

5. REPARABLE PERSONAL PROPERTY—COST TO REPAIR

When personal property has been damaged but is capable of repair, the owner is entitled to recover the cost to repair if that cost is economically feasible. When repairs are not economically feasible, the plaintiff can recover only the diminution in the value of the property—the difference in fair market value before and after the injury. This limit to recovery prevents a windfall and avoids economic waste.

Courts have struggled to determine at what point the cost of repair is no longer economically feasible. Most jurisdictions allow the plaintiff to recover the cost to repair damaged property as long as the cost to repair the property does not exceed the pre-tort fair market value of the property. Some jurisdictions provide that repairs are economically infeasible if the cost to repair exceeds the diminution in value. Thus, in these jurisdictions, the plaintiff's recovery will be limited to the diminution in value even if the repair costs would not have exceeded the pre-tort value of the property.

As a practical matter, the cost of repair and the diminution in value of property by injury are usually very close to the same amount. If a car has a dented fender, for example, its value has diminished by the cost of fixing the fender. In some situations, however, the measures will be very different. The famous case *Hewlett v. Barge Bertie*, 418 F.2d 654 (4th Cir. 1969) illustrates the issue of whether to limit recovery for damaged personal property to its diminution in value.

The plaintiff, Hewlett, owned a barge called BA–1401 which was dented by the defendant's vessel, the Barge Bertie. BA–1401 had been in an accident prior to this one and it had not been repaired. It was seaworthy, but it had only limited uses. The dent did not affect the seaworthiness of BA–1401 and no actual damages were shown. The Fourth Circuit overturned the award of nominal damages in admiralty and awarded the cost to repair the barge. Whereas repairs could be made for less than the value of the barge as scrap, the dent did not cause any diminution in the value of the barge. The court held that the cost of repair would be the appropriate measure of recovery unless the cost exceeded the fair market of the barge at the time of the injury. The dissenting judge would have awarded the plaintiff the lesser of the cost to repair or the diminution in value. The opinion notes that the plaintiff suffered no economic loss and that the cost of repairs would be economically infeasible where the cost exceeded the diminution in value.

Some courts recognize an exception to the principle of awarding the lesser of cost to repair or diminution in value where the item has some "special" or "personal" value to the owner. This exception is not intended to indirectly award excessive costs merely for sentimental purposes, but rather acknowledges that some types of personal property may have an objective reason to be repaired. An example of the type of property to which this exception might apply would be a treasured heirloom quilt that has been damaged by tortious conduct. Even if the cost to restore the quilt to its pre-tort condition may exceed the diminution in value, a court may allow damages for repair to accommodate the interests of the owner. The result would not be seen as a windfall because the owner would likely use the damages award to make the necessary repairs.

6.   LOSS OF USE

Most jurisdictions permit additional damages for the loss of the use of the injured property while it is being repaired. *See* Restatement (Second) of Torts § 928(b) (1979). Thus, the plaintiff whose car has been damaged could receive compensation for her inability to use the car while it is in the shop in addition to the repair costs. In contrast, jurisdictions historically precluded a plaintiff from recovering loss of use damages when property was destroyed. The rationale behind this prohibition was that the owner of destroyed property was essentially "selling" the property to the tortfeasor because the measure of damages is the fair market price. Continuing that analogy, no "loss of use" exists when one sells property; there is simply a payment of the cash value. Modernly, most courts permit a plaintiff to recover loss of use damages when property is destroyed. These damages are limited to loss of use for a reasonable period of time in which to replace the destroyed property, which is typically measured by fair rental value.

In *J & D Towing, LLC v. American Alternative Ins. Corp.*, 478 S.W.3d 649 (Tex. 2015), a claimant sought damages for the fair market value of a totally destroyed tow truck as well as compensation for loss of use of the vehicle. The court recognized the traditional common law rule that freely allowed loss of use damages for partially damaged but repairable property yet denied such damages when the property was completely destroyed. The court rejected that anomalous distinction and held that if personalty is totally destroyed, the owner can recover loss of use damages in addition to the fair market value of the property immediately before the injury. However, the owner cannot recover loss of use damages for a period longer than would be reasonably necessary to replace the personal property. The court observed, "That principle compels a plaintiff's diligence in remedying his loss and deters an opportunistic plaintiff from dilly-dallying at the expense of the defendant." 478 S.W.3d at 677. The measure of loss of use damages would be based on the particular loss experienced, such as the amount of lost profits, cost of renting a substitute, or the rental value of the owner's own property. This more personalized element to the loss reduces the uncertainty of the calculation and thus contributes to efficiency of settlements.

(C) REAL PROPERTY DAMAGES

Unlike personal property, different aspects of real property can be damaged or destroyed, and damages will be measured differently depending on which aspect or aspects of the property have been injured. The realty (or land) itself can be damaged. Alternatively, appurtances to the land such as buildings, trees, and minerals can be damaged, destroyed, or removed from the land. In valuing damage to real property, courts must initially determine which of these aspects of the property have been injured. Each of these types of injuries is discussed below.

1.   DAMAGE TO LAND

Courts apply two primary measures for valuing damages to realty: (1) cost to restore or repair the injured land or (2) diminution in value to the land as a result of injury.

1–(a).   Irreparable Damage to Land

If an injury to real property cannot be repaired, then the award is limited to the diminution in value of the land. The diminution in value is measured as the difference between the fair market value of the property immediately before the injury and its fair market value immediately after it. Because real property, unlike personal property, is never truly destroyed, some value remains after injury. Thus, the injured landowner recovers diminution in value rather than pre-tort fair market value.

1–(b).   Reparable Damage to Land

If the injury to realty is physically reparable, courts generally award one of two competing measures of damages: cost to restore or diminution in fair market value. The same themes and policy conflicts that affect damages for injury to personal property appear also in the law of damages for injury to real property. Specifically, courts balance concerns for compensation and economic efficiency in determining whether restoring injured land is economically feasible and, hence, whether to award restoration costs.

Some courts allow an injured landowner to recover restoration costs so long as the restoration costs do not exceed the pre-tort value of the property. Others limit recovery to the lesser of cost to repair or diminution in market value caused by the damage. This approach avoids economic waste and a windfall to the prevailing party. The theory is that if the cost to restore the land exceeds the diminution in value, the injured landowner is unlikely to restore the land and, thus, will be overcompensated if she received the restoration costs. On the other hand, a plaintiff who wishes to repair the damaged property will be undercompensated if she recovers only the difference in value and will have to pay out of pocket to make the repairs. This problem is particularly pervasive in real property because every piece of real property is unique. An injured landowner cannot simply sell the damaged property and use the proceeds from the sale as well as the damage award to buy a true substitute parcel.

The Restatement (Second) of Torts § 929 (1979) attempts to account for these competing interests. Section 929 provides that restoration cost should be ordinarily allowable as the proper measure of damages unless it is "disproportionate" to the diminution in value. Section 929 further provides that even if the restoration costs exceed the diminution in value, the landowner should be entitled to recover the reasonable restoration costs if the landowner has a personal reason for making the repairs. For example, if the damage occurs to a home that is the owner's residence, a court may allow costs of repairs even if exceeding the diminution in value.

1–(c). Temporary and Permanent Damage to Land

For remedial purposes, courts commonly distinguish between "permanent" and "temporary" injuries to land. One problem that arises, though, is that those terms have no definitive independent meaning. A court characterizes the nature and extent of the injury to land as either temporary or permanent by considering whether the injury is abatable or reversible and whether it is reasonably susceptible to restoration and repair without undue expense or hardship. There are three significant consequences that result from classification of injury to land as either permanent or temporary: (1) the measure of damages, (2) the applicable statute of limitations, and (3) the availability of equitable relief.

The award of damages for permanent harm to land is the diminution in value of the property, which is measured as the difference in the fair market value of the property immediately before and after the injury. Restatement (Second) of Torts § 929(1) (1979). This recovery takes into account past and future diminished productivity of the land. In contrast, the measure of damages for temporary harm is the reasonable cost of restoration or repair of the land to its former condition. Some courts use a fair rental value for the period of the injury to compensate for temporary harms for the loss of use of the land. Since the process of restoration of land may be difficult and costly, many courts limit recovery to the depreciated value of the land. This avoids economic waste. Further, the rule of avoidable consequences requires the injured party to diminish the loss as reasonably as possible.

If the wrongful act adversely affected the value or use of the entire parcel, courts find it appropriate to compute the damages on the basis of the total acreage and not just on the portion damaged. In some cases there may be permanent damage which occurs to one part of a tract while another portion of the parcel suffers injuries causing only temporary damage. It is proper in such instances to allow recovery for both items, provided the plaintiff does not receive double recovery.

The characterization of the injury may also affect the relevant statute of limitations. The statute of limitations period will begin running, unless tolled by equitable principles, from the date of the initial interference with the property. If the nature of the interference is a significant event that produces a permanent harm, the limitations period will be relatively predictable to calculate. A potential difficulty arises, though, where the interference with property is of a continuing character over a long period of time.

A common illustration involves a factory that is unlawfully discharging toxic effluent which leaches into the surrounding soil and contaminates an aquifer, affecting neighboring land uses. The question for landowners who seek damages for the resulting harm is whether the invasion rises to the level of a permanent harm, which then requires determining exactly when the statute of limitations began to run. Otherwise, it may be seen as a series of separate temporary harms stemming from the continuing pollution. If temporary, then the statute of limitations would run from each invasion.

Assume, for example, that the pollution continued for ten years before the landowner brought a suit for damages against the factory and further assume that the operative statute of limitations for torts is two years. If the trier of fact classifies the harm as permanent, then the landowner might be completely barred from any recovery. On the other hand, if the trier of fact classifies the injury as temporary, then the landowner would be barred from recovering damages for the first eight years of harm but still could recover for any harms occurring within the previous two year period.

Last, the characterization affects whether a party can recover injunctive relief. If the injury is classified as permanent, then courts will not issue a preventive injunction against the interference. The rationale is that the landowner is already being compensated for future harms through the diminution in value measure of damages. Therefore, an injunction to abate the harm in the future would be duplicative and overcompensate the plaintiff. In contrast, a party who sustains a temporary injury to land may benefit from an injunction. The damages given compensate for the past interference to the land and the injunction would prohibit future conduct, so no inconsistency or overlap in the recovery occurs.

In contrast to cases involving personal property, real property is never (or rarely) totally destroyed. Rather, some critical feature of the land may be injured, such as its productivity. If toxic chemicals leak into the soil or water on the land, then its productivity as farmland is injured. Consider an example where the blasting of dynamite for construction on neighboring land destroys the productivity of a well on the plaintiff's land. If the plaintiff finds it impossible to drill for water on the land after the injury, then the damage was permanent. If the plaintiff can restore the well, then repair costs are permissible, with states varying their rules about capping those damages. The most difficult question arises when the current well cannot be repaired but another well could be dug on the same land. Courts have struggled with the problem of categorization between temporary and permanent injuries.

2. DAMAGE TO STRUCTURES ON LAND

Injury to real property may also be to structures on the land. For the destruction of an improvement that has independent value separately from the land, the owner can recover its value at the time of destruction, less salvage value. If the structure is only damaged, a plaintiff can recover cost of repair and loss of use.

Some courts will limit the cost of repairs to not exceed the diminution in the value of the improvement if it has a separate value, or to the diminution in the value of the entire land if the improvement has no separate value. Thus, if a car runs off the road and crashes into a shed on the plaintiff's land, the plaintiff receives cost of repair in most jurisdictions, with a cap on the value of the shed itself if it has separate value, such as a prefabricated shed bought at a retail store.

3.   DAMAGE TO VEGETATION

Plaintiffs can also recover damages for items such as growing crops, shrubbery, or trees. Courts have employed a flexible approach to measuring such damages. This flexible approach focuses on the use of the item or its value to the land.

For example, when growing annual crops are injured, plaintiffs can recover the projected commercial market value of the crop at maturity, less costs of harvesting and transportation that the owner would have otherwise incurred. However, where crops are damaged or destroyed before maturity, the plaintiff must prove the value the crops would have had at maturity with reasonable certainty. Courts consider factors such as the nature of the season and the weather, the average yield of crops on neighboring land, and the past yield of crops in similar growing seasons. Injury to land prepared for planting, as opposed to injury to crops already planted, enables a recovery of the cost of preparation, plus rental value for the season.

Courts have employed several measures to compensate for damages for injury to or destruction of trees. At common law, injuries to fruit trees and other trees that held commercial value were measured as fair market value at the time of destruction. However, some jurisdictions enacted trespass to timber statutes that provide for recovery of treble damages or statutory damages when commercial timber was wrongfully removed from the injured landowner's property.

Some types of trees and vegetation have no true value severable from the land, such as those for shade or decorative purpose. Courts have employed several measures for injury or destruction of these types of trees and vegetation. The general rule recognizes injury to this type of property as injury to the land. Generally, the landowner is entitled to recover the cost to repair the damage only if the cost to repair the damage does not exceed the diminished value of the property as a whole.

Courts have recognized exceptions to this rule when the destroyed or injured trees have a special purpose to that land, such as for windbreak or ornamental trees. In such circumstances, some courts have allowed the landowner to recover reasonable repair or replacement costs in excess of diminution in value of the injured property. Other courts have allowed the injured plaintiff to recover the aesthetic or actual value of the trees. In order to recover replacement costs or actual value, the injured landowner must establish that the injured or destroyed trees actually provided the special value and that the damage to or the destruction of the trees interfered with the landowner's ability to use the land for the stated special purpose.

4. REMOVAL OF NATURAL RESOURCES

Damages are also recoverable for the wrongful removal of natural resources such as minerals, oil, and gas. Courts apply three different measures of damages in these cases. When the defendant has acted in good faith and removed the natural resources under a mistaken belief that she has the legal right to do so, courts award a low measure of damages such as a royalty or lost profits. A royalty would award the landowner the reasonable value the landowner would have received for leasing the mineral rights to a third party. Lost profits would be measured as the market value of the natural resource less the extraction costs. In selecting between these two measures, courts will look to factors such as whether the injured landowner possessed the expertise and intent to mine the resources herself.

When the defendant acts in bad faith or reckless disregard, some courts award a high measure of damages such as the market value of the removed resources without a deduction for exaction costs. Much like the trespass to timber statutes, some jurisdictions have enacted multiple damage statutes which allow a landowner to recover statutory damages when a defendant wrongfully removes natural resources from her property.

(D) PERSONAL INJURY DAMAGES

1.   PERSONAL INJURY DAMAGES—GENERALLY

A person who has been physically injured as a result of another's actionable conduct may recover damages that will fairly and reasonably compensate for the nature and extent of the injuries suffered. The goal is to restore the injured party, as nearly as practicable, to the position she held prior to the tort. The damages must compensate for all detriment proximately caused by the wrongdoer's conduct. Damages may include recovery for both past and future losses. Damages for personal injury need not be calculated with mathematical certainty but rather must be supported by a reasonable evidentiary foundation related to the nature and type of the interest affected. Wide latitude of discretion is necessarily left to the jury, and the award will be upheld unless determined that the amount is so excessive as to indicate that bias, passion or prejudice influenced the jury.

Although jurisdictions vary somewhat in the allowable items of personal injury damages, the most common elements include: (1) lost earnings and impaired future earning capacity; (2) physical pain and suffering and mental distress; (3) medical expenses; (4) permanent injuries, disfigurement, or lasting destruction or impairment of health and physical functions; and (5) loss of consortium. *See* Restatement (Second) of Torts § 924 (1979).

Some items are classified as "general" damages, such as pain and suffering. Others are described as "special" damages, such as future medical expenses. The difference is that special damages must be pleaded and proved with particularity and typically require expert testimony to support the evidentiary record. A trier of fact may determine general damages, on the other hand, without the aid of expert testimony based upon their own life experience and considering the nature of the injuries.

Several limitations apply to future special damages. For example, future special damages ordinarily are discounted to present value, taking into account both the projected effects of investment of the damages award and the projected effects of inflation on future costs and earnings. *See* Chapter 12, *infra*. Also, damages may be reduced by the failure of the injured party to properly mitigate by taking reasonable steps to secure prompt medical care and treatment. Prejudgment interest on some personal injury damages may be allowed, but often is governed by statute. Finally, at common law, injured parties were permitted to recover the full value of their pecuniary losses even though collateral sources, such as medical or health insurance providers, reimbursed them for these losses. As part of a larger "tort reform" movement beginning in the 1980s, many states have enacted legislative measures which limit an injured party's ability to recover damages for pecuniary losses if a collateral source such as insurance also has reimbursed the injured party for those losses. *See* Chapter 13, *infra*.

2.   MEDICAL EXPENSES

An injured party may recover damages for medical care already incurred as well as for future care and services. An injured party may recover the reasonable value of any medical care required to treat her injuries. With respect to care the injured party has already received by the time of trial, the plaintiff is entitled to recover the reasonable value of that care, provided that it was fair and reasonably necessary to treat her injuries. Plaintiffs frequently introduce their medical bills as evidence of the reasonable value of their care. However, insurance

companies and other third-party payers often
negotiate a discounted rate. The health care provider
then accepts less than the billed amount for the
services and writes-off the remainder of the bill.
Defendants often seek to introduce evidence of the
amount a plaintiff's insurance company actually pays
for the services provided to the plaintiff as evidence
of reasonable value of care.

The question of whether the injured plaintiff can
recover the "write-off" amount causes issues for
courts. Some courts apply an "actual amount paid"
approach. These courts limit recovery to the amount
actually paid to the health care provider by insurance
or otherwise. Thus, if a third-party payor such as a
private insurance company or Medicaid or Medicare
has paid for the injured party's medical expenses and
that payor has negotiated a discounted rate with the
treating provider, the injured party will be precluded
from introducing evidence of the amount the treating
provider billed.

Other courts apply the "benefit of the bargain"
approach. These courts preclude evidence of
insurance write-offs as violative of the collateral
source rule only if the plaintiff has exchanged
something of value to receive the benefit of the
insurance. Thus, these courts preclude evidence of
insurance write-offs when the plaintiff has private
insurance but may not exclude write offs when the
plaintiff receives public benefits such as Medicaid.

The majority of courts apply some version of the
"reasonable value" approach. However, courts define
reasonable value differently. Some courts adopting

this approach define "reasonable value" as the full undiscounted medical bill. These courts preclude evidence of insurance write-offs as violative of the collateral source rule and allow the plaintiff to recover the full amount billed for medical treatment. Others applying this approach allow the evidence of both the amount billed by the health care provider and the amount paid by the insurance carrier. In these states, the jury determines the reasonable value of the medical treatment based on this evidence. One court precludes the defendant from introducing evidence of the insurance write-offs to the jury but allows the court to consider such write-offs and make post-verdict adjustments. *See* Weston v. AKHappytime, LLC, 445 P.3d 1015 (Alaska 2019).

An injured plaintiff is also entitled to recover the reasonable value of any future care the plaintiff may require. The injured plaintiff must establish with reasonable certainty that she will need the care. She must also establish the cost of that care with reasonable certainty. The future medical costs for permanent injuries will be measured according to the injured party's projected life expectancy. Future medical expenses, as an item of special damages, must be proven by expert testimony and discounted to present value. On the other hand, if any estimate of future costs does not take into account the likely effect of inflation, then the award should not be discounted to present value. *See infra* Chapter 12(A), Present Value and Inflation.

Establishing the likelihood and cost of future medical expenses with reasonably certainty has proved problematic in cases where the injured plaintiff suffers a minor injury but also is exposed to the risk of a potential latent disease or injury, such as cases where the plaintiff has been exposed to a toxic substance. In such situations, the plaintiff may be able to establish an increased risk of serious injury or disease yet not be able to establish with reasonable certainty that she will probably suffer the injury or disease. Courts generally have rejected claims for increased risk of disease on the basis that the future injury may not actually occur, so the harm would be too remote or speculative to support recovery. Instead, some courts have permitted the plaintiff to recover the cost of medical monitoring where the plaintiff can show the clinical value of medical monitoring and early detection of disease.

3.   FUTURE EARNING CAPACITY AND LOST WAGES

An injured plaintiff is also entitled to recover damages for lost wages and for diminished or lost earning capacity. Lost wages differ from diminished earning capacity in that lost wages compensate the injured plaintiff for wages lost from a specific job for a period of time in which the plaintiff is unable to work because of her injuries. Future lost wages envision that the plaintiff will be able to return to that same job and not experience a loss in future opportunity for advancement. The plaintiff can recover lost wages for the period of time she has been unable to work from the point of injury until trial. If the plaintiff will not be able to return to work until some point after trial, she can also recover future lost wages.

In contrast, diminished earning capacity compensates a plaintiff for a narrowing of the range of her economic opportunities as a result of her injuries. A plaintiff can recover damages for diminished earning capacity even if she does not have a job at the time of injury or even if she is able to return to the job she held at the time of injury, so long as she can demonstrate that her injuries preclude her from other employment opportunities. For example, in *Wilburn v. Maritrans GP Inc.*, 139 F.3d 350 (3d Cir. 1998), the court awarded the plaintiff, an injured tankerman, damages for diminished earning capacity even though he returned to his position as an AB tankerman by the time of trial. The plaintiff sufficiently demonstrated that as a result of his injuries he would never acquire a promotion to barge captain.

For permanent injuries, a trier of fact calculates diminished future earning capacity for the time period of the injured party's work life expectancy. The measure takes into account both individualized factors, such as age, special skill, education, and training, as well as broader industry factors and opportunities. It seeks to replace, as accurately as possible, the lost marketability in the workplace.

4. PAIN AND SUFFERING

A trier of fact may award a victim general damages of pain and suffering. Pain and suffering encompasses many harms, including physical pain, mental suffering, depression, humiliation, anxiety, and loss of enjoyment of life. Some jurisdictions recognize recovery for "loss of enjoyment of life" as a distinct element of damages. Others award loss of enjoyment of life as part of pain and suffering. Psychological fears, such as post-traumatic stress syndrome, may also be compensable but must be reasonable and may require expert testimony to supply an evidentiary foundation.

The difficulty with allowing such recovery is providing some reasonable basis for determining an appropriate award since mental anguish and physical pain are virtually impossible to quantify. Jurisdictions provide some procedural safeguards to ensure that awards are reasonable. For example, the plaintiff must present evidence to support a claim for pain and suffering. The defendant has the opportunity to rebut the plaintiff's evidence and introduce evidence of her own.

Some jurisdictions also place limits on the types of arguments counsel can make regarding pain and suffering. For example, some jurisdictions prohibit counsel from suggesting to the jury lump sums that should be awarded for pain and suffering. *See* Parkway Co. v. Woodruff, 901 S.W.2d 434, 444 (Tex. 1995). Some jurisdictions prohibit counsel from suggesting a per diem amount that should be awarded for pain and suffering. The jury must award compensation that is fair and reasonable in light of the evidence and typically will make such judgments based upon the nature and extent of any physical injuries.

Additionally, the trial court can review an award of pain and suffering and remit or set aside the verdict if it is so excessive that it shocks the judicial conscience. Likewise, the award is subject to appellate review.

Despite these limitations, many jurisdictions have sought to enact additional limitations on damages for pain and suffering. Beginning in the 1980s, many state legislatures enacted various tort reform measures aimed at reducing verdicts awarded in personal injury cases. Most commonly, many states passed statutory caps on damages for pain and suffering. These caps limit awards to a set amount or to a set ratio between pain and suffering damages and damages for economic losses.

5. LOSS OF CONSORTIUM

The claim for loss of consortium is a derivative claim brought by a spouse or some other family member. It is primarily based on the claimant's emotional suffering as a result of the injured plaintiff's physical injuries. It includes elements such as love, companionship, affection, society, comfort, services, and solace. The claim cannot duplicate other elements of the injured party's recovery. Thus, it may include compensation for economic disadvantages or pecuniary losses only to the extent that the injured party has not already recovered for the economic disadvantage. For example, the spouse could not recover for loss of economic support if the injured party had already recovered for the lost future earnings from which the economic support would have been derived.

Some courts have expanded the class of family members who may claim loss of consortium beyond spouses. Some recognize a cause of action by a minor child or incapacitated dependent child for permanent loss of parental consortium when a parent is negligently injured by a third party. *See* Berger v. Weber, 411 Mich. 1, 17, 303 N.W.2d 424, 427 (1981). Some states also have permitted parents to claim loss of consortium for injuries to their minor children.

(E) WRONGFUL DEATH AND SURVIVAL

At early common law, the prevailing view was that the death of a tort victim extinguished all the decedent's potential claims, including those against the tortfeasor. Further, the common law did not recognize any independent claim in the decedent's dependents for their own losses. In order to alleviate the harshness of this common law doctrine and to correct the anomalous result whereby tortfeasors could effectively "profit" from their wrong by actually killing the victim rather than just injuring them, England passed Lord Campbell's Act in 1846. This Act created a new and independent remedy for wrongful death in derogation of the common law preclusion. The Act allowed the decedent's dependents to recover for their own losses occasioned by the decedent's death. The Act served as the model for numerous statutes promulgated in the United States.

...ny jurisdictions have enacted a ...al" statute which operates to ...as personal injury claims of the ...m from extinguishment under the ...n law approach. Claims under survival stat... ...mpensate for injuries suffered by the decedent rather than the losses suffered by the decedent's dependents.

Some jurisdictions merge the wrongful death action with the survival statute under a single comprehensive statutory scheme. The merger of the two types of actions provides administrative convenience and expediency in that the personal representative need only maintain one lawsuit for wrongful death. Some difficulties emerge, however, in the single statutory approach—most notably in properly identifying and separating each item of damages to avoid double recovery.

The elements and measure of damages recoverable under the "survival" portion of the statutes mirror those traditionally available had the victim lived, other than future damages. Thus, mental pain and anguish of the decedent experienced prior to death would be typically recoverable under the survival statute as would be any lost wages between the time of injury and death and any medical expenses incurred between injury and death.

Although jurisdictions differ in scope, many wrongful death statutes provide for the following elements: (1) pecuniary losses to the surviving spouse and children, (2) medical and burial expenses, and (3) loss of consortium and grief of the surviving spouse.

See 10 Del. Code § 3724. Jurisdictions divide as to whether to allow recovery for punitive damages. *Compare* Crossett v. Andrews, 277 P.2d 117 (Okla. 1954) with Boroughs v. Oliver, 226 Miss. 609, 85 So.2d 191 (1956).

The element of pecuniary loss essentially seeks to replace the financial support that the decedent would have otherwise given to their family. Accordingly, this item is calculated by taking into consideration the decedent's age, occupation, earning capacity, health habits, and probably duration of their life had the tort not occurred.

Some jurisdictions allow parents to recover for the wrongful death of an unmarried, unemancipated minor child. Recovery might include non-economic losses such as loss of companionship and grief and economic losses such as loss of financial support, if the parents can prove with reasonable certainty that the decedent child would have provided financial support to the parents if the decedent child had survived.

The wrongful death statute creates a separate and distinct right of action to the decedent's legal representative against the wrongdoer. However, that right is derivative of the decedent's right of action and is predicated on the continued viability of rights which were personal to the deceased had he lived. Thus, any defenses that would have been otherwise available to the tortfeasor against the victim are also effectively preserved and may be properly asserted in the wrongful death action. For example, a wrongful death action would be precluded if the claims of the injured party were time-barred by an applicable statute of limitations prior to death. Likewise, if the decedent's recovery would have been limited because of contributory negligence, recovery under a wrongful death action would be similarly limited.

CHAPTER 12
ADJUSTMENTS TO DAMAGES

(A) PRESENT VALUE AND INFLATION

Compensatory damages that replace future losses, such as diminished earning capacity in a personal injury action, typically are awarded in a lump sum. The first step in calculating an award for lost earnings involves estimating the projected lost stream of income over the work life expectancy of the injured party. The lost income stream ordinarily is measured by after-tax dollars, and the discount rate represents the after-tax rate of return to the injured worker. *See* Norfolk & Western R. Co. v. Liepelt, 444 U.S. 490 (1980).

The next step may involve adjusting the lump sum total by taking into account the impact of future inflation and discounting the award to present value. Both adjustments involve complex expert testimony of economic, industry, societal and individualized factors. The specific rates used for inflation and discounting may radically affect the final damages award given to the prevailing party. The selection of a higher inflation rate favors the plaintiff, while a higher discount rate would benefit the defendant.

Prevailing plaintiffs will contend that the lump sum award, which reflects future lost earnings, should be increased to take inflation into account. They would assert that an upward adjustment is necessary because otherwise the impact of inflation is to erode the purchasing power of substituted wages, resulting in under-compensation. Critics of that approach point to the speculative nature of future inflation rates and that complex economic forecasting may prove to be too difficult for jurors to assess, even with expert testimony.

Conversely, most courts recognize that some reduction of a lump sum award should be made to take into account the earning power of money. A downward reduction or discounting of the award reflects the interest that the plaintiff could earn on investing the lump sum over time. The objective of providing an award that accurately compensates, then, would be modified to approximate future earnings from those potential investments.

Several different methods have emerged for evaluating the inflation and discount rates. The "total offset" method, premised upon the rationale that predicting future rates is inherently unreliable, simply cancels out both factors. The result is that the lump sum award is not adjusted once the damages are calculated.

A second approach is the "case by case" method, where experts introduce evidence on projected wage increases related to individualized and industry factors, including an enhancement for future inflation. The trier of fact then discounts that projected future lost income stream to present value using a market interest rate, which itself includes factors such as price inflation.

The third commonly used method is called the "varied offset" or "below-market" discount method.

Evidence is considered on future hypothetical wage increases for the injured worker, taking into account both merit and industry productivity and market conditions. It effectively cancels out the inflation factor, however, both with respect to future wages and interest rates. The resulting income stream is then discounted by a below-market discount rate between 1% and 3%, which is sometimes called the "real interest rate." This method was endorsed by the Supreme Court in *Jones & Laughlin Steel Corp. v. Pfeifer*, 462 U.S. 523 (1983).

Another problem is the determination of the appropriate rate for discounting the lump sum. In *Pfeifer,* the Court stated that the discount rate should be based on the interest rate available on the "best and safest investments," which often are interpreted as federal government issued securities. The goal is to approximate the level of earnings that the money could earn through hypothetical investments that are relatively risk-free. In *Monessen Southwestern Ry. Co. v. Morgan*, 486 U.S. 330 (1988), the Court stated that parties in a private suit may stipulate to the total offset method before trial and thus avoid the inevitable battle of experts and uncertainties associated with predicting inflation and discount rates.

The calculation of future damages and adjustments to approximate interest rates and inflation necessarily present significant challenges to the parties, courts, and juries. The resulting award often may prove to be significantly higher or lower than the expert predictions in light of subsequent actual market events. In response to the potential inequity that could occur, an alternative method calls for the payment of damages in stages over the period of time that losses would be sustained. The Uniform Periodic Payment of Judgments Act provides a basic framework in which damages could be paid in installments as losses actually accrue. One advantage to the periodic payment of damages is that it alleviates the difficulties associated with making long term investment decisions of the lump sum award.

Regardless of whether the jurisdiction has approved periodic payment judgments, the parties may opt to have installment payments through private agreement, which is known as a "structured settlement." Both parties often find it more satisfactory to negotiate for such periodic payments because the defendant can often purchase an annuity for the plaintiff at less cost than the projected losses and the plaintiff then has guaranteed payments for a lifetime. Agreements can be as complex or simple as the parties choose and may take into account various market indices as reference points for purposes of assigning specific payouts.

(B) PREJUDGMENT INTEREST

Courts may award interest as an element of compensatory damages based upon statute, contract, or through equitable discretion. State and federal statutes uniformly provide for the payment of post-judgment interest to accrue on the damages awarded until paid. Parties may contract for payment of conventional interest, such as in home and automobile loans and mortgages. More difficult questions arise, however, with respect to the authorization of prejudgment interest.

The prejudgment interest component of damages compensates the prevailing party in a lawsuit for the loss of use of the money that will later be awarded at judgment. *See* City of Milwaukee v. Cement Div., National Gypsum Co., 515 U.S. 189 (1995). The award recognizes the time value of money because money itself has its own earning power. The award focuses on the period from accrual of the claim until the date of judgment. In that interim of time before damages are actually awarded, the justification for paying prejudgment interest is the recognition that the claimant should be allowed some measure of interest on the sum of money later established at judgment. Another policy reason for the award is that otherwise the liable party would be unjustly enriched by the interest earned on the funds and may delay settling or paying their obligations. Prejudgment interest is not a penalty in any sense; it is only compensation for the value of the damages ultimately awarded at trial.

Two principal issues exist with respect to prejudgment interest: entitlement and measurement. Various state and federal statutes include prejudgment interest as an allowable item of compensatory damages arising from violation of the statute. In those instances, the court often retains discretion as to whether interest should be given and to what extent. Similarly, parties have contractual freedom to incorporate a prejudgment interest component into their agreed menu of damages that would be payable to the non-breaching party in the event of a material breach of contract. The limitations on such provisions include ordinary considerations of unconscionability as well as statutory usury laws.

Apart from statute or agreement, though, courts retain considerable discretion to award prejudgment interest in order to achieve the objective of full and fair compensation. The court must evaluate a litany of factors, considering the matter from the perspective of both parties. The claimant must show the date of accrual of the claim and demonstrate that the claim may be calculated with a reasonable degree of certainty. The court will also consider whether the defendant would be unjustly enriched by not paying interest and evaluate whether the defendant may have acted to delay the trial or the payment of the claim. Good faith efforts by the defendant to resolve the dispute by offering settlement may operate to toll the running of interest as to the amount of settlement offered.

Instances where liability itself or the amount of the claim are very uncertain often may be less likely to justify a prejudgment interest award. Otherwise, the defendant may be placed in a dilemma of either being forced to pay a legitimately disputed claim or having to pay interest on the claim after judgment is rendered. As a result, courts historically espoused the notion that "liquidated" claims were proper subjects for prejudgment interest, while those which were not readily ascertainable were not. However, that distinction is not necessarily dispositive and may be overcome if other factors sufficiently justify an award of prejudgment interest to provide full compensation. Kansas v. Colorado, 533 U.S. 1 (2001). In any calculus, mathematical exactitude is not required, yet the underlying premise of showing the merits and the amount of entitlement with reasonable certainty still affects the court's discretion.

A degree of flexibility is generally employed by courts to tailor the prejudgment interest award to the nature of the claim itself. For example, in breach of contracts cases the date of the breach and measure of damages often is fairly readily calculable with relative certainty. Accordingly, prejudgment interest could be awarded with respect to the compensatory damages attributable to the breach and would not be unduly prejudicial to the breaching party. In other instances, interest may be awarded to serve the goal of just compensation. *See* Restatement (Second) of Contracts § 354.

On the other hand, with respect to various torts claims, the question of liability and amount of harm, may be less certain. Therefore, interest generally may not be awarded for emotional distress, bodily injury, pain and suffering, and injury to reputation claims. If the injury has a readily ascertainable market value, such as for destruction of personalty, prejudgment interest may be awarded. *See* Restatement (Second) of Torts § 913. Interest also is typically not awarded on punitive damages because it does not accord with the objective of compensation to the claimant. Courts also do not award prejudgment interest on future losses because they have not yet been incurred.

The second issue courts must resolve is determining the appropriate rate to use for the prejudgment interest award. Unless the applicable statute or contract delineates the rate of interest, courts will exercise their discretion guided by reference to a market-based rate. The goal is to approximate the lost opportunity that the claimant would have had to invest the funds. A common reference point is a high-grade government fixed income bond, such as United States Treasury Bills or money market rates offered by major institutions.

CHAPTER 13
LIMITATIONS ON COMPENSATORY DAMAGES

(A) FORESEEABILITY

Foreseeability is a limitation on all compensatory damages, both in contract and in tort. The doctrine of foreseeability operates as a limiting principle on entitlement and measurement of damages. Although substantive law distinctions affect the specific application of foreseeability, the principle developed to shield a wrongdoer in tort or a breaching party in contract from accountability for excessive, remote, or speculative losses. The requirement of foreseeability in contract reflects a policy of fairness in that a party will be held accountable only for those bargained-for risks of non-performance that should have been reasonably contemplated and assumed at the time of making the agreement. In tort, the doctrine of foreseeability cabins liability in the first instance to the range of harms reasonably contemplated by the actor and also functions to limit the range of damages, if liability is established.

The principles underlying the doctrine in commercial contracts were highlighted in a famous early English case, *Hadley v. Baxendale*, 9 Ex. 341, 156 Eng. Rep. 145 (1854). In that case an engine shaft in the plaintiff's mill broke, so the miller hired a common carrier to transport the part to the manufacturer in order to obtain a replacement. The carrier delayed in delivering the part to the manufacturer, causing the mill to shut down for a period of time. The plaintiff sued the carrier for lost profits associated with the stoppage of the mill. The court denied the claim on the basis that the defendant carrier did not have notice of the special circumstances involved in the contract for carriage. The court reasoned that the damages for breach must relate to what would arise naturally, either based upon the contract itself or what would reasonably be contemplated by the parties at the time of contract formation. Because the nature or terms of the contract did not provide sufficient notice of the potential liability for delayed performance, foreseeability was not satisfied.

The *Hadley* doctrine has continued in the common law as well as under the Uniform Commercial Code. It limits liability for losses that were not reasonably foreseeable by the breaching party at the time of contracting. *See* Restatement (Second) of Contracts § 351 (1981); U.C.C. § 2–715(2)(a). The doctrine inquires into what knowledge or understanding the breaching party reasonably should be charged with at the time of contract formation. *Hadley* reflects the policy choice in contract that breaching parties are held responsible only for those risks that they fairly assumed and that were contemplated as part of bargained-for exchanges. As most courts interpret it, the rule is predicated on an objective examination of the nature and purpose of the contract and the reasonable, justifiable expectations of the parties. It requires inferences of what the breaching party should have known, not what subjectively or actually might have been understood. Accordingly, evidence of the relationship of the parties, the nature and purpose of the contract, custom and trade usage, course of dealing, and sophistication of the parties may provide relevance in determining foreseeability.

The principle of foreseeability applies to all types of contract damages, although with varying restrictiveness depending on the nature of the contract and the damages sought. The common law rule provides that general damages will be awarded for harms that flow directly and immediately as a natural consequence of the kind of non-performance by the breaching party. The law conclusively presumes such damages to be reasonably contemplated by the breaching party simply by virtue of the type of breach. For example, the delivery of goods of lesser quality or quantity at variance from the contract terms obviously diminishes the value of the bargain and deserves appropriate compensation. The U.C.C. illustrates such damages in the provision allowing an aggrieved buyer to recover damages for the difference in value for accepted but non-conforming goods. *See* § 2–714.

Foreseeability presents a significant limitation in circumstances where the non-breaching party seeks special or consequential damages, such as lost profits. For example, the claimant may assert that the non-performance under one contract caused a loss of profits under a second contract with a third party. In that situation, the claimant must show that the breaching party should have contemplated or foreseen that the failure in performance in one contract caused the lost profits in the second. Under

U.C.C. § 2–715(2), recovery of consequential damages is based upon whether at the time of contracting the seller had "reason to know" of general or particular requirements of the buyer. The Code rejects the restrictive "tacit-agreement" test under older common law where the breaching party would be accountable only for non-performance terms that were specifically assumed. *See* § 2–715, cmt. 2.

The inquiry of foreseeability in contracts is determined at the time of contract formation because that is the operative time in which the parties have assumed their respective obligations and determined the nature of the performance reasonably contemplated. Subsequent events that may arise during the course of performance, such as changes in market conditions, do not impact the initial issue of foreseeability for purposes of determining accountability owed for non-performance. Rather, a court will ask whether the breaching party reasonably should have contemplated the type of risk when the bargained-for exchange occurred.

The doctrine of foreseeability also plays a significant role in tort law, although in a different fashion than in contract law. In torts, foreseeability initially functions in defining the nature and extent of the duty owed in ascertaining negligence. The assessment of foreseeability requires a hindsight analysis of whether the alleged tortfeasor should have reasonably anticipated the type of harm that would result from their actions at the time of the injury. Accordingly, it is a hypothetical construct because it asks the objective question of what a reasonable person in the tortfeasor's position should have realized about the potential consequences of their actions, not what the particular defendant actually contemplated.

In tort law of negligence, the assessment of foreseeability is evaluated at the time immediately prior to the resulting harm. The inquiry, from the alleged tortfeasor's perspective, is whether their subsequent actions or inactions would reasonably cause the category or type of injuries which ensued. Accordingly, the policy behind foreseeability in this context is a recognition that theoretically the tortfeasor should have recognized the anticipated danger and had an opportunity to adjust their conduct in a reasonable manner to avoid the harm. Since hindsight analysis of the circumstances could always lead to second-guessing and revisionist judgments, the question of foreseeability is not whether the actor technically might have averted the harm by exercising perfect care. Rather, the assessment for liability purposes considers whether a reasonable person in the situation objectively should have done so.

In the United States, the use of foreseeability to define tort duty was articulated by Justice Cardozo in the leading case, *Palsgraf v. Long Island Railroad Co.*, 248 N.Y. 339 (1928). In *Palsgraf,* a railroad employee tried to help a passenger board a moving train by pushing him from behind. The passenger dropped a small package containing fireworks, which exploded when they fell. The explosion caused a nearby scale to fall and strike the plaintiff, who was

standing nearby on a railroad platform. She sued the
railroad for negligence.

The majority opinion held that the railroad
employee's actions had negligently endangered the
passenger who was trying to board the train but did
not foreseeably place the injured plaintiff at risk.
Therefore, there was no breach of a duty owed to her.
Cardozo explained that "the orbit of the danger as
disclosed to the eye of reasonable vigilance would be
the orbit of the duty." Further, he observed "[t]he risk
reasonably to be perceived defines the duty to be
obeyed, and risk imports relation; it is risk to another
or to others within the range of apprehension."
Because the sequence of events leading to the injury
were so extraordinary, the railroad did not breach its
duty of care to the plaintiff.

The dissenting opinion by Justice Andrews in
Palsgraf objected to the majority's use of
foreseeability to limit recovery so severely. The case
is famous for presenting the opposing views on the
proper role of foreseeability in tort. The Andrews
approach, followed in many jurisdictions, is to trace
the foreseeability of consequences that flow from the
accident itself. Under this view, the plaintiff would
be able to show that she was in close enough
proximity to the explosion of fireworks to make her
injury one that flowed naturally from the events as
they unfolded.

The significance of the difference between the
Cardozo and Andrews views in *Palsgraf* is twofold.
First, the Cardozo view disfavors liability more than
the Andrews view. Second, the Cardozo approach

makes the issue of foreseeability a question of law for the court rather than a question of fact for the jury. The rejection of the duty approach by Andrews has the effect of making the question of foreseeability a factual inquiry.

The doctrine of foreseeability does not require a tortfeasor to anticipate the exact manner, means or extent of the harm. As long as the conduct is a substantial factor in producing an injury that is not too remote, the actor will be accountable for the foreseeable consequences. *See* Restatement (Second) Torts § 435 (1965). Under the "thin-skulled" or "egg-shell" plaintiff rule, a tortfeasor will be responsible for severe consequences to a particularly frail or susceptible person even if a normal person may not have experienced the same degree of harm. *See* Lancaster v. Norfolk & W. Ry. Co, 773 F.2d 807, 811 (7th Cir. 1985) The rationale is that tort liability focuses on the reasonably foreseeable type or category of harm, not the exact extent of injury produced.

In addition to the initial function of foreseeability in determining liability, the doctrine secondarily limits damages for remote injuries under the doctrine of proximate cause. *See* Restatement (Second) of Torts § 9 (1979). This restriction reflects a policy judgment that liability should not extend to unforeseeably remote injuries, even if they were caused in fact by the tortfeasor. Tort law balances the need for compensation with a concern that excessive damages would be inefficient and not socially desirable.

The tension between the goals of compensation and efficiency has resulted in a variety of treatments of proximate cause. An early leading English opinion, *In re Polemis*, 3 K.B. 560 (1921), took the extreme position in favor of compensation and held that tort liability would extend to all injuries directly caused by the negligent conduct. This rule rejected the foreseeability requirement because it imposed liability even if the actor could not have reasonably anticipated the harmful consequences.

That position was later rejected by another Commonwealth decision, known as *The Wagon Mound, No. 1* [1961] A.C. 388. In that case, Viscount Simonds observed that "it does not seem consonant with current ideas of justice or morality that for an act of negligence, however slight or venial, which results in some trivial foreseeable damage the actor should be liable for all consequences however unforeseeable and however grave, so long as they can be said to be 'direct.' " Instead, the court determined that negligence should depend on the foreseeability of the consequent harm even if it was only remotely foreseeable. In American jurisdictions courts have tended to favor rules that require "reasonable foreseeability" of the consequences of torts for the satisfaction of proximate cause.

The predominant view in modern law is that foreseeability is a significant limiting doctrine in both tort and contract. As such, foreseeability embodies notions of fairness to strike a proper balance between the goals of compensation and of limitation to keep damages within appropriate boundaries. In the absence of foreseeability requirements, tortfeasors and breaching parties would be potentially accountable for losses that they could not have reasonably contemplated. Modern law does not extend the principle of providing just compensation so far as to make breaching parties and tortfeasors absolute insurers for all losses, however remote or unexpected.

(B) CERTAINTY

A plaintiff must also prove compensatory damages with reasonable certainty. The standard is stated in terms of reasonableness rather than mathematical precision, and therefore is satisfied where a rational basis exists for computation. The requirement of certainty applies both to establishing entitlement to some recovery by meeting the substantive criteria of the claim and then, secondarily, to measure the amount of damages recoverable for the harm sustained. Once entitlement to damages is demonstrated with reasonable certainty, courts generally permit the measurement of damages to be established with less exactitude. *See* Bresler v. Wilmington Trust Co., 855 F.3d 178, 199 (4th Cir. 2017)(once personal representative of settlor's estate proved trustee's breach of contract, less precision required to show amount of resulting damages).

Several principles guide the trier-of-fact in determining whether the proof offered satisfies the plaintiff's burden regarding certainty. First, as a matter of fundamental fairness, the injured party bears the burden of demonstrating that all claimed damages are caused by and traceable to the tortious conduct at issue or the breach of contract asserted. Second, the compensatory damages must satisfy the objective of fair compensation rather than punishment for the behavior. Finally, courts recognize the reality that certain types of injuries are inherently less capable of empirical proof than others. Considerable latitude is given with respect to the certainty requirement for certain losses, such as pain and suffering or emotional distress. *See* Restatement (Second) of Torts § 912, cmt. b (1979).

In *Haines v. Comfort Keepers, Inc.*, 393 P.3d 422, 436 (Alaska 2017) an elderly woman brought various tort claims against an in-home care company based on a pattern of mistreatment and conversion of her jewelry and prescription medication by the company's care-giver. The court held that once the claimant had proven pain and suffering, it was error not to award general damages even though the measure would be difficult to establish with exact certainty.

In tort law, another reason for liberalizing the standard for certainty is the policy that the wrongdoer should not profit from the very uncertainty that their conduct created. Stated alternatively, tort law seeks to provide compensation and redress for harms but also reflects a social judgment that the tortfeasor should be held accountable for their behavior and that compensatory damages awarded may deter others in the future from similar conduct. Accordingly, once the plaintiff demonstrates entitlement to some damages, courts will generally provide a measure of leeway on the certainty limitation with regard to the amount of damages. In situations where the plaintiff establishes a violation of a right but fails to show the damages with appropriate degree of certainty, the trier of fact may limit the award to nominal damages.

Some types of losses require a more exacting level of proof to satisfy the certainty requirement. For example, a high quantum of reliable evidence is generally needed for proof of lost profits associated with breach of contract. *See* Restatement (Second) of Contracts § 352 (1981). The certainty requirement presents particular challenges to plaintiffs where they seek lost profits for breach of contract involving a new business venture.

The traditional approach disallowed recovery of such profits where no prior operating history existed on the basis that proof of damages was too speculative. This approach relied exclusively on the "before and after" method to establish lost profits. This method compares a plaintiff's profit record prior to a contract breach and following. That approach is problematic where the claimant has a limited operational history.

Today, most courts provide that where a reasonable basis of computation exists, damages may properly be given. The reasonable basis could be derived from a modified version of the "before and after" method. *See* Alaska Rent-A-Car, Inc. v. Avis Budget Group, Inc., 709 F.3d 872 (9th Cir. 2013)(lost profits awarded to new business venture based on evidence of past performance and likelihood of future success). Another method for awarding lost profits to new businesses is referred to as the "yardstick" test, which draws upon evidence of profits from comparable enterprises and makes appropriate adjustments for differences between the businesses. *See* Bigelow v. RKO Radio Pictures, 327 U.S. 251 (1946).

The Uniform Commercial Code maintains a policy of liberally applying remedies, and therefore rejects the view that "damages must be calculable with mathematical accuracy." *See* U.C.C. § 1–305, cmt. 1. Instead, the U.C.C. embraces a flexible approach where compensatory damages need only be proven in whatever manner is reasonable under the circumstances. *See* U.C.C. § 2–715, cmt. 4. Also, the Code incorporates by reference the common law doctrinal guidance of proving damages by a reasonableness standard.

(C) AVOIDABLE CONSEQUENCES

The doctrine of mitigation or avoidable consequences is another important limitation on compensatory damages. The rule operates to limit recovery when an injured party fails to take reasonable steps to avoid or limit further losses following upon incurrence of harm.

The obligation of the innocent party is often couched in terms of a "duty", but that characterization is somewhat misleading because the failure to meet the standard of reasonable mitigation does not result in a breach leading to damages. Instead, the failure to mitigate serves to exclude any damages that a plaintiff may sustain following the failure to undertake reasonable steps following the harm. Restatement (Second) of Torts § 918, cmt. a (1979). In that sense, the doctrine operates negatively by denying recovery of certain damages that a non-breaching party or the injured party in tort could have otherwise reasonably avoided without excessive risk or burden. *See* Restatement (Second) of Contracts § 350 (1981).

A modern illustration of the negative application of the mitigation principle was expressed in *Kimbrough v. Anderson*, 55 N.E.3d 325 (Ind. App. 2016) where a landowner brought a negligence suit against a neighbor for damage caused by excessive water drainage from irrigation which infiltrated their home. Upon discovery of the problem, the landowner was advised that installation of a sump pump would remove the source of the moisture and waterproofing would eliminate future water damage. The landowner did not undertake any remedial actions, however, and severe mold spread and ruined the landowner's extensive art collection. The court held that the affected landowner's failure to minimize damages after the initial injury-producing event by taking reasonable steps to mitigate the harm precluded recovery of damages for the lost art collection.

A corollary to the mitigation doctrine holds that an injured party is entitled to reimbursement of expenses reasonably incurred in attempting to mitigate losses, even if those efforts are ultimately unsuccessful. *See* Restatement (Second) of Torts

§ 919(1) (1979). Thus, if an injured party undergoes medical tests following the harm, the expenses of those tests should be ordinarily recoverable as reasonable steps attempting to limit the harm experienced. Similarly, if an employer breaches an employment contract and the non-breaching employee incurs expenses in seeking reasonable substitute employment, such costs of mitigation would typically be included in the award of compensatory damages associated with the breach. Such expenses are recoverable as compensatory damages, however, only if proven to be distinctly resulting from the harm and not merely as an inconvenience or annoyance. *See* In re Hannaford Bors. Co. Customer Data Security Breach Litigation, 4 A.3d 492, 497 (Me. 2010).

From a timing perspective, the duty of avoidance only arises following a breach of contract or the occurrence of harm from tortious conduct. The injured or non-breaching party is not required to anticipate a harm, but the law requires reasonable conduct following the injury or breach to avoid incurring additional losses. The issue of avoidance must be distinguished from entitlement to recovery of damages for a contract breach or other injury. The non-breaching party still may maintain a claim for damages associated with the breach, but the issue of avoidance may affect the ultimate measure of a damages recovery. The avoidance principle looks at the non-breaching party's conduct, not that of the breaching party and therefore advances the basic goal of providing fair compensation for losses attributable to non-performance.

The doctrine of avoidable consequences reflects three primary policy goals. First, it embodies notions of fairness to breaching parties or tortfeasors by holding them accountable only for damages resulting from their actions and not paying for losses otherwise avoidable through the exercise of reasonable care. Second, it protects the innocent party by affirmatively enabling them to undertake reasonable avoidance measures, such as seeking substitute employment or obtaining replacement goods following a contract breach, in order to secure their justifiable expectations. Finally, the rule advances a public policy of avoiding economic waste through excessive damages.

A frequent problem involves applying the standard of reasonableness for purposes of mitigation. Non-breaching or injured parties do not have to undertake extraordinary measures or suffer inconvenience or hardship in attempting to mitigate losses, nor must they necessarily be successful in the mitigation attempt. *See* Restatement (Second) of Contracts § 350 (1981). The doctrine of mitigation promotes diligence but does not necessarily require that a non-breaching party successfully obtain a replacement job or secure substitute goods, for example, but rather requires a reasonable, good faith effort to minimize loss.

The reasonableness of the duty to mitigate often is a highly fact-intensive inquiry. In *Tedd Bish Farm v. Southwest Fencing Servs.*, 867 N.W.2d 265 (Neb. 2015), a farm owner sustained a broken section of irrigation pipe due to the actions of a fencing company hired by the State's Department of Roads. The farmer complained about the damaged pipe and informed the fencing company and the State that the repairs needed to be undertaken before a specific date in order to avoid crop loss. The farmer had the financial ability to pay for the needed repairs, but declined to do so while waiting for the fencing company to admit liability. The farmer subsequently sought damages for the cost of repairs to the pipe plus the value of the lost crop. The court awarded damages for repairing the pipe but excluded damages for the lost crop, reasoning that the farmer could have reasonably paid a modest sum to make the needed repairs and thus would have avoided the much greater damages for the lost crop.

In tort law, the doctrine of mitigation obligates an injured party to exercise the care of a person of ordinary intelligence and prudence under similar circumstances. That may include undergoing surgical or medical treatment within a reasonable time to minimize damages. Whether or not a specific medical procedure is deemed reasonable for purposes of satisfying the duty to mitigate ordinarily will involve an assessment of many factors, including the nature and extent of the risks presented, the likelihood of success, alternatives to surgery, the state of medical knowledge, the pain involved in the operation, the degree of possible complications arising from the procedure, and the expenditure of money or effort required. *See* Simmons v. Erie Ins. Exchange, 891 N.E.2d 1059, 1066 (Ind. App. 2008)(insured's decision to forego surgery following auto accident deemed reasonable so did not fail to mitigate). Although an injured party is never required to undergo recommended medical treatment, such as elective surgery, a tortfeasor may not be held accountable for damages resulting from a disability or pain if medical treatment could have reasonably cured the condition. The tortfeasor bears the burden of pleading and proving failure to mitigate as an affirmative defense.

In contracts, the duty to mitigate following breach may arise in a wide range of circumstances. For instance, once a party breaches a construction contract by giving unequivocal notice of repudiation, the non-breaching party cannot recover damages for work performed following the receipt of the cancellation notice. The non-breaching party has a duty of mitigation that contemplates ceasing performance so as not to unduly increase the damages. *See* Rockingham County v. Luten Bridge Co., 35 F.2d 301 (4th Cir. 1929). Although generally the non-breaching party is expected to make reasonable efforts to mitigate damages, courts do not apply the doctrine if the contract contains a valid liquidated damages clause. The rationale for the distinction is that the liquidated sum is fixed and therefore the measure of recovery would be unaffected by the post-breach actions of the non-breaching party. *See* Queens Ballpark Co., LLC v. Vysk Communications, 226 F. Supp. 3d 254, 259 (S.D.N.Y. 2016).

The concept of what constitutes a reasonable substitute may present particular problems in the context of employment contracts. In the famous case,

Parker v. Twentieth Century-Fox Film Corp., 3 Cal.3d 176 (1970), an actress successfully claimed that it was not a reasonable substitute to accept a leading role in a western motion picture to be produced in Australia when the studio breached an employment contract for her services to perform in a musical production in California. The court reasoned that the artist was not required to seek or accept employment that was "different or inferior" in order to mitigate damages.

The Uniform Commercial Code also incorporates the doctrine of avoidable consequences, and will limit the amount of damages potentially recoverable if the non-breaching party fails to take reasonable measures to mitigate following a material breach. *See* U.C.C. § 2–715(2)(a). In *Oloffson v. Coomer*, 11 Ill. App.3d 918 (1973), for example, a grain dealer unreasonably delayed in seeking to obtain replacement goods following notice of the seller's breach. As a result, the aggrieved buyer could not recover damages that could have been avoided by purchasing substitute goods in a timely manner.

(D) COLLATERAL SOURCE RULE

Two principles of tort law that sometimes collide are that (1) responsible parties should be accountable for the losses caused by their wrongful conduct, and (2) damages should place injured parties effectively in the same position as they stood prior to the tortious conduct. When an injured party receives payment from a source other than the defendant, the second principle will be violated if there is double coverage for the same harm. If that amount from a third party is deducted from damages, however, the first principle is violated.

All payments made by the responsible party to the plaintiff, whether made prior to or following formal adjudication of liability, are credited to offset the damages owed. In some instances, the injured party may also receive payments or benefits from other sources, such as from insurance, as a direct consequence of the injury. The question then becomes whether or not such collateral or third-party payments should offset the ultimate tort liability of the wrongdoer.

The traditional formulation of the collateral source rule provides that if an injured party receives compensation or benefits from a source unaffiliated or independent from the tortfeasor, then those payments will not be deducted from the damages the plaintiff otherwise may be entitled to collect from the wrongdoer. *See* Helfend v. S. Cal. Rapid Transit Dist., 2 Cal.3d 1 (1970). The rule further operates to exclude the introduction of evidence of ancillary benefits or compensation received by the claimant as a result of the injury to avoid prejudice with the jury.

The rule has been applied in a variety of contexts, including the receipt of insurance proceeds, employment benefits, gifts of money or medical services, welfare benefits, and tax advantages. The collateral source rule generally does not apply with the same force in contract cases because the nature of the benefit of the bargain is met either by performance or payment of damages and third party insurance for nonperformance ordinarily does not come into play.

The collateral source rule has drawn considerable criticism in recent years, principally on the grounds that it could lead to a double recovery or a windfall to the injured party. If so, the rule undermines the principle of just compensation associated with the goal of placing the injured party in the same position held prior to the harm.

Supporters of the rule assert that it retains vitality for several reasons. First, an injured party should receive the full benefits of their insurance policy because they have contracted for coverage and should properly be compensated for losses associated with the risks contemplated. Otherwise, it could create a disincentive to obtain insurance coverage because an injured party would have paid premiums yet not received compensation for the very risks covered by the policy. The double recovery argument is countered by the reality that most insurance policies include a subrogation provision whereby the insurance company pays the plaintiff for their losses and then "stands in their shoes" seeking reimbursement from the tortfeasor.

Second, if any windfall does result, it should be enjoyed by the innocent party rather than the one responsible for the harm. Third, a tortfeasor should be liable for full compensatory damages, without an offset, in order to carry out the social goals of deterrence and accountability. Some have further suggested an indirect justification in that the rule provides an economic offset to the attorneys' fees owed by the plaintiff.

Complexities in applying the collateral source rule arise when determining whether or not a source should be viewed as affiliated with or independent from the tortfeasor. For example, classification of some governmental or public sector benefits, such as Medicare or unemployment compensation, have presented particular difficulties of application.

Similarly, problems emerge with the issue of whether courts should allow an injured party to recover the reasonable value of gratuitously rendered services or benefits. Some courts have held that the rule still applies and the injured party is entitled to recover the reasonable market value of medical costs, even if actually provided by a collateral source at a below market rate or gratuitously. *See* Restatement (Second) of Torts § 920A, cmt. c (1979). This approach carries out the intent of the donor to benefit the injured party rather than the tortfeasor. In contrast, other courts reason that an offset still fulfills the purposes of fair compensation and abandon a strict application of the rule for reduced damages.

In recent years, the collateral source rule has proved to be a fertile subject for state tort reform. Although states vary widely in their formulation of policy, some modifications include: allowing evidence pertaining to payments from collateral sources, requiring the jury to consider collateral benefits in assessing damages, altering the rule in medical malpractice or personal injury cases only, and reducing a damages award post-verdict.

One area that has been particularly problematic for courts has been the interplay between the collateral source rule and recovery for medical expenses. Plaintiffs frequently introduce their medical bills as evidence of the reasonable value of their care. However, insurance companies and other third-party payers often negotiate a discounted rate. The health care provider then accepts less than the billed amount for the services and writes-off the remainder of the bill. Defendants often seek to introduce evidence of the amount a plaintiff's insurance company actually pays for the services provided to the plaintiff as evidence of reasonable value of care.

In general, the extent to which a court allows the injured plaintiff to recover the "write-off" amount usually mirrors the extent to which the jurisdiction still strictly adheres to the collateral source rule. Some courts apply an "actual amount paid" approach. These courts limit recovery to the amount actually paid to the health care provider by insurance or otherwise. Thus, if a third-party payor such as a private insurance company or Medicaid or Medicare has paid for the injured party's medical expenses and that payor has negotiated a discounted rate with the treating provider, the injured party will be precluded from introducing evidence of the amount the treating provider billed. Usually, the collateral source rule has been modified or abrogated in jurisdictions adopting this approach.

Other courts apply the "benefit of the bargain" approach. These courts preclude evidence of insurance write-offs as violative of the collateral source rule only if the plaintiff has exchanged something of value to receive the benefit of the insurance. Thus, these courts preclude evidence of insurance write-offs when the plaintiff has private insurance but may not exclude write offs when the plaintiff receives public benefits such as Medicaid. Frequently, this approach mirrors the jurisdiction's approach to the collateral source rule.

The majority of courts apply some version of the "reasonable value" approach. However, courts define reasonable value differently. Some courts adopting this approach define "reasonable value" as the full undiscounted medical bill. These courts preclude evidence of insurance write-offs as violative of the collateral source rule and allow the plaintiff to recover the full amount billed for medical treatment. Others applying this approach allow the evidence of both the amount billed by the health care provider and the amount paid by the insurance carrier. In these states, the jury determines the reasonable value of the medical treatment based on this evidence. One court precludes the defendant from introducing evidence of the insurance write-offs to the jury but allows the court to consider such write-offs and make post-verdict adjustments. *See* Weston v. AKHappytime, LLC, 445 P.3d 1015 (Alaska 2019).

CHAPTER 14
DAMAGES FOR ECONOMIC LOSS OR DISTRESS ALONE

(A) INTRODUCTION

The common law historically has recognized two significant limitations to recover compensatory damages. First, damages for purely economic loss generally are not recoverable in tort absent physical injury or property damage. Second, recovery for emotional distress in the absence of physical injury is significantly limited. This chapter explores the contours of recovery in these areas and the parameters and rationales for those limits on recovery.

(B) ECONOMIC LOSS RULE

1.   ECONOMIC LOSS RULE—GENERALLY

The economic loss rule precludes a plaintiff from recovering purely economic losses in tort. Economic losses include harms such as lost profits, loss in value, reputational harm, and lost wages. A plaintiff may recover damages for economic losses in connection with physical harm to person or property only.

The rule usually operates in one of two settings. First, the economic loss rule precludes a person who is a "stranger" to the defendant from recovering damages when the defendant's tortious act causes damage to the plaintiff's economic interest rather than physical injury to the plaintiff's person or property. Second, when the plaintiff and the defendant have a contractual relationship, the economic loss rule prohibits a plaintiff from recovering economic losses such as lost profits in tort and limits the plaintiff to her remedies under the contract between the parties.

Courts have recognized several exceptions to the economic loss rule. A few courts have replaced the absolute bar approach of the economic loss rule with a foreseeability approach to claims for economic loss.

2.   ECONOMIC LOSS RULE— "STRANGER" CASES

At common law, an injured party was prohibited from recovering damages when the defendant's tortious act caused economic loss only and did not damage the plaintiff's property or cause physical injury. For example, consider a case in which a defendant tortiously obstructs the public roadway leading to the plaintiff's business. The obstruction of the roadway may cause the plaintiff to lose customers and, hence, profits but does not damage the plaintiff's property. Traditionally, the economic loss rule would preclude the plaintiff from recovering damages for the lost profits because the plaintiff's losses were economic only.

Courts advance several reasons for the economic loss rule in this setting. Some describe the economic loss rule as a rule of foreseeability and proximate cause. These courts note that the rule is necessary to limit recovery to consequences which were reasonably foreseeable. The economic loss rule also provides a bright-line limit to potentially boundless liability. Finally, some courts say the rule protects against fraudulent claims, mass litigation, and liability that is potentially disproportionate to the defendant's fault.

An early expression of the absolute bar approach was followed in the leading case of *Robins Dry Dock & Repair Co. v. Flint*, 275 U.S. 303 (1927). A steamship charterer sought to recover lost profits attributable to delays when the defendant negligently broke a vessel's propeller. The charterer contracted with the ship's owners but did not have a property interest in the ship itself. The Court denied recovery of economic losses potentially attributable to the delay, reasoning that "[t]he law does not spread its protection so far." The Restatement (Second) of Torts adopted the approach of the Court in *Robins Dry Dock*. It denies recovery for pecuniary losses resulting from a negligent interference with contractual performance (§ 766C) but allows compensation if the tortfeasor intentionally interfered with performance (§ 766A) or with prospective contractual relations (§ 766B).

In a modern setting, some courts have applied the economic loss rule to bar claims for injuries stemming from data breaches. For example, in *Community Bank of Trenton v. Schnuck Markets, Inc.*, 887 F.3d 803 (7th Cir. 2018), criminals hacked into the computer network of the defendant grocery store chain and stole credit and debit card account information from customers who shopped at the grocery store. The financial institutions that had issued the compromised credit and debit cards to the customers sued the grocery store to recover the costs to investigate claims, reissue cards, and indemnify cardholders for any fraudulent transactions. The court held that the economic loss doctrine precluded claims by financial institutions.

3. ECONOMIC LOSS RULE—CONTRACT CASES

The economic loss rule also precludes a plaintiff from recovering for purely economic losses in tort when the plaintiff and the defendant have entered into a contractual relationship. In such cases, the economic loss rule limits the plaintiff to her remedies under the contract. For example, if the defendant sells the plaintiff a truck that does not work properly such that the plaintiff cannot deliver her goods to a customer, the economic loss rule precludes the plaintiff from recovering her lost profits on the sale to the customer from the defendant as a matter of tort law. Instead, the plaintiff must seek recovery of the lost profits in an action for breach of contract.

Contract law requires that consequential losses such as lost profits must be foreseeable to the breaching party at the time of contract. Contract law also permits parties to contractually limit liability for consequential losses such as lost profits. Thus, in some cases the plaintiff may not be able to recover her lost profits in a breach of contract claim. The economic loss rule precludes the non-breaching party from evading these contractually agreed upon limits on liability through an action in tort.

Courts have offered several rationales for the operation of the economic loss rule in this context: to maintain the distinction between tort law and contract law; to protect commercial parties' freedom to allocate economic risk by contract; and to encourage the party best situated to assess the risk of economic loss to assume, allocate, or insure against the risk.

The economic loss rule does not preclude recovery in tort for economic losses when the plaintiff also suffers physical injury or property other than the object of the contract suffers damage. Thus, defective products that cause personal injury or property damage may justify compensation for damages through either negligence or strict liability theories of § 402A of the Restatement (Second) of Torts. Further, if personal injury or property damage arise as a result of the negligence, then a plaintiff may also recover pecuniary losses which are "parasitic" to the injuries. *See* Restatement (Second) of Torts § 766C, cmt. b (1979).

Courts have had difficulty determining whether the plaintiff has suffered injury to property other than the object of the contract when the defective product is a component part of a larger product. For example, in construction cases courts struggle to determine whether a defect in one part of the building gives rise to a claim for damages to the remainder of the building. One frequently arising issue involves defectively installed windows that

cause water damage to the walls and floors. *See* In re
MI Windows and Doors, Inc. Products Liability
Litigation, 914 F. Supp. 2d 744, 751 (D. S.C. 2012).

4. EXCEPTIONS TO THE
ECONOMIC LOSS RULE

Courts have recognized exceptions to the economic
loss rule in both contract cases and stranger cases.
The courts allow for recovery of purely economic loss
in limited circumstances. In an Illinois decision, a
court recognized three "traditional exceptions:
"(1) where the plaintiff sustained damage, i.e.,
personal injury or property damage, resulting from a
sudden or dangerous occurrence; (2) where the
plaintiff's damages are proximately caused by a
defendant's intentional, false representation, i.e.,
fraud; and (3) where the plaintiff's damages are
proximately caused by a negligent misrepresentation
by a defendant in the business of supplying
information for the guidance of others in their
business transactions." Mercola v. Abdou, 223
F. Supp. 3d 720 (N.D. Ill. 2016) (recognizing
exception for torts against professionals—or
extracontractual duty exception).

Similarly, a Tennessee court found that the
economic loss rule does not apply when: (1) the
parties in a case have privity of contract . . . and (2)
the action for pure economic loss is based on
negligent supervision or negligent
misrepresentation." City of Morristown v. AT&T
Corp., 206 F. Supp. 3d 1321 (E.D. Tenn. 2016). Also,
a Nevada case reasoned that exceptions to economic

loss doctrine could exist in a certain category of cases where particularly strong policy factors supported imposing liability, such as cases "where there is significant risk that 'the law would not exert significant financial pressures to avoid such negligence.' " *See* Morrison v. Quest Diagnostics Inc., 139 F. Supp. 3d 1182, 1188–89 (D. Nev. 2015).

Some courts recognize a special duty to protect from economic harm on certain classes of defendants. For example, courts have allowed for recovery of purely economic loss against certain service professionals such as auditors, surveyors, engineers, attorneys and architects. *See* Restatement (Third) Torts: Liability for Economic Harm § 4 ("A professional is subject to liability in tort for economic loss caused by the negligent performance of an undertaking to serve a client.").

Courts also recognize an exception to the economic loss doctrine when private parties assert claims for public nuisance. Thus, in *In re National Prescription Opiate Litigation*, 440 F. Supp. 3d 773 (N.D. Ohio 2020), the court allowed claims by private insurance companies to proceed against manufacturers and distributors of prescription opioids. The plaintiff insurance companies sought to recover money they paid to health care professionals to cover the cost of prescription opioids and opioid abuse treatment prescribed to their insureds. The plaintiffs alleged that the defendants had created a public nuisance. The court held that the public nuisance exception to the economic loss doctrine applied.

In the contract context, common exceptions include where damage resulted from a sudden or dangerous occurrence, where one party made intentionally false representations or fraudulent inducements, and where a party made negligent misrepresentations. *See* Schaefer v. Indymac Mortgage Servs., 731 F.3d 98, 107 (1st Cir. 2013); Tiara Condo Association v. Marsh & McLennan Companies, Inc., 110 So.3d 399 (Fla. 2013) (recognizing exception to the economic loss rule for . . . fraudulent inducement). *But see* Graham Const. Servs. v. Hammer & Steel Inc., 755 F.3d 611, 617 (8th Cir. 2014) ("Because Graham seeks purely economic damages through its negligent misrepresentation claim, we conclude that the economic loss doctrine bars recovery on that claim.") Liability for pecuniary loss caused by negligent misrepresentation is also supported by the Restatement (Second) of Torts § 552(1).

In addition to common law exceptions, statutes may also limit the stranger version of the economic loss doctrine. For example, Congress expressly provides for purely economic losses in oil spill cases as a response to several major spills in navigable waters. 33 U.S.C. § 2702(b)(2)(E) (1990); South Port Marine, LLC v. Gulf Oil Limited Partnership, 234 F.3d 58 (1st Cir. 2000) (approving recovery of a marina's lost future profits where gas spill resulted in reallocation of capital and delayed expansions); *Also see* Federal Medical Care Recovery Act. 42 U.S.C. § 2651 (2006).

5. FORESEEABILITY APPROACH
TO ECONOMIC LOSS

Some courts have replaced the absolute bar approach of the economic loss rule with a foreseeability inquiry. These courts allow a claim for purely economic loss rule when the defendant reasonably should foresee that its conduct may cause economic harm to the plaintiff. To be reasonably foreseeable, the harm must occur to a member of an identifiable class of plaintiffs. The class of plaintiffs should be identifiable in terms of the types of plaintiffs in the class; their proximity to the defendant should be reasonably ascertainable and the type of economic loss they might suffer should be predictable to the defendant.

In one leading case, the court recognized an exception to the economic loss rule when the defendants' negligence in handling a railway freight car carrying hazardous substances caused a disruption to business in the vicinity of the rail yard. In *People Express Airlines v. Consolidated Rail Corp.*, 495 A.2d 107 (N.J. 1985), the plaintiff was forced to shut down its business after a fire at a nearby freight yard forced the plaintiff to evacuate its business. The fire broke out after a tank car carrying a hazardous substance was punctured while rail workers were attempting to attach the tank car to another freight car. The plaintiff suffered no damage to its property but only lost business during the period it remained shut down. The court found that several factors made the plaintiff's economic losses foreseeable to the defendants. The court noted the plaintiff's proximity to the rail yard, the nature of the plaintiff's business was obvious to the public, the defendants were aware of the hazardous nature of the substance in the tank car and that the defendants were aware that the emergency response plan in the case of fire would require the evacuation of the plaintiff's business.

(C) DISTRESS DAMAGES

1.   DISTRESS DAMAGES—GENERALLY

Limits on the availability of damages for mental distress arise from both substantive and remedial law. Substantive law restrictions appear when the plaintiff suffers mental distress in the absence of other injury. In tort claims this issue arises frequently in two situations. First, emotional distress claims arise in "direct" claims when a plaintiff is terrorized by a situation threatening serious injury but none results. Second, emotional distress claims arise when a plaintiff is distressed by witnessing an accident involving a loved one. In contract, a party may suffer distress if a breach is anticipated but does not occur.

The general rule is that a contract claim will not support distress damages, although there are a few exceptions. The historical rule in tort held that no substantive claim for negligently caused distress could exist without physical injury. Today, most jurisdictions now recognize a claim for negligently caused emotional distress, but jurisdictions place different limitations on recovery.

2. DISTRESS DAMAGES IN CONTRACT

The general rule is that damages for mental distress or emotional disturbance are not recoverable for breach of contract. The rationale for that limitation is variously stated but generally reflects the principle that parties to a contract bargain for performance or payment in lieu of lost future promised performance. Thus, in the bargaining calculus parties would not generally contemplate potential liability for mental distress associated with a contract breach, so absent foreseeability by the breaching party at the time of contract formation such damages should be properly excluded. Further, efficient breach of contract posits that it may be economically beneficial to move goods and services to whoever values them the most, consequently contributing to the public good by maximizing resource allocation and utility. As such, courts typically do not inquire into motivations for contract breach in deciding entitlement and measure of compensatory damages, although bad faith conduct associated with a contract breach may support certain types of claims sounding in tort.

There are a few exceptions to the general rule that a breach of contract will not support damages for mental distress. The Restatement (Second) of Contracts § 353 (1981) provides for distress damages in contract only if "the breach also caused bodily harm or the contract or the breach is of such a kind that serious emotional disturbance was a particularly likely result." Examples of the latter category include (1) contracts between carriers and passengers, (2) contracts between innkeepers and guests, (3) contracts to handle dead bodies, such as for transportation or disposal, and (4) contracts for the delivery of messages concerning death. Unless a case falls within one of the narrow exceptions to distress damages for breach of contract, a plaintiff cannot recover without establishing an independent tort.

Even in circumstances involving highly personal matters, courts are reluctant to award distress damages for breach of contract. In *Repin v. State of Washington*, 392 P.3d 1174 (Wash. Ct. App. 2017), for example, the court held that, as a matter of law, a pet owner could not recover emotional disturbance, noneconomic damages resulting from a veterinarian's alleged breach of contract in euthanasia of beloved family pet. See § 32:2 Emotional injury as element of tort damages, 4 Modern Tort Law: Liability and Litigation § 32:2 (2d ed.).

However, a few courts have awarded emotional distress damages where a breach of contract interfered with a property owner's use and enjoyment of her residence. For example, in *Brown v. Compass Harbor Village Condominium Assoc.*, 2020 WL 1808375 (Me. March 5, 2020), the court awarded plaintiff condominium owners damages for mental anguish and loss of enjoyment of their units after the defendant managing association failed to maintain common areas. *See also* Matherne v. Barnum, 94 So. 3d 782 (La. Ct. App. 2012) (allowing damages for mental anguish, distress, inconvenience and aggravation in homeowners' breach of contract action against a contractor for defective workmanship in the construction of a bulkhead, boat slip and deck because the bulkhead, slip and deck were meant to be "a major source of intellectual enjoyment for the [plaintiffs] as they lived in their dream home with beautiful landscaping and water access by boat").

3.   DISTRESS DAMAGES IN TORT

Traditionally, no claim in tort existed for negligently caused distress without physical injury. Today, most jurisdictions recognize a claim for negligently caused emotional distress, but jurisdictions place different limitations on recovery.

In "direct" cases where the plaintiff suffers emotional distress because of fear of harm to herself, a common limitation restricts recovery to plaintiffs who were in the zone of danger—or placed in immediate risk of harm—and suffer some physical manifestation of emotional distress. Restatement (Third) of Torts: Phys. & Emot. Harm § 47(a) (2012). Courts have liberally construed the requirement of physical manifestation of emotional distress to include conditions traditionally considered physical symptoms such as heart attacks, ulcers, headaches, and nausea as well as psychological symptoms and conditions such as post-traumatic stress disorder, insomnia, and nightmares.

Sometimes the plaintiff suffers no risk of physical harm herself but witnesses physical harm to others. Jurisdictions limit recovery in these "bystander" claims to situations in which the bystander witnesses death or serious injury and an intimate or familiar relationship exists between the bystander and the injured or killed party. Thus, courts have precluded recovery in cases where the plaintiff witnessed injury to friends or witnessed the death of a pet. Some states limit recovery to those bystanders who were in the zone of danger of the accident. A few states allow recovery to distressed witnesses even if the claimant is not in the zone of danger if she can meet certain specific criteria, such as the plaintiff suffered severe emotional distress proximately associated with the event.

Remedial issues with distress damages arise when the plaintiff establishes an action for the invasion of another interest, such as personal injury or breach of contract. When a plaintiff has established a claim for invasion of an interest in person or property, distress damages are recoverable as "parasitic damages." The limits on such recovery are governed by the remedial limitations of foreseeability and certainty. Thus, the injured party must show a causal link between the emotional distress and the event which caused the physical injury. Courts usually interpret foreseeable distress and its consequences quite liberally in personal injury cases, whereas in fraud cases courts generally interpret foreseeability restrictively or prohibit such damages altogether.

CHAPTER 15
PUNITIVE DAMAGES

(A) ENTITLEMENT

1. PURPOSES FOR WHICH PUNITIVE DAMAGES ARE AWARDED

Punitive damages is the area of civil damages that overlaps with criminal law in its purpose and function. Unlike compensatory damages, punitive damages are not awarded to plaintiffs to compensate for their losses. Rather, punitive damages are awarded to punish defendants for egregious conduct and deter defendants and others from future offenses. Courts and scholars often refer to punitive damages as "exemplary damages" because they intend to make defendants public examples of inappropriate behavior. Punitive damages also are sometimes referred to as "smart money" because by design they hurt defendants financially.

Punitive damages hold a lengthy heritage in Anglo-American jurisprudence. American courts began to recognize punitive damage awards at least as early as 1791. Proponents argue that punitive damages are necessary to assess the true societal costs of defendants' misfeasances. An award of punitive damages also provides a fund from which plaintiffs can recover attorneys' fees and other litigation costs that are otherwise noncompensable. Despite their longstanding presence, however, punitive damages remain a controversial issue.

One of the chief criticisms of punitive damages is that they are quasi-criminal in character in punishing defendants for anti-social conduct, yet lack the benefit of traditional constitutional safeguards that apply in criminal trials. Further, the awards provide a windfall to successful plaintiffs and therefore transcend the objective of compensating for injuries. Additional concerns are that juries receive too much discretion in deciding on the entitlement and measurement of punitive awards and the incentive of receiving large punitive damage awards may encourage unnecessary litigation, further diminishing valuable judicial resources. Punitive damages pose special problems in mass disaster and products liability cases. In those cases, courts face the challenge of accommodating the goals of punishment and deterrence without imposing ruinous liability. Finally, some contend that the awards simply are ineffective in achieving the stated goals of punishment and deterrence, especially where a wrongdoer may shift the loss through insurance.

2. SCOPE OF CONDUCT SUBJECT TO PUNITIVE DAMAGES

Punitive damages are not available to redress all legal wrongs. Instead, the awards seek to punish and deter only egregious conduct. Jurisdictions vary in defining the standard of conduct that may support entitlement to punitive damages. Typically, however, punitive damages are available where the defendant acts with a malicious intent or an evil motive, such as spite, ill will, malice or the intent to injure or defraud or where the defendant acts with gross recklessness or a willful or conscious disregard for the rights of others. Generally, a defendant acts with gross recklessness when the defendant knows of the risk of harm to the injured party and either fails to take measures to avoid the harm or takes measures the defendant knows to be ineffective to prevent the harm.

The intent necessary to maintain an action for an intentional tort is not identical with the frame of mind of the wrongdoer necessary to recover punitive damages. Intentional torts are premised upon deliberate conduct that is substantially certain to invade the plaintiff's legally protected interest. The defendant need not intend harm. Indeed, the defendant may even have good intentions and yet be liable for an intentional tort. For punitive damages, however, the majority of jurisdictions require an "evil mind" or "malice." In other words, the defendant must intend to cause injury.

3. RELATIONSHIP TO CLAIM FOR COMPENSATORY DAMAGES

A claim for punitive damages is not considered an independent cause of action but is derivative in character. Therefore, a plaintiff must succeed on the underlying claim to recover punitive damages. Even if the plaintiff succeeds on the underlying claim, the plaintiff must still establish entitlement to punitive damages. Thus, even if the underlying claim does not require proof of malicious intent, such as a claim in strict liability or for negligence, the plaintiff must offer proof of the defendant's scienter or wilfulness to recover punitive damages. Where the underlying claim requires proof of malicious intent, the plaintiff need not meet a higher standard of conduct to recover punitive damages.

Although a plaintiff must establish liability to recover punitive damages, a plaintiff need not establish actual damages to recover punitive damages. In a majority of jurisdictions, a plaintiff need not recover compensatory damages to recover punitive damages. Rather, even an award of nominal damages will suffice to sustain an award for punitive damages. In contrast, equitable relief generally will not support an award of punitive damages. With the merger of law and equity, however, some courts recognize such damages in appropriate cases.

4. AVAILABILITY OF PUNITIVE DAMAGES FOR SPECIFIC CLAIMS

The prevailing rule is that punitive damages are ordinarily not recoverable for breach of a contractual obligation unless the conduct also constitutes an independent tort which would support such an award. *See* Restatement (Second) of Contracts § 355 (1981). Various justifications explain the traditional rule of denying punitive damages for breach of contract.

One rationale is that punitive damages aim to vindicate public rather than private rights. Thus, awarding punitive damages for a mere contract breach would not advance society's interest in punishing and deterring the egregious behavior that supports exemplary damages. Further, the nature of the bargain itself in contract law reflects an expectation for performance or compensation for damages resulting from breach. The underlying purpose of damages for breach of contract is to place the non-breaching party in the same position as if full performance had been rendered. Contract law does not inquire into subjective intent or attach moral blame for non-performance of promises. In addition, punitive damages could undermine the theory of efficient breach which allows a breaching party to pay damages while maximizing its own profits.

The presence of an independent tort to justify punitive damages for breach of contract is not actually an "exception" to the general rule, but rather a recognition that the same course of conduct can potentially give rise to alternative or cumulative causes of action sounding in contract or tort. In recent years, some courts have displayed an increased willingness to find sufficiently tortious conduct accompanying the contract breach to support an award of punitive damages.

A majority of jurisdictions hold that a breach of the implied covenant of good faith and fair dealing, either under common law or the Uniform Commercial Code, is not a tort sufficiently independent enough of the obligations required by the contract to allow for the imposition of punitive damages.

A growing trend recognizes an exception to the general rule to allow punitive damages predicated upon the bad faith conduct of insurance companies with respect to policy coverage or claims. These cases draw upon the public interest considerations that were expressed in an early line of cases that allowed punitive damages against common carriers and fiduciaries in limited situations. Courts consider the special relationship between insurer and insured, the unequal bargaining power of the parties, and the adhesive nature of the insurance contract as public policy reasons to support punitive damages. A handful of courts also have found similar justifications to allow employees to recover punitive damages for an employer's breach of the covenant of good faith and fair dealing implied in an employment contract.

5. VICARIOUS LIABILITY

Jurisdictions differ in opinion as to under what circumstances a principal can be held vicariously liable for punitive damages based on an agent's tortious conduct. Some jurisdictions follow the usual respondeat superior rules. Under this approach, a principal would be liable for punitive damages on the basis of the agent's conduct whenever the agent acted within the scope of employment.

The majority view follows the "complicity liability" theory articulated in the Restatement (Second) of Torts § 909 (1979). This theory more narrowly confines vicarious liability for punitive damages. Under the complicity liability theory, the principal can be vicariously liable for punitive damages only if: (1) the principal authorized, participated in, consented to, or ratified the egregious act; (2) the principal deliberately or recklessly employed an unfit agent; or (3) the agent engaged in the egregious acts while employed within a managerial capacity and acting within the scope of employment. *Accord* Restatement (Second) of Agency § 217C (1958). The rationale for the Restatement position is twofold: to encourage diligence in the selection and supervision of persons placed in management positions and to serve as a deterrent to the employment of unfit persons for important positions. Restatement (Second) of Torts § 909, cmt. b (1979).

A few jurisdictions have sought to restrict vicarious liability for punitive damages even further. For example, in Florida, the principal may be vicariously liable for punitive damages only if the principal "actively and knowingly" participated in or "knowingly condoned, ratified or consented" to the agent's misconduct. *See* Fla. Stat. Ann. § 768.72 (West 2001). Finally, a few jurisdictions prohibit vicarious liability for punitive damages altogether.

(B) MEASUREMENT OF PUNITIVE DAMAGES AND THE PROCESS FOR AWARDING PUNITIVE DAMAGES

1. FACTORS CONSIDERED IN DETERMINING THE AMOUNT OF PUNITIVE DAMAGES

A court never awards punitive damages automatically, nor as a matter of right. The trier of fact holds discretion both with respect to determining entitlement and measurement of such damages. Although jurisdictions vary in the formulation of relevant factors guiding measurement of punitive damages, certain criteria are commonly used. Those factors include: (a) the nature and reprehensibility of defendant's conduct; (b) the seriousness of the harm resulting from the misconduct; (c) the defendant's awareness and motivation regarding the potential harm; (d) the duration of the harm and any efforts to conceal the misconduct; (e) the profitability of the defendant's misconduct; (f) the defendant's net wealth; (g) the relationship between the actual harm and the amount of punitive damages; and (h) the total deterrent effect of other damages and punishment imposed upon the defendant.

In most jurisdictions, punitive damages are subject to judicial review and remittitur. Indeed, the U.S. Supreme Court indicated that judicial review of punitive damages may be constitutionally required. *See* Honda Motor Co., Ltd. v. Oberg, 512 U.S. 415 (1994). A reviewing court can set aside or reduce an award of punitive damages when it appears to be the product of passion or prejudice or shocks the judicial conscience. Jurisdictions vary in the factors by which reviewing courts are to measure the excessiveness of punitive damage awards. However, courts generally apply factors such as the reprehensibility of the defendant's conduct, the relationship between the amount of compensatory damages and punitive damages, the profitability of the defendant's conduct, the defendant's financial condition, and the amount of any criminal or civil sanctions paid by the defendant or typically imposed for comparable misconduct. *See* Pac. Mut. Life Ins. Co. v. Haslip, 499 U.S. 1 (1991).

2. FINANCIAL CONDITION

Courts find the relevance of a defendant's net wealth or financial condition in determining the amount of punitive damages a troublesome issue. One common justification advanced for allowing a jury to consider the defendant's net wealth is to ensure that any punitive damage award sufficiently punishes and deters the wrongdoer. Proponents contend that the amount necessary to deter a less wealthy wrongdoer may not be sufficient to deter a wealthier wrongdoer. Proponents also contend that consideration of financial condition is necessary to ensure that punitive damages do not exceed the defendant's ability to pay. Further, excessive punitive awards may exhaust a defendant's economic resources, rendering it incapable of paying legitimate compensatory awards to other claimants.

Some economists argue that consideration of net wealth and financial condition is irrelevant for the purpose of achieving deterrence. They note that a potential wrongdoer is likely to be deterred so long as the cost of paying compensatory and punitive damages exceeds the cost of avoiding the harm. The U.S. Supreme Court and other courts express concern that evidence of a defendant's financial condition should not be used to impose punitive damages on a defendant solely because the defendant is wealthy. *See* BMW of N. Am., Inc. v. Gore, 517 U.S. 559 (1996).

Most jurisdictions allow a plaintiff to introduce evidence of a defendant's financial condition or net worth but do not mandate that a plaintiff introduce

such evidence. *See* Restatement (Second) of Torts
§ 908, cmt. e (1979). A few jurisdictions, however,
require evidence of a defendant's financial condition
to sustain an award of punitive damages. *See*
Herman v. Sunshine Chem. Specialties, Inc., 133
N.J. 329 (1993).

Some legislative reform measures have limited
admissibility of information regarding a defendant's
financial condition. These measures generally
bifurcate the trial and require an initial finding of
entitlement to compensatory damages before a jury
may consider the derivative question of entitlement
to a punitive award. Further, entitlement to punitive
damages must be established before evidence of a
defendant's financial worth would be considered. The
policy reason for requiring a plaintiff to demonstrate
entitlement to punitive damages before offering
evidence of financial condition is to avoid prejudicing
the jury with "punitive" evidence, thus potentially
inflating a compensatory award.

3.   RELATIONSHIP BETWEEN PUNITIVE DAMAGES AND COMPENSATORY DAMAGES

Many jurisdictions require that punitive damages
bear some reasonable relationship to the underlying
compensatory damages award. However, no fixed
ratio or proportion is mandated under common law
principles. Some state legislatures, nevertheless,
impose fixed ratios or caps on punitive damages. In
one particularly noteworthy setting, the U.S.
Supreme Court imposed a fixed ratio on punitive
damages in federal maritime cases. In *Exxon*

Shipping Co. v. Baker, 554 U.S. 471 (2008), the Court held that a 1:1 ratio of punitive damages to compensatory damages was the permissible upper limit of punitive awards in the absence of evidence of exceptionally blameworthy conduct. Exceptionally blameworthy conduct would include intentional or malicious conduct or conduct motivated primarily by a desire for financial gain. Such fixed ratios and caps may create special problems in many civil rights cases where the plaintiff has not suffered pecuniary or physical harm from the violation.

4.   SPECIAL ISSUES POSED BY MULTIPLE PUNITIVE DAMAGE AWARDS

Special problems arise when multiple potential plaintiffs suffer harm by one defendant, such as in products liability cases. The wealth or poverty of the defendant is an important factor in setting the level of punitive damages because the purpose of the award is to punish and to deter the defendant and others similarly situated from such conduct in the future. In products liability cases, the financial condition of the company may be evaluated by focusing on the profits earned from marketing an unsafe product in reckless disregard of public safety. This rationale deteriorates when multiple cases seek to deprive the defendant of the same profit. At some point, the collective awards of punitive damages transcend the objective of punishment and deterrence and may threaten the viability of the enterprise. Additional concerns involve creating a "race to the courthouse" for recovery of punitive damages and substantially depleting corporate funds through multiple punitive damage awards such that some injured parties may go uncompensated for legitimate claims. As a consequence, some jurisdictions take into account previous punitive awards imposed for the same conduct.

(C) CONSTITUTIONAL LIMITS

1. EXCESSIVE FINES CLAUSE

The Supreme Court has devoted considerable attention to various constitutional questions pertaining to punitive damages. In *Browning-Ferris Indus. of Vermont, Inc. v. Kelco Disposal, Inc.*, 492 U.S. 257 (1989), the Court held that the Excessive Fines Clause of the Eighth Amendment did not apply to a jury award of punitive damages in civil cases between private parties. The Court concluded that although the goals of punishment and deterrence underlie both punitive awards and criminal law, the extent of any overlap was not sufficient to impose the same constitutional limitations.

2. SUBSTANTIVE DUE PROCESS

In contrast, the Court has recognized that the Due Process Clause of the Fourteenth Amendment imposes substantive limits on the size of punitive damage awards and procedural limitations on the process by which state courts award punitive damages. Most notably, in two cases, the Court invalidated state jury awards on the grounds that the amount of punitive damages awarded was grossly excessive in relation to the state's legitimate interest in imposing punitive damages.

First, in *BMW of North America, Inc. v. Gore*, 517 U.S. 559 (1996), the Supreme Court invalidated a $4 million punitive damage award against an automobile manufacturer for failure to disclose that a new car had been repainted prior to delivery. The manufacturer adhered to a policy of not disclosing repairs if they did not exceed three percent of the value. The Alabama jury awarded the plaintiff $4,000 in compensatory damages, which represented the difference in value between the value of the car as new and the value of the car as repainted, and $4 million in punitive damages. The Alabama Supreme Court concluded that the punitive damage award was excessive and reduced the award to $2 million.

The Supreme Court held in *Gore* that the punitive damage award violated due process because it was grossly excessive to the state's legitimate interest in punishment and deterrence. The Court began its analysis in *Gore* by identifying the narrow scope of a state's legitimate interest in imposing punitive damages. The Court noted that a state may not impose economic sanctions for violations of its laws for the purpose of changing a defendant's lawful conduct in other states. Instead, the Court explained that a state's economic penalties must be supported by that state's interest in protecting its own consumers and its own economy.

The Court then identified three "guideposts" to evaluate whether an award was grossly excessive in relation to the state's legitimate interest. Those factors are: (1) the degree of reprehensibility of the defendant's conduct; (2) the reasonableness of the ratio between the harm or potential harm suffered by the victim and his punitive damage award; and (3) the comparison of the punitive damage award and the civil or criminal penalties authorized or imposed in comparable cases.

Subsequently, in *State Farm Mutual Automobile Insurance Co. v. Campbell*, 538 U.S. 408 (2003), the Court invalidated a state punitive damage award on substantive due process grounds for a second time. *State Farm* involved an insurance bad faith claim arising out of an automobile accident. One of State Farm's insureds was at fault for an auto accident. State Farm rejected a settlement offer from the injured parties which was within the insurance policy limits. After the injured parties recovered a judgment in excess of the policy limits, State Farm initially refused to pay the excess judgment but ultimately did pay the entire judgment. Nonetheless, the insured brought suit against State Farm, alleging bad faith refusal to settle. A Utah jury awarded the insured $1 million in compensatory damages for emotional distress and $145 million in punitive damages. At trial, the insured-plaintiffs contended that State Farm refused to settle the claim against them as part of a long-standing company-wide policy designed to meet corporate profit targets by capping claims. During the course of the trial, the insured-plaintiffs introduced evidence about State Farm's claims handling practices in numerous states over a 20-year period.

In invalidating the judgment, the Court recognized the state's legitimate interest in imposing punitive damages but concluded that a state may not impose punitive damages to punish a defendant for unlawful acts committed outside of the state's jurisdiction. Additionally, the Court concluded that a state could not impose punitive damages to punish the defendant for harms to other potential plaintiffs not before the court. The Court also returned to the three guideposts it announced in *Gore*. Juries could consider evidence of misconduct directed at third parties to evaluate the reprehensibility of the defendant but only if that third-party misconduct was sufficiently similar to the misconduct directed at the injured plaintiff. With respect to the ratio of punitive damages to compensatory damages, the Court refused to articulate a "bright-line ratio" of compensatory harm to punitive damages. However, the Court concluded that "few awards exceeding a single-digit ratio between punitive to compensatory damages, to a significant degree, will satisfy due process."

Because the Court did not specify a bright-line ratio, lower courts continue to shape the contours of the due process limitations on punitive damage awards in light of Supreme Court guidance and interpreting the *Gore* factors. Lower courts have continued to allow high ratios of punitive damages in those cases where compensatory damages are especially low and where compensatory damages are substantial but do not reflect all of the potential harm. This is consistent with the Supreme Court's statement that "low awards of compensatory damages may properly support a higher ratio . . . ." *Gore,* 517 U.S. at 582.

For instance, in *Adeli v. Silverstar Automotive,* 960 F.3d 452 (8th Cir. 2020), a disappointed purchaser of a used Ferrari sued the seller for fraud, breach of warranty, and deceptive trade practices after the seller obtained a comprehensive pre-purchase safety inspection but failed to disclose all of the repairs recommended in the inspection report. Shortly after the purchase, the car developed problems with its fuel system, which was one of the recommended repair items flagged in the inspection report but never disclosed to the buyer. The defective condition could have potentially caused harmful gas to leak into the passenger cabin or caused the car to catch fire. The jury awarded the plaintiff purchaser $20,000 in compensatory damages and $5.8 million in punitive damages. The trial court reduced the award of punitive damages to $500,000.

On appeal, the Eighth Circuit upheld the 25 to 1 ratio of punitive damages to compensatory damages, rejecting a single digit limitation as not constitutionally mandated. The court reasoned, in part, that if a precise mathematical formula for due process were required, then risk assessment leading to such fraudulent conduct could turn into a calculable business decision. *Id.* at 464.

3. PROCEDURAL DUE PROCESS

In addition to these substantive safeguards, procedural safeguards are necessary to satisfy due process. Most significantly, in *Philip Morris USA v.*

Williams, 549 U.S. 346 (2007), the Court recognized expressly that juries may not impose punitive damages to punish the defendant for conduct directed at third parties. The Court also continued to recognize that evidence of third-party misconduct was relevant to establish the reprehensibility of the defendant's misconduct directed at the plaintiff. Thus, the Court held that where a significant risk exists that a jury will impose punitive damages to punish the defendant directly for misconduct directed at third parties, due process dictates that a state must adopt procedures to protect against that risk. The Court noted that a significant risk could arise as a result of the types of evidence admitted at trial or the types of arguments plaintiff's counsel made to the jury. The Court also explained that the state trial court in the case before it had refused the defendant's request for a jury instruction instructing the jury that it could not punish the defendant for the impact the defendant's misconduct had on third parties.

The Supreme Court held in *Honda Motor Co., Ltd. v. Oberg*, 512 U.S. 415 (1994), that the Due Process Clause requires meaningful judicial review of punitive damage awards to prevent the arbitrary deprivation of property through an excessive award. The Court has also held that an appellate court should review de novo a district court's evaluation of whether a punitive damage award was unconstitutionally excessive. *See* Cooper Indus., Inc. v. Leatherman Tool Grp., Inc., 532 U.S. 424 (2001).

(D) PUNITIVE DAMAGE REFORM

Increasing numbers of state legislatures have enacted statutes that regulate the availability and amount of punitive damages. Some of the most common measures include: heightening the burden of proof above the traditional preponderance of the evidence, bifurcating the proceedings involving punitive awards and compensatory damages (discussed more fully in Section B.2 of this chapter, *supra*), and placing statutory caps or ceilings on awards. These statutory measures generally have withstood constitutional challenges.

Some states have been creative in their attempts to deal with the issues. Georgia, for example, has enacted legislation aimed at addressing the problem of multiple punitive damage awards for the same conduct. The Georgia statute now permits only one plaintiff to recover a punitive damage award from a defendant for any act or omission if the plaintiff's cause of action is a product liability case. *See* GA. CODE ANN. § 51–12–5.1(e)(1).

Some other jurisdictions have enacted "extraction statutes" that require some portion of a punitive recovery be directed to the state. In one particularly unusual setting, the Ohio Supreme Court adopted an extraction requirement as a matter of common law. In *Dardinger v. Anthem Blue Cross & Blue Shield*, 781 N.E.2d 121 (Ohio 2002), a state jury awarded the husband of a cancer patient $49 million in punitive damages in a bad faith insurance case after the defendant insurance company denied his wife's claim for chemotherapy. The Ohio Supreme Court remitted the award to $30 million and directed that the award be distributed only in part to the plaintiff. Specifically, the Court directed $10 million to be paid to the plaintiff. The Court directed the remaining portion of the punitive award to be distributed first to pay the plaintiff's litigation expenses, including attorneys fees, then to establish a cancer research fund the Court ordered in the name of the deceased victim. In imposing the alternative distribution, the Court recognized the competing concerns underlying extraction statutes. The Court noted, "[t]here is a philosophical void between the reasons we award punitive damages and how the damages are distributed. The community makes the statement, while the plaintiff reaps the monetary award. . . . Clearly, we do not want to dissuade plaintiffs from moving forward with societal undertakings. The distribution of the jury's award must recognize the effort the plaintiff undertook in bringing about the award and the important role a plaintiff plays in bringing about necessary changes that society agrees need be made." 781 N.E.2d at 145–46.

Congress has previously considered, but not as yet enacted, proposals for federal legislation to regulate punitive damages. Proposed legislation sought to reduce or eliminate multiple punitive damage awards. The primary concern of Congress in this area has been the award of punitive damages in product liability cases with numerous victims.

CHAPTER 16
UNJUST ENRICHMENT

(A) THE UNJUST ENRICHMENT CONCEPT

The underlying policy of restitution is to prevent the unjust enrichment of a party who has received a benefit that in equity and good conscience should not be retained. Restitution cuts across many areas of law and equity and may arise as a remedial option in numerous situations. Equitable restitutionary remedies, such as a constructive trust or an equitable lien, may be applied where the claimant can identify and trace title to specific property in the defendant's possession. *See* Great-West Life & Annuity Ins. Co. v. Knudson, 534 U.S. 204, 213 (2002). Conversely, a legal claim for restitutionary recovery may arise where the right to possession of particular property cannot be established but a general claim against the defendant's assets is proper to prevent unjust enrichment. *See* Montanile v. Board of Trustees of Nat. Elevator Industry Health Benefit Plan, 577 U.S. 136, 143–145 (2016).

Entitlement does not hinge upon a showing of wrongful conduct on the part of the defendant, but encompasses a wide range of circumstances involving nonconsensual and nonbargained-for benefits. Unjust enrichment could support restitution in a wide range of circumstances such as for mistaken improvements of property, innocent retention of benefits, disgorging profits, breach of confidential relationships, or as an alternative remedy where agreements are found unenforceable. The central inquiry is whether the claimant is rightfully entitled to the restoration of certain benefits which would otherwise unjustly enrich the defendant.

Certain limiting principles apply to restitutionary claims. When a contract defines the obligations between two parties, the contract terms displace any inquiry into unjust enrichment. Unjust enrichment is also foreclosed when a party voluntarily confers benefits gratuitously, and an innocent party retains the freedom to refuse benefits rather than be subject to a forced exchange. *See* Restatement (Third) of Restitution and Unjust Enrichment (2011) § 2. For example, in *Birchwood Land Co., Inc. v. Krizan*, 115 A.3d 1009 (Vt. 2015) a landowner improved their property, which resulted in providing public road access and extension of utility connections to a neighbor's parcel of previously landlocked property. The developer sought restitution for enhancing the value of the neighbor's property, claiming that otherwise they would be unjustly enriched as a "free-rider." The court rejected the restitutionary claim, finding that such incidentally incurred benefits were unrequested; therefore, the landowner could not be compelled to pay in restitution.

Restitution may provide an appropriate remedy to restore benefits acquired pursuant to a failed or unenforceable agreement. Classic illustrations include contracts in violation of the Statute of Frauds or contracts entered into by a party without authority or lacking capacity. Some contracts may be deemed unenforceable at inception. *See* In re Suiter, 560 B.R.

333, 336 (D. Hawaii 2016)(quantum meruit recovery allowed to contractor for work performed even though construction contract deemed void for lack of required disclosures). Other contracts may become unenforceable due to impossibility of performance or because the defendant materially breaches and the plaintiff elects to treat the contract as ended.

Various restitutionary devices address the goal of disgorging the unjust enrichment of benefits that were originally conferred by agreement. Rescission and restitution are traditional equitable remedies available both for the breach of a contract and disgorging benefits originally bestowed under an unenforceable agreement. When courts order restitution by defendants in such cases, they also require plaintiffs to restore any benefits received pursuant to the agreement. The principle of making restitution mutually equitable is reflected by the maxim, "He who seeks equity must do equity."

Disgorgement or accounting for profits may also be appropriate as an equitable restitutionary remedy apart from agreement. Historically, courts of equity have long recognized the propriety of requiring wrongdoers to restore ill-gotten gains so that they would not profit by their wrongdoing. However, equity is not punitive in character, so courts have recognized that the nature and measure of recovery should be limited to the benefits received. *See* Liu v. S.E.C., 140 S. Ct. 1936, 1942–1943 (2020).

After determining entitlement, the second question in restitution involves properly quantifying or measuring the benefit. The restitutionary measure focuses on the gain unjustly retained by the defendant rather than the loss to the plaintiff. The difference in focus between restitution and compensatory damages often produces different dollar amounts. The Restatement (Third) of Restitution and Unjust Enrichment (2011) sets forth four possible methods to measure enrichment from the receipt of nonreturnable benefits: (1) the value of the benefit to the defendant, (2) the costs to the claimant in conferring the benefit, (3) the market value of the benefit, or the price the defendant has expressed a willingness to pay. § 49(3). The Third Restatement also provides that for an "innocent" recipient, the liability in unjust enrichment should be based on the standard that yields the smallest recovery in restitution. *See* § 50(3)(a). Claimants frequently encounter a choice of actions and, in certain cases, may elect the claim that yields the highest possible recovery.

(B) BENEFITS ACQUIRED BY AGREEMENT OR MISTAKE

1. OVERVIEW

In the law of contracts, a material mistake which undermines the integrity of the bargaining process and the fundamental assumptions of one or more parties in entering into the agreement may justify various remedies, including reformation or rescission and restitution. Similarly, in the law of equitable restitution evidence of certain types of mistakes may support disgorgement of benefits to avoid unjust enrichment.

The standards and policies involving whether mistake justifies a remedial response share some areas of commonality in the fields of traditional contract law and equity, yet significant differences exist. The remedies associated with contract law are fundamentally tailored to carrying out the benefit of the bargain, which implicitly assumes that both parties objectively agreed to the risks related to the obligations and duties of the agreement. In some contract cases where the bargain itself is the product of mistaken assumptions, courts may determine relief should be granted to invalidate the contract. In equity, on the other hand, courts focus their inquiry on whether restitution should be granted to restore property to the rightful owner and prevent unjust enrichment. The parties involved may have no contractual relationship of any kind and the benefits conferred may be the product of a mistake rather than the parties' intentions. In both law and equity, though, the remedial outcome of a material mistake may involve restitution of benefits to adjust the legal relationship of the parties.

2.   MISTAKE IN AGREEMENTS

The presence of a mistake in contractual obligations does not necessarily invalidate an otherwise valid agreement because contract law strongly favors the finality and integrity of the bargain. Consequently, the standards for setting aside agreements on the basis of mistake are stringent and do not give rise to breach or compensatory damages. Mistake, for purposes of avoidance, must be distinguished from doctrines like ambiguity or failed predictions of future market conditions.

The Restatement (Second) of Contracts § 151 (1981) defines "mistake" as a "belief that is not in accord with the facts." Not all mistaken beliefs justify contract avoidance, however. Instead, the mistake must be considered "material" and pertain to a "basic assumption on which the contract was made." *See* Restatement (Second) of Contracts §§ 152–153 (1981). The law imposes this requirement because basic assumptions affect the very nature of the bargained-for exchange, and if erroneous, may contravene the intentions of the parties in assuming risks and obligations under the agreement. The party seeking relief must not bear the risk of the mistake either according to the terms of the agreement or as allocated by the court. In other words, where the contract places the burden of the risk on a party, he or she cannot subsequently invoke a mistake. *See* Restatement (Second) of Contracts § 154 (1981).

A mistake that may justify some remedy can occur during formation, integration, or performance of the contract. The nature of the appropriate remedy will vary depending upon when the mistake occurred and whether it is classified as mutual or unilateral. Courts allow avoidance in contract law for unilateral mistakes only in very limited circumstances. The mistaken party must demonstrate either that the enforcement of the contract would be unconscionable or that the other party had reason to know of the mistake or was at fault in causing it. *See* Restatement (Second) of Contracts § 153 (1981).

To illustrate a mutual mistake in the formation of a contract, contemplate a scenario where both parties erroneous believe that the subject matter of the contract exists when in fact it has been destroyed. Such a mutual mistake in contract formation may justify an order of rescission and restitution of benefits conferred because the mistake materially affects the basic assumptions of the parties. The remaining rights and duties of the parties are terminated without obligation or consequence.

3.   MISTAKE IN EQUITY

Restitution provides a useful remedial option when one or both parties to a contract made a mistaken assumption about something material to the contract. In equity, various circumstances may justify invalidating transfers of property and subjecting the transaction to rescission and avoidance. Some commonly recognized defects in the transactional process include mistake, fraud, duress and undue influence. In each instance, courts may predicate a restitutionary award on finding flaws in the transferor's consent. The remedial solution to avoid unjust enrichment of the party holding the benefit is restitution of the property to the rightful owner. For purposes of equitable restitution, the substantive question only asks whether the retention of certain benefits by the defendant which are held as a result of the mistake would be unjust. *See* Restatement (Third) of Restitution and Unjust Enrichment § 5 (2011). As with an invalidating mistake under an express agreement, the party

seeking relief through equity must not bear the risk
of the mistake.

A mistake in integration of the agreement may
justify the equitable remedy of reformation. This
equitable device simply corrects the error to
correspond to the true intentions of the parties, but
the contract itself remains intact. In *Ranch O, LLC
v. Colorado Cattlemen's Agricultural Land Trust*, 361
P.3d 1063, 1066 (Colo. App. 2015), for example, both
parties to a conservation deed made a mutual
mistake of fact regarding the ownership of the
property. The court granted reformation of the deed
to reflect the true intentions of the parties. Finally, a
mistake by one party during the course of
performance of a contract may give rise to a claim for
restitution from the holder of the benefit who may be
otherwise unjustly enriched. Some jurisdictions
permit restitution when a party mistakenly pays the
debt of another under circumstances not amounting
to a gift or volunteer payment.

Unlike the traditional approach in contracts, the
distinction in equity between unilateral and mutual
mistake is not given weight. Rather, the inquiry
focuses on whether the claimant has conferred an
unintended benefit on the defendant under
circumstances that would result in unjust
enrichment unless a court awarded restitution. For
example, if an insurance company mistakenly pays
the proceeds of a life insurance policy to the wrong
person, the rightful beneficiary may seek a
constructive trust to require conveyance of the funds
from the recipient to avoid unjust enrichment. The

holder of the funds stands as a gratuitous donee, not a bona fide purchaser for value.

In addition to the mistaken payment of money not due, many other types of mistakes might justify restitution in equity. Some additional illustrations include mistake regarding the existence of a contractual obligation, coverage or liability, discharge of a lien due to mistake over title to property, and actions to preserve or enhance the property of another due to mistake over boundaries or ownership.

4.   MISTAKEN IMPROVEMENT OF PROPERTY

Restitution for benefits conferred through the mistaken improvement of real or personal property have a long heritage in equity. Various types of mistakes by an improver may support restitution, such as a misunderstanding over the location of boundary lines, title, the nature of the interest held, or the property owner's obligation to pay for the improvements. Restitution for mistaken improvements is never automatic and rests with the sound discretion of the court. The analysis will necessitate balancing the interest of awarding compensation to the mistaken improver for the benefits conferred with concerns of unduly prejudicing the landowner by requiring payment for unrequested improvements. *See* Restatement (Third) of Restitution and Unjust Enrichment § 10, cmt. a (2011). The balancing may consider concepts of good faith, notice, and negligence to help assess responsibility between improver and landowner.

In many instances, improvements to land cannot be easily severed by removing fixtures from the property. As a result, the innocent landowner may incur hardship if forced to compensate the improver. In a number of jurisdictions, states have enacted "betterment" statutes which provide remedies to certain classes of mistaken improvers of real property, such as persons who occupy under color of title.

Unless the owner is responsible for the improver's mistake, the measure of the restitutionary award will often be the reasonable cost of the goods and services rendered or the increase in value of the property, whichever is less. *See* Restatement (Third) of Restitution and Unjust Enrichment § 10, cmt. h (2011). Satisfaction of the award can take various forms, such as a money judgment, an equitable lien, removal of the improvement or partition of the property.

(C) MISREPRESENTATION AND FRAUD

Transfers of property induced by fraud or misrepresentation may be invalidated under traditional contract law as well as pursuant to general principles of equitable restitution. In both circumstances, the underlying principle holds that the consent of the transferor is defective.

Material misrepresentations may undermine the effectiveness of assent and consequently may prevent the formation of a contract or may make an agreement voidable. *See* Restatement (Second) of Contracts §§ 163–164 (1981). When a court finds a contract invalid, it may grant restitutionary relief to transfer any benefits conferred in the course of part performance or reliance.

The aggrieved claimant may seek to rescind the transaction based on the ineffective consent or may choose to affirm the agreement and seek damages associated with the breach of warranty. A party seeking rescission of a transfer induced by fraud is not required, however, to demonstrate that the transferee profited from the transaction nor that economic loss was experienced as a result of the deceit. Revocation of assent based on the substantive grounds of misrepresentation or fraud often does lead to mutual restoration of benefits transferred, although if the contract is entirely executory then rescission may serve an independent role. *See* Restatement (Third) of Restitution and Unjust Enrichment § 54 (2011). In many cases, restitution following rescission serves to disgorge any benefits retained by the wrongdoer and to prevent unjust enrichment. *See* Restatement (Third) of Restitution and Unjust Enrichment § 13 (2011).

Fraudulent inducement or misrepresentation in contracts potentially raises a choice of remedial alternatives for the injured party of whether to pursue a contract-based remedy for breach, the tort of deceit, or an equitable claim in restitution. In some instances, restitution may offer certain advantages to a damages claim. The substantive criteria for establishing fraud under common law tort or contract principles requires a showing of wrongful intent, for example. In contrast, a claim for restitution merely requires consideration of whether benefits would be unjustly retained.

The measure of recovery also may differ markedly. Courts can typically use two alternative methods to measure damages for fraud, both of which compensate for the plaintiff's actual loss. The "out of pocket" approach allows the difference between the price paid and the value actually received. For example, if the seller of a house fraudulently represents that a leaky roof was recently repaired, the buyer may recover the difference between the contract price and the value of the defective house. The benefit of the bargain method calculates damages by the difference between the value of the house as received compared with the value of the property as represented. In contrast, the measure of recovery in restitution focuses instead on the defendant's gains, which may prove to exceed the claimant's loss. Restitution of property *in specie* would also be highly beneficial where the defendant was insolvent.

Attorneys' fees may be available either by state statute or pursuant to the agreement but generally will not be awarded for claims sounding in tort. Certain restitutionary remedies could be classified under a jurisdiction's contract claims and allow fee-shifting, however. Also, a court may award punitive damages for a tort claim of fraudulent inducement but generally cannot in equity via restitution. Finally, a tort claim for fraud may be subject to a shorter statute of limitations than may apply to a quasi-contract claim in restitution.

(D) QUANTUM MERUIT

One restitutionary tool to achieve restitution of benefits pursuant to an unenforceable agreement or where no agreement exists is called quantum meruit. The term literally means "as much as he deserves" and comes from the historical "common counts" that functioned as quasi-contracts. The history of quantum meruit has a lengthy and checkered heritage in both contract and restitution, which has led to problems of characterization and application. *See generally* Kovacic-Fleischer, Quantum Meruit and the Restatement (Third) of Restitution and Unjust Enrichment, 27 Rev. Lit. 127 (2007); *See also* Certified Fire Prot. Inc. v. Precision Constr., 283 P.3d 250 (Nev. 2012)(quantum meruit may serve as a gap-filler to supply a missing term, such as price, in a contract implied in fact and secondarily may provide a claim in restitution to prevent unjust enrichment).

Some courts characterize the remedy as implied-in-fact, focusing on the requested or consensual nature of the benefits conferred. A common illustration of quantum meruit applied in that scenario would involve where the parties failed to agree on a price for services but otherwise manifested an intent to agree on terms. In the recent decision, *T. Musgrove Construction Co., Inc. v. Young*, 840 S.E.2d 337 (Va. 2020), a relative borrowed a commercial dump truck to haul a large load of timber. The truck was involved in an accident and overturned, spilling the logs. A towing company returned the truck to an upright position, cleaned up the accident site, hoisted the logs back into the truck, and towed the damaged vehicle to a storage site. The towing company brought a claim for its services in quantum meruit against the truck owner. The court rejected the claim, reasoning that quantum meruit was a type of contract implied in fact where work was performed at the request of another but the typically the price term was omitted, indefinite or miscommunicated. Because the truck owner had not actually requested the services, a cause of action for quantum meruit was unavailable. However, the court did find that the owner had benefitted from the towing company storing and preserving the truck, so restitution could be properly awarded in an amount not to exceed the truck's salvage value.

Other courts view quantum meruit as a fiction implied by law by the court to achieve a certain result of preventing unjust enrichment. Even if both characterizations essentially seek to prevent unjust enrichment, an important functional effect of the distinction may be a difference in the measure of the recovery obtained. Where quantum meruit is viewed as a type of implied-in-fact contract, the measure often is the reasonable value of goods and services rendered. In contrast, damage in unjust enrichment for implied-in-law contracts are based on the measure of the value of the benefit retained. *See* Paffhausen v. Balano, 708 A.2d 269, 271 (Me. 1998). Another less commonly used remedy, called quantum valebant, provides an implied-in-law claim for the reasonable value of goods sold and delivered to another.

Courts refer to such arrangements as "quasi" contracts because it describes the relationship assigned when a court imposes a duty of restoring benefits to the rightful owner. In contrast with express contracts where the intent of the parties guides and informs the determination of compensatory damages for breach, a quasi-contract is not based on adhering to such intentions nor giving the benefit of the bargain. Instead, the purpose is to provide a restitutionary vehicle to accomplish the conveyance of benefits to the claimant and preventing the unjust enrichment of the defendant. *See* Restatement (Third) of Restitution and Unjust Enrichment § 31, cmt. e (2011).

Courts vary somewhat in their formulation of the requirements for quantum meruit but common factors include: (1) the claimant furnished valuable materials or services, (2) the services were conferred for the benefit of the person sought to be charged, (3) the defendant accepted and enjoyed the benefits, and (4) the party who provided the services or materials did so with a reasonable expectation of being compensated for the benefits conferred. The premise supporting the claim would be that the retention of the benefits without payment of reasonable compensation would constitute unjust enrichment. *See* Hill v. Shamoun & Norman, LLP, 544 S.W.3d 724 (Tex. 2018). Where the goods or services are furnished gratuitously, the remedy does not apply.

A common measure of recovery is the reasonable value of the materials or services, although other courts focus on the benefits gained by the defendant.

See Mike Glynn & Co. v. Hy-Brasil Restaurants, 914
N.E.2d 103, 107 (Mass. App. Ct. 2009). The
justification for compensation is derived from an
implied promise to pay for the goods or services
rendered rather than on a bargained-for exchange.
See In the Matter of Gilbert, 346 P.3d 1018 (Colo.
2015)(attorney entitled to retain a portion of fees for
work performed under flat fee arrangement prior to
client's termination of services).

Quantum meruit is not available as an alternative
remedy where parties already completed
performance under a valid contract and all that
remains is the payment of the contract price. When
only the contract amount remains unpaid, a plaintiff
may sue for the debt with the remedy indebitatus
assumpsit. Once parties complete performance, the
contract price is a liquidated debt. Courts do not
allow an election between seeking damages for
breach of contract or an equitable claim in restitution
apart from the contract. Rather, quantum meruit
may provide an alternative basis for recovery where
no express contract governs the provision of services
or materials furnished. *See* Archon v. U.S. Shelter,
LLC, 78 N.E.3d 1067 (Ill. App. 2017)(subcontractor
not entitled to quantum meruit recovery for repairs
made to sewer installation where work was within
the scope of express contract).

(E) MONEY HAD AND RECEIVED

Another common count that developed historically
through the action of assumpsit is a claim for Money
Had and Received. The equitable doctrine is based in

restitution to recover money which in equity and good conscience rightfully belongs to the claimant.

The claim can be used to reach funds which are held by the defendant through mistake, duress, fraud, or failure of consideration. The restitutionary relief for Money Had and Received must be distinguished from an action seeking damages for breach of contract. Instead, the focus in equity is whether the party holding the money would be unjustly enriched if allowed to retain the funds. *See* Town of Stratford v. Winterbottom, 95 A.3d 538, 549 (Ct. App. 2014)(town's claim for money had and received rejected where former employee properly received cash-out payment of accrued benefits). No privity of contract between the parties is required nor any promise to pay, other than what is implied by law to avoid unjust enrichment. Also, the defendant need not come into possession of the money under an agreement to hold it for the benefit of the plaintiff.

(F) CONSTRUCTIVE TRUSTS

The constructive trust is an important and frequently used equitable restitutionary remedy designed to prevent unjust enrichment by ordering the transfer of real or personal property to the claimant asserting legal title. A broad range of substantive claims may justify imposition of a constructive trust, including breach of a fiduciary or confidential relationship, actual or constructive fraud, mistake, coercion, undue influence, duress, embezzlement, conversion, misuse or misappropriation of information, unconscionable conduct or copyright infringement. *See* Restatement (Third) of Restitution and Unjust Enrichment § 55, cmt. f (2011). The imposition of a constructive trust assumes that the claimant can establish unjust enrichment, superior title to the present holder of the specifically identifiable property, and the circumstances justify an order in equity requiring transfer of title to the rightful owner.

The equitable "trust" is created by operation of law for the purpose of conveying the subject property to the rightful owner. A constructive trust is traditionally viewed solely as an equitable remedy, not an independent substantive cause of action. The "constructive" aspect of the equitable trust only means that it operates generally like an express trust in the functional relationship of the parties where the trust *res* is held by the trustee for the beneficiary. The equitable trust differs substantively from an express trust which carries out the intentions of the settlor with respect to the fiduciary management and oversight of the trust *res* for a designated beneficiary, the *cestui que trust*. The equitable remedy instead does not rest on an agreement of the parties, and even may contravene the objectives of one of the parties.

In a constructive trust, the designation of the defendant as trustee describes the temporary role of holding specified property for the benefit of another until the conveyance can be carried out but does not carry other fiduciary responsibilities. The relationship is purely a legal fiction employed by courts of equity to achieve the transfer of title to property to the rightful owner. The fiction is particularly artificial in cases where the defendant "trustee" obtained the funds through wrongdoing, such as by fraud or embezzlement.

A close counterpart to the equitable constructive trust is the quasi-contract, which is implied-in-law. Neither are predicated on carrying out the intentions of the parties, as in an implied-in-fact or express contract, but are established by the court to accomplish the restitutionary objective of preventing unjust enrichment. An important difference between the two is that a constructive trust is imposed upon specifically identifiable property to which the claimant established a superior equitable title, while the quasi-contract claim is directed against the general assets of the defendant. A major benefit of the constructive trust is that the party may obtain property *in specie* rather than compete with other general creditors of the defendant for finding assets to satisfy their claims.

A second benefit of a constructive trust is that the successful claimant may recover property that subsequently increased in value while in the hands of the wrongdoer. The receipt of appreciated property may give the claimant a windfall in certain respects yet is not considered a penalty imposed upon the defendant. Rather, the principle holds that the wrongdoer would otherwise enjoy an unjust enrichment if allowed to profit from their misconduct and that any gain should properly belong to the innocent claimant.

(G) EQUITABLE LIENS

An equitable lien is a close cousin to the more commonly used constructive trust. The lien may arise from an express agreement between parties that fails to comply with the requirements for common law liens yet may still be enforceable in equity to carry out the express or implied intentions of the parties. The more typical illustration of an equitable lien, though, serves as an alternative restitutionary remedy in situations where a constructive trust may be inappropriate. For example, since a constructive trust provides a conveyance *in specie* of the property to the beneficiary of the trust, it assumes that a party can deliver appropriate title. In situations where property cannot be fully conveyed, such as where converted assets have been commingled with other property previously owned by a wrongdoer, a constructive trust of the whole would result in a windfall or forfeiture to the beneficiary.

An equitable lien imposes a security interest against the property to the extent necessary to prevent unjust enrichment. For example, in *Zirbel v. Ford Motor Co.*, 980 F.3d 520 (6th Cir. 2020), a retiree mistakenly received a large overpayment of retirement benefits. When the company audited its pension payments several years later it discovered the mistake and sought equitable restitution of the excess funds. The company traced the funds to one of the defendant's investment accounts. The defendant argued that the equitable lien should be extinguished because the retirement funds had been commingled with other investments. Also, in the years following the overpayment, the defendant had paid taxes, spent funds for living expenses and made gifts to children out of that account. The court upheld the equitable lien up to the amount of the overpayment, finding that the investment account had not been entirely dissipated on nontraceable items.

The party seeking an equitable lien must show that the claimant's assets have been used to improve or preserve the value of specific property of the defendant. In *Wilmington Savings Fund Society FSB v. Collart*, 980 F.3d 210 (1st Cir. 2020), a lender alleged fraudulent conveyance and sought an equitable lien against certain trust-owned property. The court denied the lien, finding no "transactional nexus" between the events giving rise to the claim and the subject property. *See* Restatement (Third) of Restitution and Unjust Enrichment § 56 (2011).

An equitable lien traditionally requires a showing of inadequacy of legal remedies, although the modern trend appears to place less emphasis on legal remedial alternatives than would be ordinarily required for issuance of injunctive relief. *See* Deluxe Building Systems, Inc. v. Constructamax, Inc., 2016 WL 4150746 (D.N.J. 2016)(equitable lien denied because claimant had adequate remedy at law of asserting a statutory mechanics lien on the subject property).

The lien and constructive trust, as equitable restitutionary devices, share certain commonalities. Since they sound in equity, both entitlement and measurement are discretionary with the court and are designed to prevent unjust enrichment. They both give the claimant rights against specifically traced real or personal property, as opposed to the general assets of the party sought to be charged. Both remedies similarly require a tracing of property, dispense with jury trial, are not effective against bona fide purchasers for value, and are enforceable with the contempt power of courts.

Important differences, both in function and practice, also exist between these two remedies. Most notably, the constructive trust involves conveyance of title, while the lien operates as a charge or encumbrance against specific property. The trust is more advantageous when the defendant is insolvent because the subject titled property is restored to the rightful owner. The lien-holder does gain a priority over general creditors with respect to the specified property, but still must obtain a further foreclosure order to satisfy the claim. The trust allows the beneficiary to obtain increases in value of the traced assets, such as where embezzled funds are invested in a profitable venture. The lien is limited to a sum certain. Apart from the issue of title, an equitable lien may be more advantageous when the property charged has declined in value. In that situation the holder can obtain a security interest in that property coupled with a deficiency money judgment against the debtor for the balance owed.

The measure of the equitable lien is governed by considerations of equitable restitution generally and will seek to prevent unjust enrichment by disgorging the benefits enjoyed by the defendant. For example, where improvements are made to realty, the court may grant an equitable lien for the enhanced value of the premises. If the improvements did not increase the market value of the property, a court may award the reasonable value of the labor or materials furnished by the party seeking restitution. The claimant will not receive a forfeiture, however, nor double recovery, even in circumstances where the defendant acted in bad faith. Restitution is not punitive but seeks simply to disgorge benefits unjustly held and to restore them to the rightful owner.

(H) WAIVER OF TORT AND SUIT IN ASSUMPSIT

Waiver of tort and suit in assumpsit is a legal restitutionary devise that disgorges unjust enrichment through quasi-contracts. Although the parties have no contract between them, a party can waive a tort claim in favor of assumpsit, which acts as an implied contract claim that requires a defendant to return unjustly held benefits to a plaintiff who should more rightfully retain them. Assumpsit applies as an alternative substantive claim to conversion and some jurisdictions permit use of the theory for profits gained from trespass. It can also apply when tortious behavior results in the defendant saving on expenses that the court deems unfair to retain. Olwell v. Nye & Nissen Co., 26 Wash. 2d 282 (1946).

This type of restitution was accomplished historically by allowing a plaintiff to use one of the old contract writs even in the absence of an express or implied contract. The writ of "money had and received" was thus used for this quasi-contract in order to create a fictional agency between the wrongdoer who converted property and its owner. As an agent, the wrongdoer was then obliged to repay the owner any proceeds from the resale of that property. Modern law retained this fiction even though it is no longer necessary to use writs.

The remedy from a suit in assumpsit is superior to compensatory damages for conversion in the situation where the defendant resold the property for a price greater than its fair market value. It is also useful in any conversion situation where the statute of limitations has expired on the tort. Assumpsit is considered an action to enforce a quasi-contract, and the statute of limitations for contract is typically longer than for tort.

Some jurisdictions have expanded this equitable action to create a fictional sale between an owner and the defendant who converted property. The quasi-contract theory then is for an implied contract of sale between these parties for purchase of the converted item at its fair market value. Historically, this result was accomplished by use of the writ for "goods sold and delivered." Felder v. Reeth, 34 F.2d 744 (9th Cir. 1929). While this action may produce the same dollar recovery as a conversion action, it has the advantage of extending the statute of limitations. See H. Russell Taylor's Fire Prevention Serv., Inc. v. Coca Cola Bottling Corp., 99 Cal. App. 3d 711 (Cal. Ct. App. 1979).

CHAPTER 17
LIMITS ON RESTITUTIONARY REMEDIES

(A) VOLUNTEERS

1. GENERALLY

A general rule in restitution is that someone who confers an unsolicited benefit to another without their knowledge or consent cannot claim that the benefit is unjust enrichment. *See* Restatement (Third) of Restitution and Unjust Enrichment (2011) § 2. In that situation, the party seeking restitution is often characterized as a "volunteer" or an "officious intermeddler." The description does not refer to wrongdoing or tortious behavior but refers to the character of the action. The action is voluntary when one renders the goods or services without invitation and when the recipient lacks a choice in their acceptance.

The rule against recovery for volunteers is based on two policy considerations. First, if the law permitted compensation for unwanted interference with another's property, it would create an incentive for intermeddling with the interests of others. Second, courts consistently recognize that public policy supports the freedom of persons to choose the circumstances and conditions upon which they enter into transactions.

A common illustration of officious intermeddling is where a volunteer makes unsolicited improvements on another's land and then demands payment. The improvements may enhance the value of the land, such as if a barn were painted or a fence erected, but the landowner is not held legally accountable for the benefits because the volunteer acted without knowledge or consent of the owner. The principle of denying restitution to officious intermeddlers applies broadly and includes providing services, making improvements to land, transferring property, or paying debts.

2.   PERFORMANCE OF ANOTHER'S DUTY

The law does recognize some limited situations in which public policy justifies awarding restitution even where knowledge or consent of the volunteered services is lacking. In these situations, the conduct of the actor is not inappropriate or "officious" but rather may further an important public interest. For example, restitution may be given for furnishing necessaries to a minor child. A parent who has a legal duty of care for the child may be held liable for the benefits conferred even if provided without their knowledge or consent. The concept of "necessaries" encompasses items like food, housing, clothing, or medicine which would be essential for the preservation and enjoyment of life. *See* Restatement (Third) of Restitution and Unjust Enrichment (2011) § 22. The person seeking restitution must have furnished the goods or services with an expectation of compensation and not gratuitously or pursuant to a contractual arrangement. Public policy favors restitution in these situations to promote protection of minors and to encourage diligence of persons responsible for their welfare. The measure of recovery generally is based upon the reasonable market value of the goods or services provided.

3.   PROTECTION OF ANOTHER PERSON

Another exception involves emergency situations where someone takes necessary action in order to prevent or alleviate another from sustaining serious personal harm or suffering. *See* Restatement (Third) of Restitution and Unjust Enrichment (2011) § 20. The public interest in preserving life or health outweighs the traditional judicial disinclination to give restitution for unsolicited benefits. The party seeking restitution must have an expectation of payment at the time the services were rendered. The rule recognizes that some persons who need emergency services may not be in a position to give consent because of age or infirmity yet presumptively would do so willingly if competent. An illustration is where an accident leaves a person unconscious and a Good Samaritan physician subsequently stops and renders life-saving medical treatment. The ultimate outcome of such treatment, however, is not determinative regarding entitlement to restitution as the law presumes that medically necessary services are beneficial. *See* Restatement (Third) of Restitution and Unjust Enrichment (2011) § 20, cmt. c.

4.   PROTECTION OF PROPERTY

In contrast, services volunteered to preserve someone else's property are gratuitous acts of kindness that may create a moral obligation of payment but not a legal one. This philosophy was articulated in a well-known early case, *Bartholomew v. Jackson,* 20 Johns. 28 (N.Y. Sup. Ct. 1822). The opinion observed: "If a man humanely bestows his labor, and even risks his life, in voluntarily aiding to preserve his neighbor's house from destruction by fire, the law considers the service rendered as gratuitous, and it, therefore, forms no ground of action."

Despite judicial reluctance to compensate voluntary preservation of personal property, recovery is permitted in limited situations. Courts have somewhat relaxed the standards for entitlement since *Bartholomew*, though they remain considerably higher than where providing necessary assistance to protect a person's health and safety. The requirements include an intent to charge for the services rendered and lack of an opportunity to communicate with the owner. Further, the actions must be necessary for protection of the property, and unlike the health and safety exception, the owner must receive an actual benefit. *See* Restatement (Third) of Restitution and Unjust Enrichment (2011) § 21. Restitution is measured by the lesser of the loss avoided or by the reasonable value of the services provided for preservation of the property. The rationale for stricter standards for restitution in this circumstance is the paramount value of human life over property interests.

5.   BENEFITS CONFERRED BY MISTAKE

As discussed in Chapter 16, *infra*, restitution may be awarded when benefits are conferred upon another by mistake. For example, a bank error accidentally crediting the wrong account with funds is not voluntarily bestowing a benefit. A party who mistakenly discharges a financial obligation of another also is not considered an officious intermeddler because they acted without any intent to confer a benefit upon a third party. Some jurisdictions are reluctant to permit a substitution of creditors, however, and refuse restitution on that basis.

In situations involving mistaken improvements to land, courts must balance the doctrine of unjust enrichment against forcing an involuntary exchange on the landowner. Courts may base recovery in restitution on whether the improvements are fixtures or capable of removal. Where the landowner has a choice of accepting the benefit, such as where a fence or shed could be removed, restitution is allowed when the owner retains the improvement. If the improvement cannot be severed, such as a coat of paint on a barn, the court will consider the equities and balance the hardships in deciding both entitlement and measurement in restitution.

These cases are not without difficulty, however, especially in regard to calculating the valuation of the benefit conferred. If a court awards restitution, the landowner still bears responsibility of paying for something not bargained for and that may actually interfere with other potential uses of the land. If denied, the mistaken improver confers a benefit with no countervailing compensation. Along with these competing considerations, other factors include the knowledge of the parties and the extent of the benefit conferred. The measure of any recovery is typically the lesser of the objectively measurable increase in value of the property or the value of labor and materials used in making the improvements. *See* Restatement (Third) of Restitution and Unjust Enrichment (2011) § 10.

(B) TRACING

1. OVERVIEW

Equity limits a claimant's ability to obtain restitution against particular property by requiring the claimant to identify or "trace" misappropriated property through the transactional sequence into its substituted product. *See* Restatement (Third) of Restitution and Unjust Enrichment (2011) § 58. The tracing rules apply broadly to various equitable restitutionary claims, including constructive trusts, equitable liens or rights of subrogation. The use of tracing to achieve equitable restitution has a long history, originating in suits against trustees and fiduciaries, but also involving cases of fraud, conversion, mistake or breach of contract. *See* Palmer on Restitution § 2.14. The restitutionary remedy may further allow the rightful owner to seek recourse either from the wrongdoer, an innocent donee, gratuitous transferee, holders of property received by mistake, or a recipient other than a bona fide third party purchaser, including a subsequent transferee.

The claimant bears the burden of establishing the trail of exchanged or transferred property but may do so through unlimited transactions. The inability to trace exchanged property will defeat entitlement to equitable restitution even though the claimant still retains full legal remedies. An illustration of the tracing limitation occurred in *In re Hayward*, 480 S.W.3d 48, 52 (Tex.App. 2015). In that case, a partner in a publishing company sought to obtain a constructive trust to recover her share of royalties and profits for the sale of certain publications. The court denied the constructive trust because the claimant failed to show an identifiable res that could be traced back to the proceeds of the original property. The loss of the equitable remedy may be very significant, however. With a constructive trust, for example, a claimant may be able to recover traced property *in specie* and thus benefit from an increase in value of the property. As explained in *Estate of Cowling v. Estate of Cowling*, 847 N.E.2d 405, 412 (Ohio 2006):

A constructive trust is an equitable remedy that must be imposed on particular assets, not on a value. For example, if a party is inequitably deprived of 100 shares of stock that are valued at $10,000, a constructive trust should be imposed over 100 shares of stock, not $10,000. The value of the stock may decrease to $9,000 through no fault of the present possessor. In that instance, it would be inequitable to impose a constructive trust for a higher dollar amount than the stock's new value. Similarly, should the stock rise, the beneficiary of a constructive trust should not be deprived of that increase in value.

An equitable lien, on the other hand, does not capture any increased value, but like the constructive trust, it offers priority over general unsecured creditors. This advantage is particularly significant when the wrongdoer is insolvent. An inability to trace would defeat these beneficial remedies.

Equitable restitution also enables the claimant to reach certain property that would otherwise be unavailable to satisfy a claim at law. For example, if a wrongdoer misappropriates funds and uses the proceeds to acquire a homestead property, it would be considered exempt from a judgment creditor yet potentially available for imposing an equitable lien. The principles of equity to prevent unjust enrichment may outweigh the statutory policy of a homestead exemption. This result depends upon the ability of the claimant to trace the embezzled funds into that particular property.

When claimants trace property to funds used to make improvements upon land or chattels already owned by another, they may be entitled to either a common law or statutory lien or an equitable lien. A constructive trust is not available, however, because the conveyance of the entire property would result in a windfall to the claimant and exceed the objective of preventing unjust enrichment.

A claimant's ability to trace and recover specific assets through equitable restitution is particularly significant where the wrongdoer is insolvent. The

Restatement (Third) of Restitution and Unjust Enrichment (2011) allows a claimant to reach traced property and enforce specific restitution even against an insolvent wrongdoer. It requires tracing of the legal or equitable interest. Recovery is generally limited to the claimant's loss when an award of property in excess of the loss would be at the expense of an innocent third party such as an unpaid creditor or a surviving dependent. *See* § 61(a).

Equitable restitution may reach not only traced property but also its product, so long as that recovery is not grossly disproportionate and does not come at the expense of dependents or creditors. For example, if a wrongdoer purchases stock with embezzled funds, a constructive trust may be used to convey the stock itself as well as any dividends received from the stock shares. Some courts limit recovery of profits to situations involving a showing of moral blame or "conscious wrongdoing," and limit the liability of an innocent converter to the value of the property held.

2.   COMMINGLED FUNDS

A difficult tracing problem arises when a person wrongfully commingles property belonging to another with personal assets, such as depositing embezzled funds in the wrongdoer's pre-existing bank account. Although the misappropriated money losses its separate identity in the commingled account, courts will impose an equitable lien on the account to allow restitution of the amount which rightfully belongs to the plaintiff. The claimant would be unjustly enriched if the court granted restitution of the entire fund; conversely, a wrongdoer should not be able to foreclose restitution simply by the act of commingling funds. In situations involving a series of deposits and withdrawals, the burden of tracing and identifying specific funds becomes factually impossible. As a result, courts have adopted various default rules designed to liberalize the tracing requirement so as not to unfairly or fortuitously shield a wrongdoer from restitution or permit them to receive a windfall simply because they commingled misappropriated funds.

In an early English decision known as *Clayton's Case, Devaynes v. Noble,* 1 Mer. 572 (1816), the court created a presumption that the first money put into an account would be the first money withdrawn. The rule was predicated on the idea that the claimant would probably benefit by being able to reach the funds remaining in an account because the wrongdoer would have deposited and subsequently withdrawn personal funds first. Under this "first in, first out" approach, the claimant's recovery would depend upon the fortuity of the timing of when the various funds and their product were either dissipated or profitably invested.

A later English decision, *In re Hallett's Estate,* 13 Ch. Div. 696 (1879) modified the rule in *Clayton's Case* by holding that a court should presumptively treat the first withdrawals from a commingled fund as belonging to the wrongdoer, leaving the remaining funds available to imposition of the claimant's equitable interest. Known as the rule of Jessel's Bag, referring to a member of the court, Sir George Jessel, this method would often benefit the claimant because typically the first moneys withdrawn by a wrongdoer from a commingled fund would be dissipated and therefore unreachable. The money left in the account would be available for satisfying equitable claims. The tracing fictions were further refined by *In re Oatway,* 2 Ch.Div. 356 (1903) where the court allowed the claimant the choice between following the withdrawn funds or those remaining in an account, reasoning that the order of priority of deposits and withdrawals should be immaterial.

The previous Restatement of Restitution rejected all of the tracing fictions and provided a rule of proportionality that allowed the claimant to reach a share of both withdrawals and any funds remaining in an account in the proportion of the misappropriated funds to the whole at the time of withdrawal. *See* Restatement of Restitution (1937) §§ 210–211. Under the Restatement approach, the sequence or timing of deposits and withdrawals did not dictate the choice of remedy In cases involving "conscious wrongdoing", the Restatement allowed the claimant an option of a proportionate share both of the remaining funds and the property withdrawn. The rules applied uniformly irrespective of whether the funds were physically commingled, deposited in an existing bank account, or used to pay some premiums upon a life insurance policy. That approach provided partial protection to the wrongdoer by limiting recovery to the proportion that the claimant's property bore to the wrongdoer's own property.

The Restatement (Third) of Restitution and Unjust Enrichment (2011) § 59(2)(a) departs from this approach, instead providing a dual presumption in favor of the claimant. First, those withdrawals that are either untraceable or unprofitable are allocated to the wrongdoer. Second, the claimant retains the ability to elect tracing and obtaining restitution of the product of withdrawn funds where that may yield an advantageous result. To avoid these presumptions from harming innocent parties, the Restatement (Third) limits recovery by a claimant to the actual loss where a recovery in excess of the loss would otherwise go to an innocent party (§ 59) or a protected third-party (§ 61).

Additional tracing issues occur when a wrongdoer makes withdrawals from a commingled account, dissipates those funds and then later makes additional deposits of personal funds into the same account. Should a court treat the deposits as a restoration of the claimant's money or instead as belonging to the wrongdoer? Where the wrongdoer replaces funds in the account, the Restatement (Third) adopts the view that subsequent contributions into a commingled account do not restore the claimant's misappropriated property unless evidence shows an affirmative intention by the wrongdoer to effectuate that result. *See* Restatement (Third) of Restitution and Unjust Enrichment (2011) § 59(2)(b). This presumption effectively preserves funds added into the account for the benefit of the account holder and other creditors. Similarly, the Restatement (Third) does not allow traceable product to exceed the commingled account's "lowest intermediate balance." Restatement (Third) of Restitution and Unjust Enrichment (2011) § 59(2)(c).

(C) BONA FIDE PURCHASER

1. OVERVIEW

A bona fide purchaser is a party who acts in good faith and pays value for legal title to property without notice of an outstanding equitable interest. The law protects a bona fide purchaser against prior equitable claims. The primary justification for this rule protecting certain transferees is to ensure certainty and to protect the integrity of commercial transactions. In short, the law effectively gives the buyer who acts in good faith and without actual or constructive knowledge of equitable the legal assurance that the title obtained will be honored. Another rationale underlying the bona fide purchaser doctrine is that legal title historically has been considered superior to equitable title. Finally, the doctrine is consistent with the view that, as between two innocent parties, the loss should not fall on the one who paid value. The bona fide purchaser doctrine, though, is limited by the nature of the underlying property rights held by the grantor. Although the doctrine protects against adverse claims when no record notice exists of a prior inconsistent interest, the bona fide purchaser cannot acquire greater rights than the grantor. *See* Graves v. Wayman, 859 N.W.2d 791, 801 (Minn. 2015)(bank could not assert bona fide purchaser status where grantor's underlying deed was void).

In order to claim bona fide purchaser status, a party must meet several requirements: the party must acquire legal title, for value, and without notice of prior equitable interests. The lack of any element will suffice to defeat the protected status. The defense applies to virtually any type of property rights, including realty, personalty, and negotiable instruments. The application of the defense will vary, however, depending on the nature of the property interest at stake and the overlay of various statutes. For example, the recording statutes pertaining to real property impose a requirement that the deed or mortgage be filed in a central location which itself serves as constructive notice to the world of that interest. The Uniform Commercial Code contains various provisions that affect the bona fide purchaser rules, such as section 1–204 regarding what constitutes paying "value."

Consider the following illustration: A wrongfully transfers legal title to property held in trust to B, who has no notice that the transfer violates the trust agreement nor of the interest of the true beneficiary, C. If B has paid value for the property, however, B would be protected as a bona fide purchaser against the equitable interest asserted by the beneficiary in the trust *res*. C could maintain an action for fraud or breach of the trust agreement against A, but could not seek reconveyance from B through equitable restitution. On the other hand, if B did not pay value, such as if B were classified as an innocent donee, then C would prevail because all of the required elements of the bona fide purchaser defense were not met.

2. NOTICE

The notice that can defeat bona fide purchaser status can be either actual or constructive. Constructive notice is satisfied, for example, when a deed, will, mortgage, or other instrument has been duly recorded in a public office under state law recording statutes. *See* Restatement (Third) of Restitution and Unjust Enrichment (2011) § 69. Thus, a purchaser of real estate is given a safe harbor of protection by reliance on recorded titles and will ordinarily not be subordinated to unrecorded equities of which the purchaser has no actual or constructive knowledge.

Constructive notice may arise in other ways as well. A court may charge a principal with the knowledge of an agent acquired during the agency relationship. Also, a court may impute notice to a transferee in situations where the prior equitable claim would have been discovered by the exercise of reasonable due diligence. Even a fact such as a very low purchase price of property may suffice to place the potential buyer on notice that the property has an outstanding equitable claim against it.

The U.C.C. provides a greater latitude to a holder of negotiable instruments, who will take free of equitable claims if value was paid in good faith even where the holder failed to satisfy a duty of objective due diligence to discover a fraud. *See* U.C.C. §§ 1–201(20); 1–202; 3–304; 8–304. The U.C.C. gives this heightened protection to the holder of negotiable instruments because it promotes certainty in commercial transactions.

3.   VALUE

A transferee must also give "value," or an exchange of consideration, for the acquired property in order to receive bona fide purchaser status. The concept of sufficient value is reasonably flexible, based on the nature of the property at issue. Mathematical precision is not required. A person receiving property gratuitously will not meet the standard. Typically, a party cannot object that consideration was "inadequate." As a result, consideration that is more than nominal but less than fair market value will support the claim of purchase for value. Nevertheless, a purchase price substantially below market value may be relevant to the issue of notice. *See* Restatement (Third) of Restitution and Unjust Enrichment (2011) § 68, cmt. h. The U.C.C. § 1–204 defines value as "any consideration sufficient to support a simple contract."

The satisfaction of an antecedent debt constitutes giving value sufficient to cut off the beneficial interest in a constructive trust unless the constructive trust property consists of an interest in land, but not against the beneficiary of an express trust. Whether a person receiving property as security for or in satisfaction of a pre-existing obligation is considered a purchaser for value varies subject to local precedent. *See* Restatement (Third) of Restitution and Unjust Enrichment (2011) § 68(2).

In re Marriage of Allen, 724 P.2d 651 (Colo. 1986) illustrates the requirement that a bona fide purchaser must have given value for the property. In that case a husband used embezzled funds to make home improvements and then the property interest was included in a divorce settlement agreement. The employer traced the proceeds to a portion of the wife's share of the settlement arrangement and sought a constructive trust to convey the misappropriated assets. Although the wife was not charged with notice of the embezzlement, she was not accorded bona fide purchaser status because she did not give value for the property. Instead, the wife maintained only innocent donee or gratuitous transferee status.

4. LEGAL TITLE

A transferee, in addition to giving value and acquiring property without notice of equitable claims, must obtain legal title rather than equitable title in order to prevail as a bona fide purchaser over the competing equitable interests. A bona fide purchaser's rights are superior to prior equitable interests. In contrast, a judgment creditor possessing a statutory lien on property is not accorded the same priority status over previous equitable claims even though the creditor had no notice of such equitable interest. *See* Restatement (Third) of Restitution and Unjust Enrichment (2011) § 60, cmt. b.

(D) CHANGE IN POSITION

Another defense to restitution is known as "change in position." It provides that a court of equity may exercise its discretion to withhold or limit restitution if the recipient of the property was without notice and if an order of restitution would result in a substantial hardship due to changed circumstances of the defendant. *See* Restatement (Third) of Restitution and Unjust Enrichment (2011) § 65. The defense has been applied sparingly because the standard for its application is especially rigorous. Because this defense defeats an otherwise meritorious claim for restitution, the change in the defendant's position must be compelling. Many courts find relevant whether the claimant acted in a negligent manner and the recipient of the property was blameworthy, such as in the case of mistaken payments.

This defense reflects the traditional discretion of a court of equity to fashion its orders based upon the relative hardships of the affected parties. Consequently, although one party has held or enjoyed a benefit that ordinarily may justify disgorgement, subsequent events may influence the willingness of a court to order restitution. For example, if goods are destroyed by fire, without tortious conduct or fault by the holder, a court may decide not to require restitution. A common example of the change of position defense is where a person mistakenly delivers goods to another and then the goods are lost or destroyed without the fault of the recipient. Assuming that the holder of the mistakenly delivered property did not have a duty of care toward the property or its rightful owner, the change in position defense can apply.

The application of the defense requires an inquiry into the degree of hardship and the materiality of the change in position. The court also will examine the defendant's own conduct toward the property before asserting the defense. If the defendant committed a tort or was substantially more at fault than the claimant, the defense is unavailable. The defendant must show that the change in circumstances occurred prior to learning the relevant facts and before obtaining an opportunity to make restitution. Finally, the nature of the loss or destruction of the property is relevant. If the recipient exercised reasonable reliance or if a long period of time elapsed since acquiring the property interest, a court may give that party more latitude in asserting the defense.

An interesting example of these principles at work is *Alexander Hamilton Life Ins. Co. of Am. v. Lewis,* 550 S.W.2d 558 (Ky. 1977). In that case the plaintiff insurance company paid proceeds on a life insurance policy to the defendant beneficiaries in the mutually mistaken belief that the insured was deceased. The recipients of the funds had not committed wrongdoing and had spent the funds for ordinary living expenses, home improvements, medical expenses and for purchase of an automobile prior to receiving notice of the true status of the insured. The court did not accept the change in position defense and ordered equitable restitution of the funds. The court reasoned that the defense did not apply to prevent restoration of the mistakenly paid funds because of the balance of respective hardships on the parties and the types of expenses incurred. Dissipation of funds in normal living expenses, without more, is not generally considered a change in position that discharges an obligation to repay. *See* Restatement (Third) of Restitution and Unjust Enrichment (2011) § 65, cmt. c. Instead, the recipient

must show a direct causal relationship between the
receipt of the funds and the expenditure.

Courts interpret the defense of change in position
in a manner consistent with the general principles
underlying equitable restitution. Someone who
acquires property to which they have no legal claim
has a duty to restore it to its owner unless the
property has been a gift or otherwise acquired under
circumstances that do not make it unjust to retain.
The duty of restitution does not arise until the
recipient learns the facts that make restitution
appropriate. Therefore, if the goods are consumed,
lost, stolen, transferred or destroyed in the interim,
their duty of restitution is limited to the extent of the
benefit enjoyed.

CHAPTER 18
JURY TRIALS

(A) SOURCE OF THE RIGHT
TO A JURY TRIAL

The right to trial by jury in civil cases arises from two main sources: statutes and the federal and state constitutions. Congress and state legislatures can grant a right to trial by jury for any civil claim by statute. Assuming no statutory right to a trial by jury, the right to a trial by jury arises as a matter of constitutional law. The Seventh Amendment to the U.S. Constitution preserves the right to a trial by jury "[i]n Suits at common law." Because the Seventh Amendment has not been incorporated to the states through the Fourteenth Amendment, the Seventh Amendment does not apply to states. Pearson v. Yewdall, 95 U.S. 294 (1877). As a result, the Seventh Amendment governs the right to a trial by jury in federal court only. The applicable state constitution governs the right to a jury trial in state court.

The Seventh Amendment and all state constitutions preserve the right to a jury trial in cases at common law only. Courts interpret this to mean that the right to a jury trial exists in cases at law only and not to cases in equity. Thus, the characterization of a remedy and the claim as legal or equitable is central to whether the right to a jury trial attaches to the claim.

(B) SCOPE OF THE RIGHT
TO A JURY TRIAL

1.   SCOPE OF THE RIGHT TO
A JURY TRIAL—GENERALLY

Absent a statutory grant of a right to a jury trial, state and federal constitutions preserve the right to a jury trial in "suits at common law." The U.S. Supreme Court as well as state courts recognize that the right does not extend to those suits in which only equitable rights exist and equitable remedies are administered. The courts, however, also recognize that the right to a jury trial is not limited to only those cases that raise claims which were cognizable at common law. Instead, this language preserves the right to a jury trial in any proceedings in which legal rights are ascertained. *See* Feltner v. Columbia Pictures Television Inc., 523 U.S. 340 (1998).

The right to a jury trial clearly attaches in those cases in which the parties assert only claims which were recognized by the English common law courts and seek only legal remedies available in English common law courts. The quintessential example of such a case would be a case in which a plaintiff seeks compensatory damages for breach of contract.

Likewise, the parties clearly do not have a right to a jury trial in those cases in which the parties seek only equitable remedies not available in the English common law courts. The quintessential example of such a case would be a case in which the plaintiff sought specific performance for a breach of contract.

Determining whether the parties have a right to a jury trial becomes more problematic in other areas. A few of the difficult areas involve cases in which the parties assert statutory causes of action that did not exist at common law; cases in which the parties assert claims arising in substantive equity, and cases in which parties assert mixed claims of law and equity. Determining which specific issues must be submitted to the jury in claims to which the right to a jury trial attaches also gives courts trouble.

2. NOVEL STATUTORY CLAIMS

The U.S. Supreme Court has adopted a historical analog test for determining whether the parties have a right to a jury trial in cases asserting statutory claims that were unknown at common law. Under the historical analog test, the Court attempts to determine whether the cause of action is more analogous to a claim tried in common law courts than a claim tried in courts of equity in the 18th century. To do so, the Court looks at both the nature of the substantive rights being asserted and the nature of the remedy to see whether the claim is more analogous to a claim asserting legal rights. However, the Court generally places more emphasis on the nature of the remedy.

For example, in *Chauffeurs, Teamsters & Helpers Local 391 v. Terry*, 494 U.S. 558 (1990), the Court concluded that the parties had a right to a jury trial in a claim brought by a union member seeking backpay from a union for breach of the duty of fair representation. A plurality of the Court concluded that the substantive claim for breach of a duty of fair representation was most analogous to a claim against a trustee for breach of fiduciary duty. The plurality acknowledged that a trust claim fell within the exclusive jurisdiction of courts of equity. However, the plurality still found the right to a jury trial to attach to the claim for breach of a duty of fair representation because the backpay that the plaintiff sought was legal in nature.

3.   SUBSTANTIVE EQUITY

Historically, the courts of equity took two types of cases. In the first type of case, the remedy at law was inadequate. This basis was explored through the inadequacy rule covered in Chapters 3 and 4, *supra*. The second type of case involved substantive equity. For instance, cases involving trusts, mortgages, and shareholder derivative actions were a matter of substantive equity rather than remedial equity because only equity recognized these claims. The courts at law had no effective way of handling these substantive claims, so equity devised means of dealing with these areas. Thus, any case concerning these substantive matters came under equitable jurisdiction regardless of the type of remedy sought in these claims.

Most states retain the rule that there is no right to a jury trial for a claim brought in equity. This rule applies to substantive equity as well as remedial equity. Therefore, if a shareholder derivative action is tried in state court, there is no right to a jury trial in most states. It does not matter if the complaint seeks legal remedies, such as damages for alleged fraud by the company's officers. Unlike remedial equity, it is the nature of the claim that makes such a case an equitable one.

The Supreme Court changed that rule for cases of substantive equity brought in federal court. In *Ross v. Bernhard*, 396 U.S. 531 (1970), the Court addressed whether shareholders were entitled to a jury trial in a derivative suit under the federal guarantee of a right to a jury trial embodied in the Seventh Amendment. The Court faced the problem of how to reconcile the historical development of substantive equity with the commands of the Seventh Amendment which provides for a right to jury trial in matters "at law." The Court decided to ignore the "historical accident" of substantive equity and to focus instead upon the legal or equitable nature of the remedy sought in the underlying claim. As the Court stated later in *Dairy Queen, Inc. v. Wood*, 369 U.S. 469, 477–78 (1962), "the constitutional right to trial by jury cannot be made to depend upon the choice of words used in pleadings." Therefore, because the plaintiffs in *Ross* sought damages, there was a right to a jury trial.

The Court's conclusion in *Ross* applies only to federal jury trial rights because the Seventh Amendment does not apply to the states. Some states have been persuaded by the Supreme Court's analysis and have interpreted their own state Constitutional guarantees in the same manner. Most states have not followed the Supreme Court's approach and have retained the rule that claims in substantive equity do not support a right to a jury trial.

(C) MIXED CLAIMS OF LAW AND EQUITY

1. EQUITABLE CLEAN-UP

The merger of law and equity in the twentieth century brought the reform that mixed claims of law and equity could be brought in one claim and before one judge. The merger was procedural only and did not change the substantive differences between law and equity.

When a plaintiff seeks purely legal relief in a merged court, a right to a jury trial attaches. Therefore, a claim seeking damages for breach of contract supports a right to a jury trial in the merged court. There is no such right when the claim is purely equitable relief, such as one for specific performance.

Problems arise when the plaintiff brings a mixed claim that seeks both legal and equitable relief, or when a plaintiff brings one type of claim and the defendant counterclaims with a different type. Historically, courts handled this situation with the doctrine called "equitable clean up." Under this doctrine, if a case is primarily equitable in nature, the parties have no right to a jury trial, and the judge can resolve the legal issues without a jury. For example, consider a nuisance claim where a plaintiff seeks an injunction to prevent future loss as well as damages for past losses. If the injunction issue predominates, then the trial judge can decide the equitable remedy issues and then decide the damages issues. The parties have no right to a jury trial because the judge can "clean up" the remaining legal issues after deciding the equitable ones. Most states still follow the clean-up doctrine today. In seeking to determine whether the equitable issues predominate courts consider factors such as the extent to which the legal and factual issues in the equitable claims and legal claims overlap.

2.   FEDERAL APPROACH TO MIXED CLAIMS

The Supreme Court rejected the equitable clean-up approach for federal courts. The Court held that the Seventh Amendment guarantee to a right to a jury trial in matters "at law" applies to mixed claims of law and equity. In *Dairy Queen, Inc. v. Wood*, 369 U.S. 469 (1962), the Court held that the clean-up doctrine violates the Seventh Amendment right to a jury trial in cases at law. Consequently, a federal court must first try any legal issues before a jury, unless the parties waive that right. After the determination of the legal issues, the judge may then resolve any equitable issues in a manner not inconsistent with the verdict.

For example, consider a hypothetical case in which an employee sues her former employer, alleging that her employer wrongfully discharged her after she refused her supervisor's sexual advances. The plaintiff employee asserts a common law claim for intentional infliction of emotional distress for which she seeks compensatory damages. She also asserts a claim for reinstatement and backpay under Title VII of the Civil Rights Act. Because the plaintiff seeks only equitable relief for her claim under Title VII, the parties would not be entitled to a jury trial had she brought her Title VII claim in a separate lawsuit. However, the parties are entitled to jury trial on her claim for intentional infliction of emotional distress.

Under the federal approach, if either party demands a jury trial, the court must try the common law claim to a jury first. The court can then resolve the Title VII claim without a jury. However, it may not resolve any of the equitable issues in a manner that is inconsistent with the jury verdict on the common law claims. Thus, if the jury finds that the supervisor did make sexual advances toward the plaintiff, the court cannot conclude that the supervisor did not make sexual advances. The court could still deny equitable relief if it had other sufficient legal grounds for doing so. For example, if the court concludes that reinstatement is not practicable or that the employer had a legitimate employment reason for termination and that the plaintiff's refusal of the sexual advances was not the reason for her termination, the court could deny equitable relief consistent with the jury verdict.

(D) SUBSTANCE OF THE RIGHT TO A JURY TRIAL

Even if the parties possess a right to a jury trial, the Supreme Court and state courts recognize that not all issues arising in a case need be submitted to a jury. Instead, some issues are reserved for the court. Thus, for example, in *Tull v. United States*, 481 U.S. 412 (1987), the Court found that the defendant had a right to a jury trial in a civil enforcement action under the federal Clean Water Act. However, the Court also held that Congress could constitutionally require the trial court rather than the jury to fix the amount of the civil penalties imposed in the enforcement action.

The Supreme Court has explained that issues arising within a legal claim must be submitted to the jury only if jury resolution is necessary to preserve the substance of the common law right of trial by jury. However, determining which issues are essential to preserve the substance of the right proves problematic. The Supreme Court looks to historical antecedents to determine which issues were tried by the jury at common law. The Court also takes into account "functional considerations." In so doing, the Court examines the nature of the issue to be resolved, the type of evidence involved in resolving the issue and the relevant expertise and experiences of the judge and jury in determining whether the judge or the jury is better suited to resolve the issue.

For example, in *Markman v. Westview Instruments*, 517 U.S. 370 (1996), the Court held that, even though the parties had a right to a jury trial in patent infringement cases, the construction and interpretation of the patent at issue need not be submitted to the jury. Instead, the Court held that the trial court could construe the patent as a matter of law. In contrast, in *Hana Fin., Inc. v. Hana Bank*, 574 U.S. 418 (2015), the Court concluded that the issue of whether multiple versions of a trademark give the same impression to consumers such that they can "tacked" must be submitted to the jury. In her opinion, Justice Sotomayor noted that this sort of inquiry is not "one of those things that judges often do" better than jurors.

Likewise, the Court has relied on functional considerations in deciding the extent to which the Seventh Amendment limits the scope of appellate review. For example, in *Teva Pharmaceuticals USA v. Sandoz, Inc.*, 574 U.S. 318 (2015), the Court determined that an appellate court should apply a clearly erroneous standard when reviewing facts. In contrast, in *Cooper Industries, Inc. v. Leatherman Tool Group, Inc.*, 532 U.S. 424 (2001), the Court held that an award of punitive damages is not a finding of fact, and thus can be reviewed by the court of appeals de novo. Describing the exercise of setting punitive damages as a "finely tuned exercise" in which "juries do not normally engage," the Court was persuaded by the superior "institutional competence" of judges.

CHAPTER 19
ATTORNEYS' FEES

(A) INTRODUCTION

The traditional study of remedies often devotes primary attention to the substantive and procedural requirements pertaining to claims involving injunctions, damages, restitution and declaratory judgments. The entitlement, fashioning and measurement of such claims are central themes to an understanding of the efficacy and preferences in evaluating the merits and advantages of various remedial options. A complementary remedial issue which may significantly impact the effectual nature of recovery is whether costs of litigation, such as attorneys' fees, may be awarded to a prevailing party.

The default approach under common law regarding attorneys' fees is the American Rule, which holds that each party bears its own costs of litigation. It is distinguished from the English approach that allows the prevailing party to recover litigation costs as a matter of course from the losing party. Such litigation expenses include attorney's fees, and the rule applies equally to prevailing plaintiffs and defendants.

Several policy considerations support the American Rule. The primary justification for refusing attorneys' fees to the winning party is to avoid penalizing a party for its reasonable claim or defense. The party that loses on the merits is not considered a wrongdoer, and to impose fees may discourage the legitimate use of the court system. A handful of courts have also justified the rule by pointing to the potential difficulties and burden of proving what constitutes a reasonable fee.

The American Rule draws sharp criticism on several grounds as well. A primary objection is that a prevailing party can only be "made whole" upon being reimbursed their litigation expenses in addition to any other form of relief granted. For example, where the prevailing party only obtains injunctive relief or the claim produces a relatively small pool of damages, such as in vindicating certain civil rights claims, then the lack of monetary compensation may serve as a disincentive to pursue otherwise valid claims. Another objection to the rule is that it indirectly contributes to the burdens on the already taxed judicial system because unsuccessful litigants are not generally held accountable for the costs associated with bringing claims with little chance of prevailing on the merits.

A number of exceptions to the American Rule have developed through contract, statutes, and in equity. Some reflect dissatisfaction with the potential inequity in bearing litigation costs, while others are designed to encourage certain types of litigation in the public interest. Illustrative state and federal statutes which often contain provisions authorizing fee awards to successful litigants include consumer protection, environmental, privacy, and civil rights laws.

One major exception to the American Rule is that parties may stipulate by contract to the payment of attorneys' fees when a non-breaching party must enforce the agreement. Such contractual fee-shifting provisions are generally upheld provided they are not unconscionable. Commercial agreements commonly include attorneys' fee provisions, such as bank loans and leases. Also, some states have enacted statutes that provide for the award of attorneys' fees to secure compensation for breach of contract. Parties may not, on the other hand, contract out of procedural fee-shifting or the court's equitable authority to award attorneys' fees for abuse of judicial process.

(B) EQUITABLE EXCEPTIONS TO THE AMERICAN RULE

1.   BAD FAITH LITIGATION

A court has inherent equitable power to award reasonable attorney fees to the prevailing party when the losing party has acted in acted in "bad faith, vexatiously, wantonly, or for oppressive reasons" in the course of the litigation. Chambers v. NASCO, Inc., 501 U.S. 32 (1991). In *Chambers*, the buyer of a television station sought to compel completion of the transaction, but the seller engaged in a series of delay and obstruction tactics to prevent enforcement of the court's orders. The Supreme Court upheld the fee award imposed by the district court based upon the bad faith exception to the American Rule. The Court observed that the award of fees for bad faith litigation serves the dual purpose of vindicating the integrity of the court and making the prevailing party whole for expenses caused by the opponent's misconduct. The Court further found that the bad faith equity exception could be used even if other rules also provided sanctions. Finally, the opinion approved the award of fees by federal courts sitting in diversity even when the applicable state law did not recognize the bad faith exception to the American Rule.

In *Goodyear Tire & Rubber v. Haeger*, 137 S. Ct. 1178 (2017), the Court reaffirmed the inherent power of federal courts to manage their affairs to achieve the orderly and efficient administration of justice by fashioning sanctions for litigation misconduct, which includes awarding attorney's fees against offending litigants. The Court held, though, that such fee awards must be compensatory and not punitive in nature, so could go no further than to redress the specific losses sustained by the injured party. Therefore, when a court uses its inherent sanctioning authority to shift fees the claimant must show a causal link between the misconduct and the fees incurred. The Court styled the necessary causal connection as a "but-for" test. Federal courts, then, have discretion to allocate litigation expenses to sanction bad faith conduct but may allocate only those litigation expenses directly related to the misconduct.

While the Supreme Court has yet to clearly define bad faith, the standard under this rule requires more than simply showing that the claim, defense, or appeal had a weak foundation. Instead, the claim must have been frivolous or without merit.

2.   COMMON FUND

Another exception to the American Rule may arise where litigation produces a common fund for the benefit of a group of claimants, such as produced in a successful class action. The doctrine provides that someone who creates, preserves, or increases the value of a fund in which others have a beneficial interest may obtain reimbursement from the fund for their litigation expenses. *See* Sprague v. Ticonic Nat'l Bank, 307 U.S. 161 (1939).

Pursuant to the "common fund" or "equitable fund" approach, attorneys' fees are actually taken directly out of a pool of damages paid by a defendant before the sums are distributed to the successful claimants. As such, it is not a true exception to the American Rule because the fees are not directly shifted to the losing party but are instead drawn from the fund of damages. The plaintiff class shares its recovery with the attorneys in a manner similar to contingency fee arrangements.

The common fund doctrine reflects the equitable restitutionary principle that prevailing parties would otherwise be unjustly enriched if they received the benefits of a lawsuit without sharing in the costs. *See* Boeing v. Van Gemert, 444 U.S. 472 (1980). Because of this underlying equitable purpose, courts will generally refuse to apply the doctrine when there is no inequitable outcome, for instance where the claimants already receive attorney fees through a fee-shifting statute.

3.   SUBSTANTIAL BENEFIT THEORY

Another recognized but rarely used exception to the American Rule is the "substantial benefit" theory. This theory applies only where litigation produces a substantial benefit for a certain class of beneficiaries, such as where an attorney obtains a favorable litigation outcome for her client that subsequently benefits another group. In contrast with the common fund exception, the nature of the benefits produced may be intangible or non-monetary rather than leading to creation of a specific fund.

One difficulty with imposing attorneys' fees against the benefit recipients is that they do not have a choice in accepting or refusing the benefits conferred. Further, quantifying the benefits of an intangible nature, such as greater corporate accountability or institutional honesty, are inherently difficult to determine.

The requirements for satisfying the substantial benefits doctrine are: (1) the plaintiff must confer a substantial benefit; (2) the class of recipients must be readily identifiable and ascertainable; (3) the benefits must be traceable to the class; and (4) a reasonable basis must exist to ensure that the costs are proportionally spread among the benefitting class. The Supreme Court has characterized the substantial benefit theory as a derivation of the common fund exception and concluded that the benefit must accrue to the defendant responsible for paying any fees. *See* Alyeska Pipeline Serv. Co. v. Wilderness Soc'y, 421 U.S. 240 (1975).

4.   PRIVATE ATTORNEY GENERAL

Another exception to the American Rule provides for fee awards to a successful litigant who acts in a capacity as "private attorney general" with respect to a matter promoting the public interest. The doctrine recognizes that the government necessarily has limited resources to ensure full enforcement of the laws. Therefore, in limited situations private parties may fulfill a quasi-governmental role by pursuing litigation to carry out enforcement of laws that reflect strong public policy, such as civil rights or environmental protection. Because the private citizen's action benefits the public good, the rationale is that they should be reimbursed for their litigation costs. Further, plaintiffs in such cases often seek only injunctive relief, resulting in no fund of damages to offset the expenses incurred. Courts justify the authority to award fees based upon their inherent equitable powers to carry out the interests of justice.

Numerous states accept the private attorney general theory, but the Supreme Court specifically rejected it as a matter of federal common law in *Alyeska Pipeline Service Co. v. Wilderness Society,* 421 U.S. 240 (1975). In *Alyeska,* environmental organizations sought declaratory and injunctive relief that the government's plans for issuance of permits necessary for construction of the Alaskan pipeline violated various federal environmental protection statutes. The plaintiff organizations prevailed, and the Court of Appeals awarded attorneys' fees against the pipeline company based upon theory that they were acting as private attorneys' general. The Supreme Court reversed, reasoning that federal courts should not impose fee awards without express statutory authority. In response to the decision, Congress promptly enacted the Civil Rights Attorney's Fees Awards Act, 42 U.S.C.A. § 1988, to authorize the recovery of attorneys' fees to prevailing parties under a wide variety of civil rights, environmental, and other statutes involving matters of public interest.

Alyeska does not affect the availability of the private attorney general theory under state common law. In *Serrano v. Priest,* 20 Cal. 3d 25 (1977) the California Supreme Court held that attorneys' fees could properly be awarded under a state common law theory of private attorney general. The plaintiff there successfully challenged the California public school financing system as being in violation of state constitutional provisions guaranteeing equal protection of the laws. The doctrine was later codified by state statute. Cal. Civ. Proc. Code § 1021.5.

(C) FEDERAL FEE-SHIFTING STATUTES

1. ENTITLEMENT TO FEE AWARDS

One of the foremost criticisms raised regarding the American Rule has been that a successful claimant would not be made whole where the amount of damages recovered would not offset their litigation expenses. If the prevailing party only obtained declaratory and injunctive relief, the problem was compounded. Heightened public attention to the issue arose following *Alyeska,* as many expressed concern that the American Rule could undermine the willingness of private parties to pursue legitimate claims in the public interest. In response to these concerns, Congress actively passed various fee-shifting statutes, particularly with respect to environmental and civil rights. An important illustration is the Civil Rights Attorney's Fees Awards Act of 1976, 42 U.S.C. § 1988, which provides that the court, in its discretion, may allow the prevailing party to recover a reasonable attorney's fee as part of the costs. Courts presumptively allow recovery of fees to the successful party pursuant to such statutory authorizations and do not require a further showing of bad faith. *See* Newman v. Piggie Park Enterprises, Inc., 390 U.S. 400 (1968).

The federal fee-shifting statutes typically provide for the recovery of attorney fees to the "prevailing party" or "prevailing plaintiff" although some statutory schemes leave the issue of fee-shifting to judicial discretion. The Supreme Court outlined in *Hensley v. Eckerhart,* 461 U.S. 424 (1983) a basic approach for fee eligibility under The Civil Rights Attorney's Fees Awards Act, 42 U.S.C. § 1988. The Court concluded, as a threshold matter, that a plaintiff is a prevailing party upon succeeding on a significant issue in litigation which achieves some of the objectives the parties sought in bringing suit. Beyond that initial determination, the reasonableness of the fee would turn on various evidentiary factors, including the nature and extent of the success achieved. Justice Powell, writing for the Court, admonished that the request for attorneys' fees should not result in a second major litigation. 461 U.S. at 437.

In *Texas State Teachers Ass'n v. Garland Independent School District*, 489 U.S. 782 (1989), the Court refined the *Hensley* test for attorney fee awards. The issue in that case was how to interpret "prevailing" when the plaintiff achieved only partial success on the merits. In *Garland*, several teachers' unions brought constitutional challenges concerning various school board policies limiting union activities and communications. The Court held that fee eligibility was predicated on demonstrating success on a "significant" issue in litigation but did not require that a plaintiff prevail on the "central" issue in dispute. The Court explained that the principal consideration for fee eligibility is whether the legal relationship of the parties was "materially altered" in a manner consistent with the intentions of Congress in the fee-shifting statute. The degree of overall success relates to the measurement of the fee. Consequently, no fees would be awarded where the plaintiff achieved only technical or *de minimis* success.

The Supreme Court explained these standards further in *Farrar v. Hobby,* 506 U.S. 103 (1992). The Court held there that a civil rights plaintiff who receives a nominal damages award was a "prevailing party" eligible to receive attorney's fees under 42 U.S.C. § 1988. The Court explained that "a material alteration of the legal relationship occurs [when] the plaintiff becomes entitled to enforce a judgment, consent decree, or settlement against the defendant."

506 U.S. at 113. The Court curtailed this expansive interpretation a few years later in *Buckhannon Board and Care Home, Inc. v. West Virginia Dept. of Health and Human Resources,* 532 U.S. 598 (2001). In that case, the Court rejected the so-called "catalyst" theory and held that mere voluntary changes in behavior, without securing an enforceable judgement, did not suffice for a fee award.

Although many federal fee-shifting statutes provide for the recovery of attorney fees to the "prevailing party," many courts apply a more rigorous standard for awarding fees to successful defendants. In *Christiansburg Garment Co. v. Equal Employment Opportunity Commission,* 434 U.S. 412 (1978), the Court distinguished between prevailing plaintiffs and prevailing defendants for purposes of fee eligibility. It held that a prevailing plaintiff in a Title VII discrimination case under the Civil Rights Act of 1964 ordinarily receives a fee award absent special circumstances, but a prevailing defendant could recover fees only by showing that the plaintiff's claim was "frivolous, unreasonable, or groundless" even if not brought in bad faith. 434 U.S. at 422. The Court reasoned that a dual standard for eligibility was justified in order to encourage private attorney general suits to protect civil rights while also to shield such claimants from potential fee liability when the suit was meritorious yet unsuccessful.

The Court expanded on *Christianburg Garment* and addressed the proper allocation of attorneys' fees in the context of complex litigation which involved both frivolous and non-frivolous claims. In *Fox v.*

Vice, 563 U.S. 826 (2011), the Court determined that a defendant prevailing on the frivolous claims may be entitled to recover attorney's fees only to the extent that the costs were incurred by work related directly to the frivolous claims and which would not have been incurred but for those specific claims. The Court reasoned that the policy behind § 1988 supports the defendant receiving attorney's fees only for the marginal cost incurred as a result of the particular claim and that defendants should not receive a pecuniary benefit as a result of the plaintiff pleading more broadly than warranted.

In *CRST Van Expedited, Inc. v. E.E.O.C.,* 136 S. Ct. 1642 (2016), the Supreme Court further clarified that a favorable ruling on the merits is not a necessary predicate to find that a defendant has prevailed for purposes of awarding fees under a federal fee-shifting statute. The Court reasoned that although a plaintiff seeks to effectuate a material alteration in its legal relationship between the parties, a defendant may "prevail" by vindicating its position or also simply by rebuffing the plaintiff's claims. Thus, a court's final judgment rejecting a plaintiff's claims for non-merits reasons should not prevent recovery of attorneys' fees for defending against frivolous claims. Further, the Court noted that the congressional policy giving district courts discretion whether to award fees and the statutory fee-shifting language itself did not distinguish between merits-based and non-merits-based judgments.

2. MEASUREMENT OF FEES

The standard approach for calculating attorneys' fees is called the "lodestar" method. The lodestar is calculated by multiplying a reasonable hourly rate for each attorney times the number of hours reasonably spent on the litigation. A court may adjust this amount up or down in light of the "degree of success obtained" in the litigation. *See* Hensley v. Eckerhart, 461 U.S. 424 (1983). The claimant must provide a specific, evidentiary basis to justify recovery of fees, and the lack of appropriate documentation may result in reduction or denial of the award.

The Supreme Court treats the lodestar figure as presumptively reasonable, subject to adjustment only in rare or exceptional circumstances. Applicants seeking to depart from the lodestar bear a heavy burden to show why an adjustment is necessary. For example, in *City of Burlington v. Dague,* 505 U.S. 557 (1992), the Court rejected an enhancement of a fee award for the risk of non-recovery under a contingency fee arrangement. The Court found that such an enhancement would likely duplicate factors already reflected in the lodestar calculation.

The Court recently reiterated the general sufficiency of the lodestar figure in *Perdue v. Kenny,* 559 U.S. 542 (2010), noting that the policy behind fee-shifting statutes is to enable the claim to be litigated, not to enrich attorneys. The Court held that most factors, including the novelty and complexity of the case and the quality of an attorney's performance, are already reflected in the lodestar calculation. Further, financial factors known at the start of representation, such as contingency fee arrangements and the advancement of litigation expenses by counsel, are not a basis for adjustment.

In exceptionally rare circumstances where the attorney can demonstrate that the lodestar calculation does not adequately measure the attorney's value, a court may enhance the lodestar amount, provided an objective basis is given for doing so. For example, if there is undue delay in reimbursement of fees or expenses, especially when caused by the defense, a court may enhance the value of attorneys' fees by applying a standard rate of interest.

Many lower courts consider additional factors to determine the reasonableness of and subsequent adjustments to the attorneys' fees under the Lodestar Method. For instance, the Fourth, Fifth, Sixth, Eighth, Tenth, and Eleventh Circuits utilize some form of the factors set forth in *Johnson v. Georgia Highway Expl. Inc.*, 488 F.2d 714 (5th Cir. 1974). These criteria include the time, labor, and skill required, difficulty of the legal issue, and customary fees, among others. Nevertheless, courts continue to struggle with reconciling which of these factors are subsumed within the initial lodestar calculation.

An award of attorneys' fees under 42 U.S.C. § 1988 does not necessarily need to be proportionate to the amount of damages recovered by the plaintiff in the underlying civil rights action. Rather, the amount of damages is only one of many factors that a court should consider in calculating a reasonable fee under the statute. The Supreme Court noted in *City of Riverside v. Rivera*, 477 U.S. 561 (1986) that claims seeking to vindicate civil and constitutional rights may produce relatively small monetary damages yet serve an important public function. A contingent fee limitation would undermine Congressional intent in promoting protection of civil rights by making it harder for individuals to obtain legal representation.

The fee awarded pursuant to § 1988 may nevertheless differ from amounts owed under a contractual obligation between attorney and client. In *Blanchard v. Bergeron*, 489 U.S. 87 (1989), the Court held that the fees awarded under the civil rights fee-shifting statute were not automatically governed by or restricted to the amount designated in a contingent fee contract. Although the terms of a contingency fee arrangement were relevant, it did not necessarily dictate what constituted a "reasonable fee" under § 1988. To illustrate, in *Venegas v. Mitchell*, 495 U.S. 82 (1990), an attorney who successfully represented a client in a civil rights suit sought to recover his contractual contingency fee which significantly exceeded the amount awarded under the fee-shifting statute. The Court upheld the validity of the contractual arrangement, finding that a "reasonable fee" under the statute does not override or replace otherwise valid contractual terms. The Court reasoned that Congress established fee-shifting statutes to benefit the party rather than the lawyer, leaving clients free to bargain on whatever terms they choose to obtain counsel of their choice.

(D) EQUAL ACCESS TO JUSTICE ACT

The Equal Access to Justice Act contains provisions for awarding attorneys' fees to private parties who prevail in civil suits against the United States. 28 U.S.C. § 2412. The Act serves as a limited waiver of sovereign immunity and is strictly construed. The purpose of the EAJA is to reduce the disadvantage in economic resources faced by private parties who challenge unreasonable governmental actions.

The Act contains two alternative scenarios for prevailing private parties to recover fees. Under one section, the Act gives the court discretion to impose fees against the federal government to the same extent as private parties pursuant to either common law or statutory authority. 28 U.S.C. § 2412(b). For example, the court may draw upon equitable principles and impose a fee award where the government acted in bad faith in the conduct of litigation.

The second provision provides for a mandatory assessment of fees in a non-tort civil action unless the court finds that the position of the United States was substantially justified or that special circumstances make an award unjust. 28 U.S.C. § 2412(d)(1)(A). *See* Pierce v. Underwood, 487 U.S. 552, 566 (1988). Therefore, the Act effectively creates a presumption in favor of a prevailing private party and shifts the burden to the government to demonstrate that its actions were reasonable. The Act specifies that fee calculations must be based upon "prevailing market rates" but places a ceiling of $125 per hour on fees absent an adjustment for inflation. 28 U.S.C. § 2412(d)(2)(A)(ii). Additionally, the statute provides that the designated hourly cap may be increased upon a showing of a "special factor." In *Kathrens v. Bernhardt*, 2020 WL 7093919 (D. Or. 2020), for example, the claimant successfully challenged certain decisions by the Bureau of Land Management taken pursuant to a federal environmental statute. The court found that a higher hourly rate was justified under the EAJA where the attorney for the plaintiff possessed special expertise and skill in the field of environmental litigation which aided them in successfully litigating the claims.

(E) COSTS UNDER FEDERAL RULES

Courts may also rely upon Rule 11 under the Federal Rules of Civil Procedure as a vehicle to impose sanctions for abusive litigation practices and thus facilitate the efficient administration and procedure of the federal courts. Thus, fees awarded pursuant to Rule 11 must be distinguished from eligibility for fees under fee-shifting statutes. Under such statutes, fees are linked to the merits or outcome of the underlying litigation. Rule 11 fee awards, in contrast, are not related to success as a prevailing party but instead focus on deterring abusive litigation practices. Consequently, sanctions are limited to those expenses directly caused by improper filings. *See* Cooter & Gell v. Hartmarx Corp., 496 U.S. 385 (1990). The rule may be implicated where non-discovery pleadings or motions lack a sufficient factual or legal basis or are filed for improper reasons. Commonly recognized improper purposes have included harassment, delay or increasing costs of litigation. Once a determination is made that certain filings violate Rule 11, the court has discretion to assess reasonable attorney fees and expenses. *See* Continental Casualty Co. v. Marshall Granger & Co., LLP, 2017 WL 1901969 (S.D.N.Y. 2017).

One function of the rule is to shift the costs of litigation and compensate a party for expenses directly resulting from abusive practices. The rule also serves educational and rehabilitative purposes in that it allows the court to use monetary sanctions to punish and deter attorneys responsible for violating the federal rules. A party seeking sanctions must first serve a motion on the alleged violator describing the offending conduct and then, within a 21 day safe harbor period, the violator may avoid sanctions by withdrawing or appropriately correcting the paper in question. The safe harbor provision does not apply, however, if the court initiates the sanctions process *sua sponte*.

Several other statutory and procedural provisions are available to a court to deter litigation abuse. For example, 28 U.S.C. § 1927 permits a court to assess litigation costs against an attorney who "multiplies the proceedings" in a case "unreasonably and vexatiously." The amount of fees awarded must relate directly to the excess proceedings. Fed. R. Civ. P. 37 permits sanctions against parties or persons who unjustifiably resist discovery. Appellate courts, pursuant to Fed. R. App. P. 38, may impose cost sanctions against an appellant for bringing a frivolous appeal.

CHAPTER 20
DECLARATORY REMEDIES

(A) NOMINAL DAMAGES

The relationship between substantive rights and remedies has been a theme throughout this Nutshell. Because a right is only as great as the remedy that vindicates it, the variety of remedies available for particular rights contributes to their importance. Moreover, if there is no remedy for a right, then the right is a "paper tiger" without means of enforcement.

An award of nominal damages is not an insignificant remedy in this context, however, even though it provides no monetary recovery to the plaintiff other than a token amount. The award carries significance in that it serves as a declaration of the plaintiff's victory on the substantive claim. That remedy is a limited one, but not an entirely empty one.

A court awards nominal damages when a plaintiff establishes the violation of a legal right but cannot establish the requirements of remedies that would otherwise be available, typically because no substantial injury or loss has occurred. Most case law and state statutes limit the amount of nominal damages recoverable to one dollar, but in other cases the award should not exceed $100, lest the nature of the sanction morph from nominal to compensatory. A court may use nominal damages in a trespass case, for example, when the owner of the land cannot prove any actual loss from the defendant's invasion. In such cases, nominal damages serve the function of ascertaining the rights of the parties and providing a foundation for a court to issue potential injunctive relief to prevent future violations of that interest.

Nominal damages also serve an important role in civil rights litigation. In *Carey v. Piphus*, 435 U.S. 247 (1978) the Supreme Court declined to endorse presumed damages for violations of due process rights, but did permit nominal damages in cases where no loss can be established. The significance of the nominal damages in this context is that they can support an award of attorneys' fees under The Civil Rights Attorney's Fees Awards Act of 1976. Without such an incentive to vindicate civil rights, most plaintiffs would find it difficult to pursue a claim. The other significance of a nominal damages award is that an award of damages, even nominal ones, can serve as the basis for punitive damages if other circumstances are met in some jurisdictions.

(B) DECLARATORY JUDGMENTS

1. OVERVIEW AND FUNCTION

The declaratory judgment is a statutory remedy available under modern state and federal law. It gives courts the power to determine the rights or legal relations of parties to a justiciable controversy. This statutory remedy developed in response to a gap in the common law that no specific means existed to declare the status or rights of parties to resolve certain types of disputes. Apart from several specialized declaratory remedies, such as bills to quiet title or cancellation of instruments, the closest counterpart under common law was nominal damages. Those remedies were much more limited in scope and application than subsequent declaratory judgment statutory schemes.

A declaratory judgment is unique among remedies in that it does not provide monetary compensation nor does it mandate or prohibit specific actions. In contrast with equitable decrees such as injunctions, it is not considered an extraordinary remedy and therefore does not require a showing that other remedies are inadequate. A declaration of rights does not coerce or bind parties *in personam*, therefore it cannot be the basis for a finding of contempt. Once a declaratory judgment establishes rights, however, it may pragmatically influence parties to tailor their subsequent actions to correspond to the decree.

A court can issue a declaratory judgment as an independent order, or in combination with other orders. For example, if a landowner plans to erect a fence and an adjoining neighbor disputes the location of the boundary line, a declaratory judgment can resolve the controversy over the property rights. If the construction of the fence is imminent, the court may also issue a prohibitory injunction to prevent its installation. In the exercise of its discretion, the court may stay its hand in issuing a declaratory judgment unless all property owners potentially affected by the decree were parties to the suit. Further, some courts disfavor issuance of a declaratory judgment where the claimant uses it principally to preempt other disputed issues or gain a tactical litigation advantage.

Declaratory relief with respect to defining statutory coverage has been used in various civil and criminal contexts, such as determining the scope and applicability of a licensing statute. Although the declaratory judgment does not order a party to comply directly with the statute, it carries an indirect coercive effect by setting forth the scope of the statutory requirements and effectively giving notice that non-compliance risks violation of the law.

Parties to intellectual property disputes commonly prefer declaratory relief as a remedy because it allows parties to determine rights prior to engaging in an infringement action. The Supreme Court adopted a liberal "totality of the circumstances" view of what constitutes a case or controversy sufficient for maintaining a declaratory judgment in the intellectual property context. In *MedImmune, Inc. v. Genentech, Inc.*, 549 U.S. 118 (2007) the Court held that a patent licensee could seek a declaratory judgment in federal court to establish non-liability even prior to terminating or breaching its licensing agreement. The Court found that the Constitution's Article III requirement of a case or controversy was satisfied even when a party complied with a challenged coercive or involuntary claim of right. Actual noncompliance with rights claimed under a patent or trademark was not required to render a claim justiciable.

In *Medtronic, Inc. v. Mirowski Family Ventures*, 571 U.S. 191 (2014), a licensee sought a declaratory judgment against a patentee to establish non-infringement. Because a patentee ordinarily bears the burden of proving infringement, the question was whether the burden of proof should shift when the roles of the parties were reversed. The Court observed that the operation of the Declaratory Judgment Act was procedural, leaving substantive rights unaltered. Consequently, because the burden of proof was a substantive aspect of a claim, the Court held that the burden of proving infringement remains with the patentee. Otherwise, reasoned the Court, the purpose of the Declaratory Judgement Act would be undermined as the licensee would face the dilemma of either abandoning rights or risking suit.

2. THE FEDERAL DECLARATORY JUDGMENT ACT

The Federal Declaratory Judgment Act, codified at 28 U.S.C. §§ 2201, 2202, provides a procedural mechanism for the issuance of declaratory relief by federal courts without reference to the availability or sufficiency of other remedies, such as money damages or injunctions. The Act therefore expands the remedial authority of federal courts but does not create new rights. Nor does the statutory authorization for declaratory relief confer or expand the subject matter jurisdiction of federal courts—it still requires an independent basis for the court to assert its jurisdiction. Rather, the Act serves an enabling purpose, which confers a discretion on courts rather than an absolute right upon litigants. *See* Public Service Comm'n of Utah v. Wycoff Co., Inc., 344 U.S. 237 (1952). The Act specifically excludes certain actions, such as those involving federal taxes or tariffs, and may not apply if another statute provides procedures and remedies limited to a particular type of cases. The orders are reviewable as final judgments and have *res judicata* effect.

Federal Rule of Civil Procedure 57 implements the Act and incorporates Rules 38 and 39 with respect to the jury trial. Rule 57 and the Act do not independently establish the right to jury trial, however, so federal courts must ascertain whether or not such rights exists by reference to traditional norms of equity and law. A party may supplement a declaratory judgment remedy in federal court with further relief, such as money damages or an injunction. Such additional relief may be awarded pursuant to Federal Rule 54(c) even if the party has not demanded that relief in its pleadings.

Constitutional and prudential considerations also affect the power and propriety of federal courts to issue declaratory judgments. The Declaratory Judgment statute itself specifically requires that a case or controversy exist in order to satisfy constitutional standards for the exercise of judicial power. *See* 28 U.S.C. § 2201. The dispute must involve genuinely conflicting claims rather than a hypothetical concern or an advisory opinion. No bright line exists between an abstract question and a constitutionally sufficient controversy; rather, courts consider whether a substantial and immediate controversy exists between parties with adverse legal interests. *See* Aetna Life Ins. Co. of Hartford, Conn. v. Haworth, 300 U.S. 227 (1937). Courts also retain considerable discretion with respect to issuance of declaratory judgments and may refuse to render a decree if it would not terminate the controversy or serve a useful purpose.

3.   TIMING

One of the principal advantages to a declaratory judgment remedy is to ascertain rights or legal relations, such as under a contract or coverage of a statute, prior to incurring a breach or violation. Because federal courts do not render advisory opinions, a concrete dispute must already exist in order to justify the court's action. Further, if the breach or violation has already occurred, a court may decide that a declaratory order would not serve a useful purpose and decline to exercise its discretion. Accordingly, issues related to the timeliness of seeking relief are some of the most heavily litigated and contested aspects of declaratory judgments.

In *Dyer v. Maryland State Board of Education*, 685 Fed. Appx. 261 (4th Cir. 2017), a State Board of Education instituted removal proceedings against an official for misconduct, and the official subsequently sought a declaratory judgment in federal district court that the removal process was illegal. When the official lost a bid for re-election, the court granted the Board's motion to dismiss, reasoning that a live case or controversy no longer existed.

A court also may decline to issue declaratory relief if its timeliness has already passed. For example, if criminal proceedings have already been initiated, a court will likely refuse to order a declaratory judgment regarding the scope of the applicable penal statute. In refusing to exercise jurisdiction, the court may appropriately cite reasons of judicial economy, respect for the ongoing proceedings, and recognition that the claimant may raise the same issues of statutory coverage as a defense in the criminal trial.

4.   FEDERALISM AND ABSTENTION

The prevailing practice of federal courts strongly favors the exercise of jurisdiction over disputes within their statutory province. Concomitantly, courts may selectively choose to abstain from hearing cases otherwise within their subject matter jurisdiction in limited circumstances. The traditional factors informing the abstention doctrine in federal courts holds special application in the declaratory judgment context because the Federal Declaratory Judgment Act is specifically couched in terms of discretion. The broad discretion conferred on federal courts regarding the propriety of exercising jurisdiction under the Act was described by the Court in *Wilton v. Seven Falls Co.,* 515 U.S. 277 (1995): "Congress sought to place a remedial arrow in the district court's quiver; it created an opportunity, rather than a duty, to grant a new form of relief to qualifying litigants." 515 U.S. at 288.

Consequently, federal courts which otherwise possess subject matter jurisdiction over a dispute may decline to exercise that jurisdiction in deference to a state forum. In *Brillhart v. Excess, Inc.,* 316 U.S. 491, 494–495 (1942), the Court held that when another proceeding was pending in state court which could fully adjudicate the matters in controversy between the parties, then a federal court should abstain from exercising jurisdiction to consider a declaratory judgment claim. The Court explained that it would be "uneconomical as well as vexatious" for the federal court to proceed as it would otherwise gratuitously interfere with the "orderly and comprehensive disposition" of the state court proceeding.

Strong considerations of federalism, comity, and judicial economy affect the exercise of discretion by a federal court in situations where a pending state court proceeding involves matters related to a federal suit. A federal court may abstain from exercising jurisdiction in order to allow a state court to decide important matters of state law. However, the mere existence of a related state proceeding does not automatically preclude a federal declaratory judgment action. Rather, federal courts generally consider a number of factors in exercising discretion when concurrent state proceedings are pending.

For example, in *Kelly v. Maxum Specialty Ins. Group*, 868 F.3d 274 (3d Cir. 2017), two related lawsuits were pending in state and federal court. The state suit involved a claim for damages associated with an automobile accident. The federal action sought a declaratory judgment regarding whether the insurance company had an obligation to defend and indemnify the defendant. The federal district court dismissed the declaratory judgment suit, reasoning that it had discretion to abstain where the proceedings had the potential to dispose of the same claims. The Third Circuit Court of Appeals reversed, finding that standard for parallel proceedings too restrictive. Instead, the court reasoned that discretion for federal abstention properly could be exercised when substantial similarity existed in parties and issues between the pending proceedings.

In addition to basic principles of comity and federalism, courts take into account whether declaratory relief would settle the controversy and serve a useful purpose, the convenience of parties and witnesses, whether the declaratory remedy is being used merely for the purpose of "procedural fencing" or a race for *res judicata*, if the dispute presents novel or complex state law issues better resolved by state court, judicial economy in avoiding duplicative or piecemeal litigation, discouragement of forum shopping, the effectiveness of alternative remedies, and potential inequities in permitting the plaintiff to gain precedence in time and forum.

An illustration of these principles was addressed in *Mueller Systems, LLC v. Robert Teti and Itet Corp.*, 199 F. Supp. 3d 270 (D. Mass. 2016) where a Canadian corporation brought an action in Canada against a Delaware corporation claiming misappropriation of confidential information and intellectual property. The corporation subsequently brought suit in federal district court in the United States seeking a declaratory judgment that it did not misappropriate trade secrets. The court determined that the exercise of personal jurisdiction over the foreign corporation was justified but observed that the suit was a "near mirror-image" of the pending suit in Canada. The court followed a multi-factor abstention analysis, including concerns for increasing friction between sovereign legal systems, and declined to exercise its discretion to hear the declaratory judgment claim.

Also, under the abstention doctrine recognized in *Younger v. Harris*, 401 U.S. 37 (1971), federal courts ordinarily refrain from hearing declaratory judgment actions regarding state criminal statutes when the plaintiff is the subject of ongoing criminal proceedings pursuant to that statute. Lower courts have set forth three specific situations where abstention under *Younger* is appropriate in ongoing state court proceedings: (1) when there are ongoing judicial state proceedings, (2) when the state proceedings implicate important state interests, and (3) when state proceedings afford an adequate opportunity to raise federal claims. *See* Rossi v. Gemma, 489 F.3d 26 (1st Cir. 2007). Further, in *Steffel v. Thompson*, 415 U.S. 452 (1974) the Court found that declaratory relief was not necessarily precluded where a state prosecution had been threatened but was not yet pending and a federal plaintiff demonstrated a genuine threat of enforcement of a state criminal statute. Nevertheless, a threat of prosecution cannot rest on imaginary or speculative fears. *Also see* Google, Inc. v. Hood, 822 F.3d 212, 223 (5th Cir. 2016)(mere investigation, without probable cause and service of formal charges, is not enough to apply the *Younger* abstention doctrine).

INDEX

References are to Pages